The Commitments

This book examines *The Commitments* (Parker, 1991) for the first time as a film, rather than an adaptation of Roddy Doyle's bestselling novel, and as a significant cultural event in 1990s Ireland.

A major hit in Ireland and around the world, the film depicts the short-lived attempts of an ensemble of young working-class Dubliners to achieve success as a soul covers band, playing the hits of Aretha Franklin, Otis Redding, and others, on a mission to 'bring soul back to Dublin'. Drawing upon interviews with key figures involved in the film and its music, including Roddy Doyle, Angeline Ball, and Bronagh Gallagher, as well as archival research of director Alan Parker's papers, the book explores questions of authenticity associated with youth, music, class, and culture, and assesses the film's legacy for the Irish film industry, Irish music scenes, and Irish youth. It also examines the film's status as a truly transnational production.

This concise, yet interdisciplinary case study will be of interest to students and researchers in popular music, cultural studies, and sociology, as well as film and media studies.

Nessa Johnston is Senior Lecturer in Media, Film and Television at Edge Hill University, UK. Her research is about sound and music in screen media, cult cinema, media technologies, and media industries.

Cinema and Youth Cultures

Cinema and Youth Cultures engages with well-known youth films from American cinema as well as the cinemas of other countries. Using a variety of methodological and critical approaches, the series volumes provide informed accounts of how young people have been represented in film, while also exploring the ways in which young people engage with films made for and about them. In doing this, the Cinema and Youth Cultures series contributes to important and long-standing debates about youth cultures, how these are mobilized and articulated in influential film texts, and the impact that these texts have had on popular culture at large.
Series Editors: Siân Lincoln and Yannis Tzioumakis

The Beatles and Film
From Youth Culture to Counterculture
Stephen Glynn

Clerks
'Over the Counter' Culture and Youth Cinema
Peter Templeton

Moonlight
Screening Black Queer Youth
Maria Flood

The Commitments
Youth, Music, and Authenticity in 1990s Ireland
Nessa Johnston

Precious
Identity, Adaptation and the African American Youth Film
Katherine Whitehurst

For more information about this series, please visit: https://www.routledge .com/Cinema-and-Youth-Cultures/book-series/CYC

The Commitments

Youth, Music, and Authenticity in 1990s Ireland

Nessa Johnston

LONDON AND NEW YORK

First published 2022
by Routledge
2 Park Square, Milton Park, Abingdon, Oxon OX14 4RN

and by Routledge
605 Third Avenue, New York, NY 10158

Routledge is an imprint of the Taylor & Francis Group, an informa business

British Library Cataloguing-in-Publication Data
A catalogue record for this book is available from the British Library

Library of Congress Cataloging-in-Publication Data
Names: Johnston, Nessa, author.
Title: The Commitments : youth, music, and authenticity in 1990s Ireland / Nessa Johnston.
Description: Abingdon, Oxon ; New York : Routledge, 2022. | Series: Cinema and youth cultures | Includes bibliographical references and index.
Identifiers: LCCN 2021037235 (print) | LCCN 2021037236 (ebook) | ISBN 9780367273125 (hardback) | ISBN 9781032189710 (paperback) | ISBN 9780429296048 (ebook)
Subjects: LCSH: Commitments (Motion picture) | Motion pictures and music. | Youth--Ireland--Social conditions--20th century. | Music--Social aspects--Ireland. | Popular culture--Ireland--History--20th century.
Classification: LCC PN1997.C7485 J66 2022 (print) | LCC PN1997.C7485 (ebook) | DDC 791.43/72--dc23
LC record available at https://lccn.loc.gov/2021037235
LC ebook record available at https://lccn.loc.gov/2021037236

ISBN: 978-0-367-27312-5 (hbk)
ISBN: 978-1-032-18971-0 (pbk)
ISBN: 978-0-429-29604-8 (ebk)

DOI: 10.4324/9780429296048

Typeset in Times New Roman
by Deanta Global Publishing Services, Chennai, India

Contents

Figures

Series editors' introduction

Despite the high visibility of youth films in the global media marketplace, especially since the 1980s when Conglomerate Hollywood realized that such films were not only strong box office performers but also the starting point for ancillary sales in other media markets as well as for franchise building, academic studies that focussed specifically on such films were slow to materialize. Arguably the most important factor behind academia's reluctance to engage with youth films was a (then) widespread perception within the Film and Media Studies communities that such films held little cultural value and significance, and therefore were not worthy of serious scholarly research and examination. Just like the young subjects they represented, whose interests and cultural practices have been routinely deemed transitional and transitory, so were the films that represented them perceived as fleeting and easily digestible, destined to be forgotten quickly, as soon as the next youth film arrived in cinema screens a week later.

Under these circumstances, and despite a small number of pioneering studies in the 1980s and early 1990s, the field of 'youth film studies' did not really start blossoming and attracting significant scholarly attention until the 2000s and in combination with similar developments in cognate areas such as 'girl studies'. However, because of the paucity of material in the previous decades, the majority of these new studies in the 2000s focussed primarily on charting the field and therefore steered clear of long, in-depth examinations of youth films or were exemplified by edited collections that chose particular films to highlight certain issues to the detriment of others. In other words, despite providing often wonderfully rich accounts of youth cultures as these have been captured by key films, these studies could not have possibly dedicated sufficient space to engage with more than just a few key aspects of youth films.

In more recent (post-2010) years, a number of academic studies started delimiting their focus and therefore providing more space for in-depth examinations of key types of youth films, such as slasher films and biker films, or examining youth films in particular historical periods. From that point on, it was a matter of time for the first publications that focussed exclusively on key youth films from a number of perspectives to appear (*Mamma Mia! The Movie*, *Twilight*, and *Dirty Dancing* are among the first films to receive this treatment). Conceived primarily as edited collections, these studies provided a multifaceted analysis of these films, focussing on such issues as the politics of representing youth, the stylistic and narrative choices that characterize these films and the extent to which they are representative of a youth cinema, the ways these films address their audiences, the ways youth audiences engage with these films, the films' industrial location, and other relevant issues.

It is within this increasingly maturing and expanding academic environment that the Cinema and Youth Cultures volumes arrive, aiming to consolidate existing knowledge, provide new perspectives, apply innovative methodological approaches, offer sustained and in-depth analyses of key films, and therefore become the 'go to' resource for students and scholars interested in theoretically informed, authoritative accounts of youth cultures in film. As editors, we have tried to be as inclusive as possible in our selection of key examples of youth films by commissioning volumes on films that span the history of cinema, including the silent film era; that portray contemporary youth cultures as well as ones associated with particular historical periods; that represent examples of mainstream and independent cinema; that originate in American cinema and the cinemas of other nations; that attracted significant critical attention and commercial success during their initial release; and that were 'rediscovered' after an unpromising initial critical reception. Together these volumes are going to advance youth film studies while also being able to offer extremely detailed examinations of films that are now considered significant contributions to cinema and our cultural life more broadly.

We hope readers will enjoy the series.

Siân Lincoln & Yannis Tzioumakis
Cinema & Youth Cultures Series Editors

Acknowledgements

This book would not exist without the advice, assistance, and support I received right from the beginning and throughout the research and writing period. In particular I am grateful to: Lisa Moran Parker, Roger Shannon, Tim Anderson, Maria Pramaggiore, Justin Wyatt, Storm Patterson and staff at BFI Special Collections, Raven Cooke and Leanne Ledwidge at the Irish Film Archive, Brian McMahon (Brand New Retro), staff at the National Archive of Ireland, staff at Dublin City Library and Archive, colleagues at Edge Hill University, and colleagues and friends in Dublin especially Jane Cullen, Luke McManus, Elizabeth Smith, Denis Murphy, and Ruth Barton. I am very grateful indeed to the series editors, Yannis Tzioumakis and Siân Lincoln, and to Philip Drake and Liz Greene, especially for reading early drafts and providing invaluable feedback. I would also like to thank Melanie Selfe and Maria Antonia Vélez-Serna for encouraging me to spend more time in archives.

I am profoundly grateful to my interviewees and would like to thank for their time, encouragement, and conversation: Roddy Doyle, Lynda Myles, Bronagh Gallagher, Angeline Ball, Blaise Smith, Lance Daly, Hugh Linehan, Paul Bushnell, and Kevin Killen.

I would also like to thank my mother, Janice Johnston, for all her love, support, and encouragement, for passing on to me her enthusiasm for cinema, and not minding my repeated trips to the Stella, Classic, and Savoy to see *The Commitments*.

This book is dedicated in loving memory of my father, Roy Johnston (1929–2019)

Introduction

Beyond text, beyond film:
The Commitments as event

Released three decades ago in 1991, *The Commitments* is a generation-defining film, capturing a youthful Ireland on the brink of profound social change. A major hit in Ireland and beyond, it depicts the short-lived attempts of an ensemble of young working-class Dubliners to achieve success as a soul covers band, playing the hits of Aretha Franklin, Otis Redding, Wilson Pickett, and others, on a mission to 'bring soul back to Dublin'. Adapted from the bestselling debut novel by Roddy Doyle, and directed by Alan Parker (*Bugsy Malone* [1976], *Fame* [1980]), the film made famous a group of mainly unknown young musicians turned actors, launched two bestselling soundtrack albums, and most recently a stage adaptation by Doyle. Eschewing the traditionally rural settings of Irish cinema and shot on location in inner city and suburban Dublin, it depicted urban working-class Ireland vividly, capturing a depressed and dilapidated early 1990s Dublin that was nonetheless youthful and energetic. Filmed and released during a transformative period in Irish society, with entrenched poverty and mass emigration, yet on the cusp of the new European single market in 1992 and the Celtic Tiger economic revival (from the mid-1990s to 2007), the film reflects the reservations and aspirations of a young generation looking increasingly outward and beyond the social repression of the Catholic Church.

The plot follows a music-obsessed young Dubliner, Jimmy Rabbitte (Robert Arkins), who forms and manages a soul covers band, initially with his friends Outspan (Glen Hansard) and Derek (Ken McCluskey) on guitar and bass, and the arrogant but talented vocalist Deco (Andrew Strong). Taking out a newspaper ad, he auditions hundreds of local musicians, before forming the full band – saxophonist Dean (Félim Gormley), drummer Billy (Dick Massey), pianist Steven (Michael Ahearne), and the much older and more experienced Joey "The Lips" Fagan (Johnny Murphy) on trumpet. With the addition of three backing singers, Imelda (Angeline Ball), Bernie (Bronagh Gallagher), and Natalie (Maria Doyle Kennedy), and some

DOI: 10.4324/9780429296048-1

haphazard initial rehearsals, the band The Commitments is born. Despite the success of their first gig at a local community centre, and increasing musical accomplishment as they gain further live experience, backstage tensions threaten to derail the band. Ultimately, despite local press and record label interest, and a possible near miss encounter with Wilson Pickett, The Commitments fall apart and the various members follow new projects, but not before Jimmy has succeeded in raising their spirits and expanding their horizons.

In this book I am concerned with the film beyond its status as an adaptation from a bestselling novel by Ireland's most significant living writer, Roddy Doyle, and beyond director-centred criticism's focus on the authorship of Alan Parker. As a popular comedy musical, it is easy to dismiss the film for lacking profundity or not engaging with its social themes in any depth. Despite winning four BAFTAs, including Best Film, and broadly favourable press coverage, many critics were dismissive of *The Commitments*, and none took it particularly seriously. For example, writing in October 1991, the critic Adrian Martin expressed his disappointment:

> Parker's career in cinema has been single-mindedly devoted to the pursuit of overwhelming, moment-by-moment spectacle, with no opportunity for a quick dramatic frisson or a cheap laugh ever passed up. [...] Once *The Commitments* reaches its plateau of spectacle with the band on a succession of stages, the interesting themes and questions start ebbing away, and all that remains are the cheap shots.
>
> (Martin 1991)

Similarly, academics tend to treat the film as an inferior adaptation of Doyle's book. Despite *The Commitments'* commercial success and significant popular appeal, particularly with youth audiences, the major book-length academic studies on Irish cinema have little to say about it. Lance Pettitt devotes a single page to it in a section titled 'Box office Irish' and compares it somewhat unfavourably with Doyle's novel despite successfully capturing Dublin's 'urban working class milieu' (Pettitt 2000: 126). Similarly, Martin McLoone declares the film and television adaptations of Doyle's Barrytown trilogy as the 'most consistent vision of urban Ireland'; yet points to *The Commitments*'s 'Hollywood clichés' that deviate from the spirit of the novel, and compares it negatively with the British TV-film adaptations of the second and third parts of the trilogy, *The Snapper* and *The Van* (McLoone 2000: 205). Ruth Barton makes no mention of the film in *Irish National Cinema* (2004) but mentions it briefly in *Irish Cinema in the Twenty-First Century* (2019). Most intriguingly, Barton and O'Brien's edited collection *Keeping It Real: Irish Film and Television* (2004) features a still from *The Commitments* on the cover, despite none of the chapters discussing the film, not even in passing. A footnote in Barton's 2019 book states that

> so determining of Irish cinema was *The Commitments* that when Harvey O'Brien and I co-edited a collection of essays on the subject, none of which mentioned the Parker film, the publisher insisted on illustrating the volume with an image from it.
>
> (Barton 2019: 221, n.2)

While I sympathise with Barton's frustrations, this demonstrates how academic analysis of national cinemas can be out of step with the cultural reach of popular cinema, particularly youth cinema. A lack of serious engagement with the film in Irish academic circles, despite its commercial success and cultural impact, suggests that the film's popular legacy has been almost too all-encompassing to be considered worthy of serious scholarly investigation.

Meanwhile, *The Commitments* has been analysed extensively in Irish literature contexts, with Doyle's book as the primary object of enquiry. Published in 1987, it was a bestseller, propelling the 29-year-old author and schoolteacher to sudden fame. It strikingly captured the sounds and music of working-class urban Irish youth in a way which resonated widely, and news of a film adaptation was greeted with excitement and anticipation. However, in literary contexts, any mention of the 1991 film is framed as mere adaptation of the primary text. For example, Timothy D. Taylor devotes much of his essay on class and soul in *The Commitments* to the book, then on one page compares and contrasts the film with the book, mostly negatively (Taylor 1998: 298). A standout work in this mould is Michael Cronin's *The Barrytown Trilogy* (2006), which provides an excellent analysis of Doyle's three novels and their associated films, but again, Cronin's treatment of the works is primarily literary, describing each iteration as 'novel/film', putting *The Commitments* film in dialogue with the novel. In contrast, this book treats the film as the primary object of enquiry, providing an in-depth analysis of its cinematic qualities and contexts. Any references made to the novel will consciously avoid treating it as an *urtext*. This is not to undermine Doyle's importance or authorship, but to allow a fresh examination of the film unencumbered by traditions of literary analysis.

In the rest of this introduction, as well as an overview of this book I will provide a reappraisal of the film, focussing on the pre-production, release, and reaction from critics and audiences, investigating the extent that the process entered into dialogue with Dublin, its culture, and its inhabitants. Beyond its young ensemble cast, the city can be understood as a key character in *The Commitments*, and a representational move away from the rural settings previously typical of Ireland on screen. The crew shot forty-four locations in the Dublin area in just fifty-three days, working six-day weeks, and Parker repeatedly stated that it was the most fun shoot he ever experienced (Parker 2016). The film's open casting call gave 1,500 young hopefuls the opportunity to audition for parts; casting agents Ros and John Hubbard scouted the Dublin live music scene for suitable musicians alongside using their usual contacts in the acting world; and the use of Dublin for location shooting meant that an unusual proportion of the general public were aware of the film and eager to see the city in which they lived depicted cinematically. The film's budget of US$12 million (Pettitt 2000: 41) may have been small by Hollywood standards, but by Irish film industry standards it was colossal; reflected in the scale of the film, the energy of its musical set pieces, and the marshalling of its young cast and extras into an impactful cinematic experience of Dublin on screen not seen before. More than just a film, and more than just an adaptation, for a great many Dubliners *The Commitments* was an event.

My approach not only treats the film as the primary object of enquiry, it embraces its broader popular cultural significance, and moves beyond the film text to explore *The Commitments* as an event in 1990s Ireland, borrowing from Rick Altman's notion of 'cinema as event' as opposed to 'film as text' (Altman 1992: 2). 'Cinema as event' favours examination of a film's production and reception as subsets of culture at large, and the text (i.e. the film itself) as a point of interchange rather than the focal point (1–14). Hence, the four chapters of this book and the conclusion take different thematic approaches in order to appraise *The Commitments* not only as a film text, but also as a set of processes and shifting discursive formations. Rather than suggesting that the film text is reflective of its contexts (which is the traditional 'criticism and interpretation' route), the point of this event-focussed analysis is to think about *The Commitments* event as more encompassing, and arguably more interesting, than *The Commitments* text.

'I wanna tell you a story': An overview of this book

Though not a teen movie, *The Commitments* shares with teen movies a concern with 'reversing age-defined privileges' (Speed 1998: 24). Upon its release, half of Ireland's population was twenty-five or under (Oaks 1998: 134), yet high unemployment meant that many school leavers could not adopt the trappings of adulthood associated with economic independence. In the film the characters' ages are not specified but it is assumed that they are in their early twenties, and Jimmy's continued residence with his parents and younger siblings is a source of humorous low-level masculine sparring with his father and irritation for his mother. The living situations of the rest of the band are not always directly specified, although drummer Billy mentions that he can rehearse all he likes because his father is dead and all his brothers are younger, 'so there's nobody to tell me to shut the fuck up'; and singer Bernie shares her modest high-rise flat with her mother and younger siblings. Even Joey "The Lips", the older trumpet player, who Jimmy pointedly tells 'you're the same age as me da' in their first meeting, states that he has returned to Ireland from the US because 'me mammy isn't very well'. The humour of the band members' dependency upon these types of domestic arrangements is inevitably laced with frustration.

The band members with jobs have traditionally low-paid ones: Bassist Derek works in an abattoir, singer Natalie in a fish processing plant, Bernie in a chip van, Deco as a bus conductor. Pianist Steven is a medical student, differentiating him from the others. More educated, more religious, and most likely middle-class, he has a clearer route into upward mobility and less at stake in The Commitments' success. The group might not be teenagers anymore but their economic situation keeps them in a despondent liminal state between the dependence of childhood and the independence of adulthood. As predominantly working-class youth, economic and social barriers further narrow their options. Yet they are too young to be invested in the project of Irish independence and nation-building that began in the 1920s, growing up in the shadow of the 'Troubles' in Northern Ireland and the IRA's campaign on mainland Britain, neutering the post-imperial project's rebellious idealism. As Cronin points out, these young characters are instead subject to a stratified and hierarchical Irish state with its interests entwined with the (then) impenetrably powerful Catholic Church, represented in the film by priests, journalists, and labour exchange clerks:

> anyone who is invested with even a modicum of authority speaks differently. The problem faced by Jimmy and most of his friends is not the occupying force of a foreign army but the hermetic exclusivism of indigenous class privilege and the social apartheid of the city.
>
> (Cronin 2006: 38)

By putting the tribulations of Jimmy and his band front and centre, the film reverses an age-defined privilege specific to the Ireland of the time. Furthermore, it is American musical culture that promises liberation from the chokehold of Irish church-state oppression.[1]

Thinking of *The Commitments* as a youth film, rather than a teen film, is more accurate, even if the youth of the film is more in the casting than the authorship. At that time, Doyle's novel was seen as giving voice to Dublin's working-class youth, having been inspired by his time as a schoolteacher, however, none of the characters are of school going age. Doyle was twenty-nine when the novel was published and thirty-three when the film was released. The distance between him and the youngsters he taught in Greendale Community School, in Kilbarrack (a suburb on Dublin's Northside), was negligible: 'I was 21 when I started teaching in 1979, and I was teaching 17-year-olds, so there wasn't a huge gap in age' (Doyle 2021). Parker was fourteen years older than Doyle, making Parker a generation older than the cast of *The Commitments*, with Doyle's age providing a bridge between the two generations. With a flair for putting vibrant musical performance on screen, Parker's track record included directing a number of significant, commercially successful, youth-oriented musicals. His debut feature, *Bugsy Malone*, reimagined 1930s and 1940s gangster films with an all-child cast, and his 1982 film *Pink Floyd: The Wall* is also a significant work of music-driven film, though not regarded as a musical possibly for reasons of rock snobbery. *Fame* (1980) followed ambitious teenagers at a New York performing arts academy, and offers the closest comparison with *The Commitments*. Indeed, with Parker's name attached to the film, it was described in some quarters as '*Fame* on the Liffey' (O'Sullivan 1992: 4) helping to publicise an open audition process that mirrored that of *Fame*.

The Commitments is a musical youth film, but is it an *Irish* musical youth film, or Irish youth musical? While the film has recognisable specificity as Irish through its Irish cast and Dublin shooting locations, using just one set (built nearby at Ardmore Studios), it won BAFTAs and all the key personnel apart from Doyle were British, making it a British film. Given the fraught state of Anglo-Irish political relations at the time, there is much at stake in this aspect of the production's identity. Following the scrapping of the Irish Film Board in 1987, and until its reinstatement in 1993, the Irish film industry was in the doldrums with little activity that was not funded with British or American money. Nevertheless, the process of casting and making *The Commitments* generated activity in Dublin that was integral to the energy of the film itself, as well as renewing enthusiasm for film in the city. What makes *The Commitments* an Irish film in spite of everything was the dedication to location shooting, and the emphasis upon casting unknown Irish talent, with the involvement of the city and its communities.

Considering *The Commitments* as an event, therefore, helps to solve this paradox at the heart of the film's Irishness and the film's authorship. Chapter 1 considers these issues in more detail, exploring the transnational contexts of the film's financing and production. Chapter 2 is the most textually focussed of all the chapters, exploring questions of race, class, and gender and the politics of representation of the film, with an emphasis on screen performance and comedy. The second half of the book is more focussed on music and sound; Chapter 3 explores music scenes, music industry, and the film's relationship to the musical genre, with Chapter 4 looking more closely at the recording of the two soundtrack albums, musicianship, and discourses of authenticity relating to soul and sound mediation. The Conclusion considers the afterlife of the film and its legacy.

2020 regrettably marked the passing of Alan Parker, and this book offers a reappraisal of his previously underestimated contribution to Irish cultural life. On the 1st of August 2020, Doyle paid tribute to Parker with a humorous yet touching Facebook post. Written in the style of his 'Dublin dialogues' between two unspecified male characters of Doyle's age as though exchanged over a pint of Guinness, it finishes with:

-Jack Charlton an' Alan Parker – the two Englishmen who changed the face of Ireland.
-It's gas, isn't it?

This highlights a synchronicity of the time – the filming of *The Commitments* in Dublin in 1990 took place in the immediate aftermath of the men's football World Cup, Italia '90, in which the Ireland squad managed by Charlton made history by getting to the quarter finals, a major boost for a small country still in economic difficulty. And given the poor state of Anglo-Irish relations at the time, the contribution of both Parker and Charlton demonstrates an inflection point which could be rationalised thirty years on as building to Ireland's emergence out of Britain's imperial shadow. My own engagement with this project has involved sifting through memories that are distant enough to be sometimes suspect, yet not so long ago that they might lose credibility. Despite Parker's unfortunate passing, the young people involved with the film are still with us, although now middle-aged. Inevitably, a notable feature of this project of recall is how different accounts contradict each other. For instance, a 1991 interview with Parker suggests he had the musically multi-talented Robert Arkins in mind for four parts, including the lead singer Deco. However, Arkins stated in 2016 that he 'always read for Jimmy, no other part' (Milton 2016). While sifting fact from fiction can be difficult, the manner in which the film attracts slightly contradictory accounts of its production is part of its fascination.

As well as analysis of the film, this book interrogates the film's reception by academics, critics, and audiences, and its pre-production, shoot, and post-production, all of which are interconnected. While aspects of production have been covered by the press and the promotional machine of the film, this book draws additional detail from archival research and interviews. A particularly important resource referenced throughout this book is Alan Parker's papers, the 'Parkive', held at the British Film Institute. As they contained little information on the rehearsal, recording, and mixing of the music which is the focus of Chapter 4, detail concerning these processes was gleaned from interviews with musician and arranger Paul Bushnell and engineer Kevin Killen. Sadly, Parker passed away during the early research period of the book, but I am very grateful to his wife Lisa Moran Parker for her invaluable assistance and input. Securing generous interviews with Doyle, Bronagh Gallagher and Angeline Ball closer to the end of the project gave me the opportunity to explore issues with them that have previously gained little press interest. With youth as a core theme, I also focussed on interviewing people who were in their teens and twenties when the film was made, and I myself was a twelve-year-old Dubliner on its release, aligning my own perspective more closely with that of the younger people involved. This makes this project not only about youth, but also memory of youth, and a reflection upon the excitement of the project at the time, and the period of change that has unfolded since.

Pre-production and release of *The Commitments*

What is striking about revisiting press coverage of *The Commitments* is the extent that the casting and production of the film was excitedly anticipated. For example, an *Irish Times* interview with Parker in June 1990 publicises the open auditions (Dwyer 1990a: 3), and the main feature article of the paper's 'Weekend' supplement on 11 August 1990 details the final casting decisions and the shooting dates (Dwyer 1990b: 1–2). The article repeatedly emphasises the scale of the operation: 'Literally thousands of aspirant movie stars, not to mention all the members of 64 different bands, were considered by Alan Parker and his team for his film "The Commitments"'. Furthermore, it is reported as an unfolding story: 'Work has started on the soundtrack, locations are being chosen all over Dublin and "The Commitments" is set to go before the cameras a fortnight from Monday. It will be shooting for nine weeks, entirely in the Dublin area'. Parker gives particular credit to the film's casting directors, the Hubbards:

> 'I was very lucky to have John and Ros help me with the casting', he says. 'They've been scouring every gig in Dublin for months. They even went on the wagon to get through four pubs a night. They had their first drink last week when I gave them the list of my final decisions'. (Ibid.)

A native of Dublin, Ros Hubbard and her husband John, as Hubbard Casting, have cast a significant number of Irish and international film and television productions, working in Los Angeles, New York, and London as well as Dublin.

Parker's mention of the alcohol and the pub culture in which Dublin's music scene is embedded further iterates notions of authenticity and working with insiders. The level of publicity and hype was not limited to the *Irish Times* – there were similar pieces in the *Evening Herald*, *Irish Press*, *Irish Independent*, *Irish Examiner*, *Sunday Independent*, and *Sunday Tribune*, and in local newspapers such as the *Connaught Sentinel*, *Southern Star*, *Western People*, and *Dundalk Democrat*. Years later, Parker reiterated the Hubbards' importance, praising their 'remarkable job', which involved seeing thousands of people before he arrived (Parker 2016). Furthermore, Parker's assertion that he would look at 'anybody' has been reiterated anecdotally by several people I spoke to in relation to this project. Beyond the press coverage, people in Dublin, especially young people, were aware of the film and the possibilities that the auditions represented. A then fifteen-year-old Lance Daly (Kid with Harmonica, now a film director), who was pursuing acting at the time and was invited to audition, mentioned that even the invited auditions were on a huge scale.

> I just remember there was a lot of excitement […] I think everyone was really positive about the book, and were excited that Alan Parker was coming to make this movie. There were a lot of associations with *Fame* I remember – the guy who made *Fame* is coming, no mention of the other great movies he's made.
>
> (Daly 2020)

The hype spread to other parts of the country, and papers based outside Dublin even ran stories about local youths travelling to Dublin to audition. A particularly whimsical example of this type from the Cork-based *Irish Examiner*, 'Aidan thankful for chance meeting', describes how a twenty-one-year-old County Cork 'youth with a dream' took the train to Dublin after his parents showed him the newspaper ad for the auditions. When he got off the train, he asked a passer-by for directions to the casting agency, and upon arrival discovered that the passer-by was actually Alan Parker (Ryan 1991: 9). This story was run to coincide with the release of the film, describing events from a year earlier, demonstrating how the excitement surrounding the audition process remained an integral aspect of the unfolding story.

After several months of talent scouting and invited auditions, the open casting took place in June 1990 in the Mansion House in Dublin's city centre, which is the official residence of the Lord Mayor of Dublin. These open auditions attracted a great deal of attention. Thousands queued, with many drawn in merely by the presence of the queue. Blaise Smith (now an artist) had no acting experience but was in contention to play the part of Jimmy, and was eventually cast as the pool hall manager (Parker 2016; Sweeney

2006: 17; Smith 2020). He had no idea about the auditions until by chance he passed the queue on Dawson Street into the Mansion House:

> I saw loads of people who were in my dole queue […] because every-one was signing on at the time. Then I saw this friend […] and asked her, what's going on here? And she told me that they had an open cast-ing for a film […] So I snook into the queue with her […] cutting out about four hundred people behind.
>
> (Smith 2020)

Once inside, Smith described a live audition situation, in which auditioners sang for everyone in the room, including those in the queue. Coincidentally, he recalls that Michael Aherne, who was eventually cast as pianist Steven Clifford, auditioned while Smith was queuing and was received with excited, good-natured applause.

> I remember the whole day being a bit of a laugh, and you know when you're 21, you're floating around, there's no deadline, you're rolling from one cup of coffee to the next, to somebody's house to call in. […] I was on a year out [from art college] so really just floating around with this great mass of unemployed people under 30, if they hadn't already left the country. (Ibid.)

A less publicised aspect of the film's production, but a significant feature of the film, is the sheer number of extras that appear in street scenes in work-ing-class neighbourhoods such as Ballymun and Darndale, and in crowd scenes such as at the labour exchange. The extras in these scenes were not bussed in, rather they were locals recruited via community representatives, which required careful negotiation and cooperation, including hiring local security (Linehan 2020; Ball 2021).

Dwyer's *Irish Times* feature states that Parker himself read with and videotaped 1,500 contenders. The short-listed candidates were called back to re-read four or five times and to participate in music auditions with a specially assembled band of Irish session musicians.

> 'I must say I was astonished at the young talent here in Dublin', [Parker] says, now that the arduous search is completed. 'It's been a difficult and painful process for me, not just choosing the final group, but agonising over who would be left out'.
>
> (Dwyer 1990b: 1–2)

This hype recurs in other popular accounts, emphasising musical talent over acting talent: 'None had much in the way of acting experience prior to making *The Commitments*, but they more than made up for it in freshness and sheer exuberance' (Gray 1999: 198). The repeated emphasis is upon Parker as an intrepid prospector in a Wild West of raw performance talent, patiently panning for undiscovered musical gold:

> I also saw all of the established young actors in Dublin, particularly those who were also musicians. [...] In the book and the film the band members take their first steps hesitantly — being downright awful in their early rehearsals, but gradually improving, culminating in their brief success at the end of our story. Our musicians therefore had to have a certain degree of competence in order to be able to bridge this transition from bad to good. The conventional wisdom being that it was a lot easier for a good musician to play badly than the converse!
>
> (Parker n.d.)

This extensive press coverage meant that the cinema release of *The Commitments* in September 1991 was much anticipated in Ireland. As a former advertising executive, Parker was involved with the marketing and promotion of *The Commitments* from pre-production all the way through to its release, using a strategy that tapped heavily into notions of authenticity. The press kit provided background to the origins of the novel, the making of the film (especially the casting process), and included a little booklet called 'A Tosser's Glossary' with dictionary-like definitions of some of the film's more colourful terminology (Beacon Communications 1991a). This was reported to the extent that Irish audiences were aware of it and amused by it. For example, state broadcaster RTÉ's report from the film's Dublin premiere includes a vox pop in which an excited attendee says 'In America they gave out a little booklet to [help them] understand – you'd better give that to those on the Southside as well!' ('The Commitments Premiere' 1991). 20th Century Fox organised a press event in Dublin in August 1991, ensuring maximum local and national coverage of the film prior to its gala opening in the Savoy Cinema on Dublin's O'Connell Street in September of the same year (see Figure 0.1). A few weeks after its premiere at the Cinerama Dome in Los Angeles, journalists were flown in from LA to cover the Dublin premiere. As well as Doyle, Alan Parker, and the cast, the event was attended by John Hurt, John Boorman, Brenda Fricker (who had recently appeared with Daniel Day Lewis in the much acclaimed and highly successful *My Left Foot* [Sheridan 1989]), Gabriel Byrne, Adam Clayton of U2, and musicians Liam Ó Maonlaí and Mary Coughlan. The *Irish Times* reported that additional tickets had been put on sale for the general public ten days earlier at an affordable £5 each (an idea Parker had run by Doyle and which Doyle supported enthusiastically [Doyle 2021]) and had sold out in just ten minutes, with people queuing from

Figure 0.1 Audition poster, Hubbard Casting

early in the morning (Dwyer 1991: 26). The premieres in LA and Dublin were synergistic, with the glamour of LA appropriate for an international release, feeding into the excitement of the Dublin premiere (see Figure 0.2), which in turn authenticated the film's Irishness and the cast's Dublin-ness for the benefit of international critics and audiences.

Figure 0.2 RTÉ television coverage of *The Commitments* premiere, Savoy Cinema, Dublin

Grossing a respectable $13.9 million dollars in the US over two months (*The Numbers* n.d.), the film played for at least six months in Irish cinemas, was the first film in Ireland to gross more than £2 million ('The Last Real Showman' 2000), and it continued to earn as a VHS release throughout the 1990s. The soundtrack album went triple platinum (*BPI* n.d.), remaining in the charts in the US, UK, and Ireland for a considerable period ('*Commitments*' n.d.; 'Billboard 200 ...' n.d.), and was inescapable throughout cafes and shops in Dublin and beyond in the years that followed. Its success led to the release in 1992 of *The Commitments Vol. 2*, featuring additional songs recorded for the film. Meanwhile, minor controversies flared up regarding the gritty depiction of actual Dublin locations, with residents voicing their concerns via RTÉ Radio's *Liveline*,[2] and a songwriter attempted unsuccessfully to sue for royalties after recognising lines from a song she had written in the film's audition sequence ('Singer Fails ...' 2000). The film launched the music career of sixteen-year-old singer Andrew Strong (lead singer Deco) and helped to promote Glen Hansard (guitarist Outspan) and his newly signed band The Frames, Maria Doyle Kennedy (singer Natalie) and her band The Black Velvet Band, as well as the careers of the rest of the cast with varying degrees of success. In the years that followed, talk of a sequel rumbled on but never materialised. Some members of the original cast continue to this day to tour as 'The Stars from the Commitments', and in 2013 Doyle adapted the book as a West End stage musical (still scheduled to tour in 2021 and 2022), in the same year that Irish film director Jim Sheridan adapted it as a radio play for the BBC.

In retrospect, *The Commitments* can be viewed as transitioning between the slick 1990s Celtic Tiger Irish cinema, and the 1980s type of socio-politically inclined popular comedies of the Dublin-based Passion Machine theatre company, with which Doyle collaborated with *Brownbread* (1987), in which three youngsters from Barrytown (Doyle's fictitious Dublin suburb) kidnap a bishop. Doyle has stated that his initial idea for *The Commitments* was to follow young people forming a football team rather than a band, but that Passion Machine founder Paul Mercier got there first with the popular play *Studs* in 1986 ('Roddy Doyle' 1992). One by-product of a lack of a fully fledged film industry in 1980s Ireland, and a lack of production of British-style TV films, meant that popular theatre provided a forum for Ireland's equivalent to the British TV work of Alan Bleasdale, Ken Loach, and indeed Stephen Frears, who went on to direct adaptations of Doyle's novels *The Snapper* and *The Van*. *Brownbread* demonstrated early on Doyle's talents for tapping into a listless anti-establishment mood amongst Dublin's youth at the time and foreshadowed the crumbling of the Catholic Church's authority in the 1990s.[3]

Parker, meanwhile, has been described by many of his collaborators as being at the height of his powers in his directing of *The Commitments* (Linehan 2020; Myles 2020; Ball 2021). Despite the generation gap between Parker and his young cast, and some simmering creative conflicts with Doyle, Parker's suitability and competence for the film as a music-led project has rarely been questioned. Nevertheless, while the film could not have been realised without the work of Parker or Doyle's novel, it is not a mere product of Parker's directorial mind, or Doyle's writerly imagination; instead it developed a life of its own through the energies of its cast and location. Even Doyle acknowledges how his novels and associated films have circulated amongst the Irish population in a manner beyond his initial authorial control, resonating

> with working-class people in Ireland in a way that was quite extraordinary. They claimed ownership, really, of *The Commitments* and *The Snapper* and *The Van* [...]. Lines from those books became spoken lines, characters became well-known, in a way that would never happen with a book that I would write in Britain for example or in Italy, even if they are well-received.
>
> (Doyle, quoted in Giambona 2019: 254)

Unlike *The Commitments* text, *The Commitments* film belongs to Dublin, in a way that nobody involved in the making of the film could have anticipated.

Notes

1 For an expanded discussion of the relationship between American culture and postcolonial, yet socially conservative, Irish society, see McLoone (with McLaughlin) (2008).
2 I was unable to locate any recordings of these phone-ins from 1991, and am relying upon my and other listeners' memories of them.
3 I am grateful to Hugh Linehan for highlighting these contexts during my interview with him.

1 A commitment to Dublin?

From transnational co-production to locational specificity

The stark white-on-black opening titles roll along to the upbeat opening number 'Treat Her Right', leading into the first shot of *The Commitments*, a bustling market in a drab, bricked-up graffitied street, accompanied by voiceover narration by Jimmy Rabbitte (Robert Arkins). We are visually introduced to the young man of the voiceover, just one of many in the crowded market, trying and failing to sell bootleg cassettes, videos, and t-shirts. The voiceover recounts 'how it all began', as though teleologically justifying an implied later success, asserting that he 'was always in the music business, but more on the sales side'. Fresh-faced and intense, he is both of the market and slightly detached from it; his dark quiffed hair and black clothes are stylishly retro. The scene is dominated by greys, blues, and browns, and the setting is unquestionably urban. As well as Jimmy's unmistakable Dublin accent in the voiceover, the soundtrack tells us in the most cliched way possible that this is Ireland – in the background a man scratches out a traditional Irish jig on his fiddle. Jimmy's voice and perspective is to the fore throughout *The Commitments*, despite the strong ensemble dynamic and distinct cast of characters. It is he who sets the agenda, and the other band members who riff off his pronouncements, support him, disagree with him. His voice therefore maps most closely onto the authorial voice of the text, emphasised through the use of voiceover narration. The irony that his narration of this success story is a fantasy, sent up vividly in a later scene by the sight of Jimmy sitting in the bath, shower cap on his head, and speaking into the shower head as though it were a microphone (see Figure 1.1), makes his earnestness more palatable. Despite the global success of U2, Bob Geldof, and Sinéad O'Connor, all earnest, serious-minded musical artists, Ireland is not comfortable with this type of seriousness. Jimmy's pretensions to seriousness in his musical endeavours can never be entirely taken at face value.

From the opening onwards, it is apparent that we are witnessing an Irish story captured in an Irish location, narrated by a previously unknown Irish

DOI: 10.4324/9780429296048-2

Figure 1.1 Jimmy Rabbitte's 'interview'

actor rather than an established star. Nonetheless, such a cast and setting do not necessarily make *The Commitments* an Irish film. While it regularly features in polls and lists of 'best ever' Irish films, a 1999 BFI poll ranked it 38th out of '100 best British films of the century' ('Best 100 British Films ...' 1999), highlighting the film's industrial status as an international co-production despite its Irish cast and recognisable Dublin locations. This chapter explores this paradox at the heart of the film's Irishness, focussing on two main interlocking themes. It examines the film's development and financing, highlighting the relevant wider industrial contexts of its production, then analyses its construction of a cinematic Dublin. Running through this chapter is a concern with youth, especially an Irish generational shift; discourses of authenticity; and the mobility of capital, culture, and people.

The tendency of academics and critics to compare the film unfavourably with the book as a 'dilution' of Doyle's text tends to be bolstered by the British and American aspects of the film's production, or in other words, the notion that authentic Irish stories can only be told by Irish authors. Yet my analysis will demonstrate a subtler (if insidious) logic of 'trickle down economics' at work. In my desire to put the film first, the genesis of the characters and story in Doyle's novel, his involvement with the screenplay, and the relationship between the film and its source novel will be considered. However, this chapter will move beyond a literary conception of authorship which posits the film as 'mere' adaptation via a spectre of 'dilution' or 'interference' (e.g. 'Hollywood' or 'Alan Parker'), without ignoring the adaptation process. Instead, I will demonstrate a number of competing currents at work that contributed to the development and creation of the film, which hinge upon shifting discourses of authenticity, in which questions of authorship are played out. Throughout, I explore *The Commitments* as a case study of transnational film production, the machinations of which serve to illustrate broader currents in Irish cultural determination. I also discuss the marketability of the film's conspicuous localism, despite its thematic emphasis upon the globalised Anglo-American popular culture of soul music.

Tony Tracy and Roddy Flynn argue for the need to look again at contemporary Irish film using a transnational lens, and move away from the more traditional preoccupation of Irish film scholars with Irish film as a 'national cinema'. Using the example of *The Lobster* (Lanthimos 2015) – a film that is held up as an Irish film industry success despite it not being recognisably 'Irish' and only two of the eighteen production entities involved in it being Irish – they demonstrate the limitations of confining analysis of Irish cinema to a narrow preoccupation with textual analysis that maps themes and ideas in films onto an understanding of the Irish nation and its history. In contrast, the transnational approach they advocate:

> opens a route out of a narrowly cultural conception of national cinema—a paradigm that was never fully adequate to the complex history of Ireland on screen anyway—while nevertheless maintaining one eye on the shifting status of the nation as a persistent but also multidimensional and dynamic site of identity formation and patron of cultural production.
>
> (Tracy and Flynn 2017: 172)

By using this transnational approach it is possible to retrospectively accommodate *The Commitments* despite its British-American production contexts and its dismissal as a 'lesser' adaptation or populist crowd pleaser. What is perhaps odd about *The Commitments*'s previous neglect in Irish film studies is that it does in fact exude a strong sense of place, an identifiable Irish setting, and 'markers of Irishness' (ibid.), therefore making it ripe for the very type of analysis Tracy and Flynn highlight as overly dominating the field.

A British-American-Irish film: *The Commitments* and its production contexts

Despite the commercial success of *The Commitments*, its status as an Irish success has been debated from early on. An article from *Newsweek* in 1992 referenced a number of ostensibly Irish box office draws of the time, including *The Commitments, My Left Foot* (1989), *The Field* (Sheridan

1990), *Hear My Song* (Chelsom 1991), and *The Playboys* (MacKinnon 1992), and made the point that as these films were typically financed from outside Ireland, their resulting box office receipts did not enrich Ireland. The same article quotes director Neil Jordan, who sums up such non-Irish Irish productions as follows: 'They make films that portray this quaint, magical country where everyone is eccentric and lives outside time with no material concerns' (Foote 1992: 46).

Intriguingly, the article lays the blame on a lack of investment at Irish government level, and quotes by way of explanation David Kavanagh, then head of the Irish Film Institute: 'The funds don't exist in Ireland to sustain a film industry [...] So this intense interest in things Irish is an opportunity that is exploited by non-Irish filmmakers who have the capital' (ibid.). The figures presented in this 1992 article are stark, with the Arts Council of Ireland funding the Abbey Theatre (the Irish national theatre) at the time about four times as much as all Irish film production combined. Kavanagh ascribes this to a lack of cultural value attached to film in Ireland: 'There is a history of film being seen by certain forces in Ireland as a foreign and pernicious influence [...] There is still an underlying lack of sympathy for the industry among politicians and civil servants' (ibid.). Hence, questions around identity are bound up with film finance and cultural value.

Indeed, *The Commitments* was nominated for, and won, several BAFTAs, and was eligible to do so because it qualifies as a British film, with all the key creative personnel being British. While Doyle wrote an early draft of the screenplay and has a screenwriting credit, it was further adapted by British screenwriters Dick Clement and Ian La Frenais, known for Hollywood screenplays as well as quintessentially British TV sitcoms such as *The Likely Lads* (BBC2, 1964–6) and *Porridge* (BBC1, 1974–77). The line producer was David Wimbury, the Director of Photography was Gale Tattersall, the costume designer was Penny Rose, the editor was Gerry Hambling – all British. In terms of top-level authorship and upper-level crew, it was a very British production. From the perspective of the young Dubliners appearing in the film, key personnel working on set had a noticeably British identity, all older than Parker, with 'that Ealing kind of accent, slightly cockney. These were the kind of people who were probably dynastically involved since the time of David Lean in filmmaking' (Smith 2020).

At the same time, the main financiers were American – the film was executive produced by Marc Abraham and Armyan Bernstein of Beacon Pictures in Los Angeles, and Parker, Clement, and La Frenais were all based in LA. This conspicuously Irish film adapted from a conspicuously Irish novel was, in essence, an American independent film made by LA-based Brits, and distributed by the very Hollywood 20th Century Fox. This is a sensitive issue and as Michael Cronin points out, 'For an English director to put Ireland on screen in the context of continuing political tensions and violence was not going to be seen as a wholly innocent or neutral engagement' (Cronin 2006: 17). Cronin refers also to Pettitt's description of film funding in Ireland after the closure of the Irish Film Board in 1987 as a period of 'Anglo-American film interests [...] mov[-ing] into the gap to support (and profit from) Irish-themed films' (Pettitt 2000: 124). The film's British status, therefore, has deeply uneasy colonial connotations, though paradoxically its Hollywood studio backing also makes its British status questionable.

While Parker's Britishness might be considered a dilution of the film's Irishness, Doyle is generous in his assessment of Parker and of Stephen Frears (director of *The Snapper* and *The Van*) and credits both British directors as 'sensitive to the fact that they weren't Irish. Neither of them assumed that Dublin was a British city with a different accent' (Doyle 2021). Furthermore, Doyle never imagined the film being directed by an Irish director, partly due to their scarcity at the time:

> If you threw a stone in Dublin, you wouldn't have hit a film director, put it that way [...] You could admire Thaddeus O'Sullivan without thinking he's the man for this particular job [...] I think I would have been a bit nervous with an Irish director as well [...] that somehow they'd mess with it, which is maybe unfair. Or maybe not!
>
> (ibid.)

It might seem paradoxical, but both Doyle and Scottish producer Lynda Myles felt that an Irish director might have been less loyal to Doyle's creation than Parker, despite his Britishness (Myles 2020; Doyle 2021). And although Doyle did not choose Parker as a director, he was not resistant to the idea:

> To find out the guy who directed *Birdy* [1984] – which I thought was brilliant – and *Mississippi Burning* [1988] was going to be directing *The Commitments*, I wasn't going to say, I'd much rather it was directed by such-and-such who'd done a short [...] When you look at the variety of things that he did, creatively successfully, it's extraordinary really.
>
> (Doyle 2021)

Moreover, crew in more junior roles were Irish, with notable examples including location assistants Robert Walpole (now a film and TV producer, *The Stag* [Butler 2013], *Shrooms* [Breathnach 2007]) and Hugh Linehan (now a senior *Irish Times* arts journalist). A teenage actor in the minor role of 'Kid with Harmonica', Lance Daly, is now an acclaimed director himself.

Paul Bushnell and Kevin Killen, who were heavily involved with the film's music, were both young Dubliners who went on to establish themselves in Los Angeles and New York and have significant international music careers. The generational aspects of the film's production are striking and in parallel with the trajectory of the youthful cast and characters; many involved in making *The Commitments* were young Irish getting their 'break'. There is an element of paternalism mapped onto the colonial connotations of this stratification, but it would be reductive to think of this entirely in such terms. While the cast have given many interviews looking back on their career trajectories since the film, there has been less acknowledgement made of others who got their start behind the scenes or in minor roles.

Furthermore, the pre-production and financing of *The Commitments* demonstrate a very specific dynamic that was at work in late 1980s/early 1990s Hollywood and its relationship with Britain and Ireland, centred upon Los Angeles, London, and Dublin. As mentioned in the Introduction, the lack of a fully fledged film and TV drama industry in Ireland at that time meant that Doyle's earlier ideas for comedy-drama such as *Brownbread* (1987) had been produced for theatre, and any attempts at film production necessitated collaboration with UK- and US-based industry professionals. The eventual success of the films of *The Commitments*, *The Snapper*, and *The Van*, alongside Doyle's Booker nomination for his novel *The Van*, demonstrate how Doyle required some engagement with British cultural industries in order to get his 'break'. This idea of fame in Irish cultural terms being bound up with a British cultural and entertainment ecosystem is just as prevalent as the mythologised idea of 'Hollywood', and is reflected in the film itself through Jimmy's fantasy interviews – he addresses the interviewer as 'Terry', a clear reference to Terry Wogan, the Irish-born BBC broadcaster.

The genesis of the film preceded Alan Parker's involvement by several years. Initially, it was Lynda Myles who was interested in a film of Doyle's book, as early as 1988, after two different people had sent it to her. She contacted another producer, Roger Randall-Cutler, suggesting they collaborate on it. After a meeting with Doyle in London in which he was 'sort of auditioning people for it', Doyle agreed they could option it (Myles 2020). Doyle credits Myles with pivotal support and professional development, while articulating a strong sense of his ownership of the work from early on.

> I didn't see the book as a film until other people came to me really [...] There was interest, even when the book was self-published. It quickly made me a bit cagey, but one Irish producer was going to superimpose the band onto New York, and I thought that was a hideous idea [...] I had a very strong sense that I owned it.
>
> (Doyle 2021)

When on a tour of the UK organised by his publisher Heinemann (during mid-term break, given that Doyle was still teaching full time), the publishers set up a meeting with four sets of producers in the Groucho Club. 'I didn't like what they [*the producers*] were saying. And the last person I met was Lynda Myles, and it was different immediately' (ibid.). Doyle describes a meeting of minds with Myles, regarding authenticity of language, absence of stars, and a Dublin setting.

Myles and Randall-Cutler were turned down for script development money by agencies in Britain, including the National Film Development Fund, and eventually secured some money privately from Souter Harris, a commercials producer, for Doyle to draft a screenplay, which gave Harris an executive producer credit on *The Commitments*. Myles mentored Doyle, inspiring his reinterpretation of the book in cinematic terms:

> I remember Lynda strongly recommended that I watch *The Big Chill* [1983]. It was about bringing people together. The excuse to bring people together. […] I suppose, the type of writing I was doing at the time lent itself more to Alan Bleasdale. *Boys from the Blackstuff* […] Structurally different, but the world was the same. And Ken Loach films. That was the type of world I was thinking in terms of. A lot of the biopics that came later, the Ray Charles one, they weren't there. So I don't recall seeing any music films. But I remember, *The Big Chill*, I remember Lynda recommending strongly I watch it, which I did, again and again. […] And Bill Forsyth, and Lynda knew him personally […] That working-class world. That was the kind of ambition I had. And Alan [Parker] was different. Alan got that, and got it well, but managed to make it bigger. The way the music was depicted, that's I think where a lot of the glory of the film – if I remember it right – is.
>
> (Doyle 2021)

Nevertheless, the producers felt that Doyle's initial draft required additional input, and brought in Dick Clement and Ian La Frenais to develop a second draft. In Doyle's words: 'I had a bash at writing the script. But it was never a plan. Never an ambition'. He felt a slight disappointment at the involvement of co-writers, even though he loved their work.

> It felt a little bit like failure perhaps that I hadn't got it over the finishing line myself. But I must have learnt a lot because when it came to *The Snapper* later on then, I mean, it was virtually the first draft that was filmed, and I learnt an awful lot, thanks to Lynda in large part, doing drafts and seeing what works and what doesn't.
>
> (Doyle 2021)

Meanwhile, over lunch with Alan Parker in Los Angeles, Clement and La Frenais informed him of the project and elicited his enthusiasm (Clement and La Frenais 2019: 183). At that point he had agreed with TriStar to direct a US$40 million adaptation of *Les Miserables*; however, feeling 'much more passionate about *The Commitments'* he opted for the smaller Dublin-based project instead (Dwyer 1990a: 3). With Parker on board as director, several offers of finance were made, and Myles and Randall-Cutler chose the offer from Beacon Pictures, a newly formed independent, financed privately by Beacon chairman Tom Rosenberg, whose previous career was in real estate. With Beacon on board, a distribution deal with 20th Century Fox was put in place, which concurrently had the rights to distribute Parker's *Come See the Paradise* (1990) (Gritten 1991; Myles 2020).

The budget has been reported at around US$12 million, a huge sum of money compared with productions financed in Ireland during the Irish Film Board years, or in the UK in the late 1980s and early 1990s. Yet it was posited in the press as a much smaller scale project than Parker's *Mississippi Burning* and *Come See the Paradise*. Hence *The Commitments*, with its smaller budget and lack of stars, would have been considered more personal and 'grittier' compared to his preceding projects. Despite his British identity, Parker was at this point well-established and settled in Hollywood, having purchased a house above Sunset Strip in 1987 for US$840,000, more recently valued at US$4.25 million (David 2015). Both Myles and Parker had followed in the footsteps of British producer David Puttnam, who had moved from producing popular British cinema with Enigma Films in the 1980s, most notably *Chariots of Fire* (Hudson 1981), as well as more Hollywood-orientated productions, including Parker's *Midnight Express* (1978), to becoming chairman and CEO of Columbia Pictures in 1986. Myles was also a senior vice-president of European production for Columbia Pictures in the 1980s. This push-pull relationship between attempts to revive and sustain a self-contained commercial British film industry with some overseas co-production is a context described somewhat scathingly by Peter Wollen as 'the fabulous collapse of Puttnamism and the flight of its leader to Hollywood' (Wollen 2006: 41).

Alan Parker's papers at the BFI reveal how embedded he was in Hollywood by that time (Parker 1991), containing a paper trail of promotional events such as industry screenings and 'thank you' notes, and even a 1991 letter from the Motion Picture Association of America President Jack Valenti enthusiastically singing *The Commitments'* praises, despite stating that he is not typically given to writing fan letters (Valenti 1991). The majority of the 'thank you' notes and cards were communicated via Parker's agent Rosalie Swedlin, of the Creative Artists Agency in Beverly Hills, a powerful agency headed by Michael Ovitz and Ron Meyer. Now a producer, Swedlin was influential and well-respected, also representing Martin Scorsese, Barry Levinson, and Sydney Pollack. She was described as soft spoken and untemperamental compared with other agents, and it was noted that (unusually for the business) 'she also reads' (Weinraub 1991). Despite the fairly modest commercial success of *The Commitments* in the US, where it grossed US$13.9 million, this relatively small film had the full muscle of the Hollywood promotion and distribution machine, opening in 555 US theatres and in third place in its first week of release on 13 September 1991, dropping out of the top ten in the third week (*The Numbers* n.d.). Full page ads were taken out in *Variety* and *Hollywood Reporter* in December 1990, before the film was even completed.

Parker's base in Hollywood and his transatlantic identity has made him an uneasy fit for British critics and academics who tend to damn him with faint praise, and bind up his transatlantic identity with his commercial sensibility, linking it with his previous work as a director of television commercials. This excerpt from Robert Shail's book on British film directors is a pertinent example:

> In Parker's best films he has shown an ability to anchor a progressive message within accessible, audience-pleasing entertainments. This has led to unsurprising accusations of philistinism which tend to underestimate the skill required to successfully pull off what he attempts to do. He is certainly a director with visual panache and one who isn't afraid to speak his mind. It's a pity that circumstances and personal inclination have so often taken his talents away from his native industry.
>
> (Shail 2007: 162)

Shail is critical of the British filmmaking establishment for not accommodating a talent such as Parker. It also hints at what an outspoken commentator Parker has been throughout his career, frequently critical of British film style and traditions, and articulating discomfort with the label of British filmmaker, seeing himself instead as a Brit based in Hollywood who makes movies. In an entertaining critical intervention, Parker presented *A Turnip Head's Guide to the British Cinema* for Thames television in 1986, which gave him space to rail against British film style and its shortcomings:

> Most of our directors learn their trade on the small screen or small stage. Also, too many have been brought up on the notion of film, not movies, with the consequence that most contemporary British films have admirable depth but no cinematic width – what's been called 'talking head cinema'.
>
> (Parker 1986)

Here Parker demonstrates a clear link between taste hierarchies and class politics, and later sends up auteur theory and director-centred criticism by including a contribution by David Puttnam in praise of the films of the 1930s: 'They absolutely understood that the brains behind the entire thing was the writer, that the energy – creative energy – was the producer, and if he had a brother-in-law who could deport himself reasonably then he became the director' (ibid.).

Parker further articulates a mix of self-deprecation and self-aggrandisement:

> one of the greatest myths in film is the auteur theory, invented by the French in the Fifties. The myth was that film was the work of only one person, the director. This myth was rather perpetuated by critics and of course the vanities and egos of us directors. The auteur theory has been described as the art of making invisible the producer, and the screen-writer, and the cast, and the cinematographer, and the art director, editor, costume designer, composer, not to mention 140 technicians, making the whole lot of them entirely disappear, including the projectionist.
>
> (Parker 1986)

What is interesting about this programme in relation to authorship of *The Commitments* is how it illustrates Parker's strong belief in filmmaking as a team effort, rather than director-centred. Furthermore, for Parker, the critics' obsession with the director is bound up in cultural snobbery and a distrust of entertainment: 'we seem to polarize everything in this country, in this case, art at one end and entertainment at the other, so that we're almost ashamed to admit that we're part of showbusiness' (Parker 1986). What is clear is that Parker's pride in his working-class identity strongly influences his criticism of a British film culture he considers stultified by class snobbery. Two other points his documentary makes include critiquing the disdain of film critics for his commercial background, and problematizing the notion that films have a national identity. It is striking how a lot of these points foreshadow the critical reception of *The Commitments* five years later.

Elsewhere Parker articulates a strong sense of identification with the young casts of *Fame* and *The Commitments*:

> 'Fame' was about the American Dream, and it was about young kids who almost expected success. The kids in 'The Commitments' were raised to believe they were going to be failures. They came from large families, mostly, and the sort of background where if they put on airs and graces, they'd be put down. I liked that about them.
>
> (Parker, quoted in Gritten 1991)

His commentary track on the Blu-ray release of *The Commitments* reiterates this point over a scene between Jimmy and Bernie in Bernie's high-rise flat: 'It's about working-class kids from a similar background to where I [Parker] grew up, using music to escape. As Joey says, "it's poetry"' (Parker 2016). He positions his class background as an uneasy fit for an industry which is partly about money but also partly about cultural value, as with notions of cultural value come notions of snobbery. In this case, then, the filmmaker's commercial sensibility is interlinked with his class background.

Parker's pride in his working-class identity was further manifested in a belief in building the world of *The Commitments* through a dedication to Dublin and casting young working-class Dubliners. Working with Ros and John Hubbard as casting agents based in Dublin meant tapping into local knowledge and networks necessary to make the open casting calls and audition processes successful, as did working with young local crew. However, this dedication to Dublin was prefigured in Doyle's approach to potential producers and financiers, and in Lynda Myles's steering of *The Commitments* project prior to Parker coming on board. According to Myles, Doyle:

> wanted to write the script and I said, no question. It was so much his voice, to me, it was insane but, apparently other producers had other ideas. The authorial voice was so clear. [...] Another question he had was, where would we shoot it? I looked at him like he was crazy, and said 'where you wrote it'. And apparently other people wanted to relocate it.
>
> (Myles 2020)

In this way, the dedication to Dublin and Doyle's authorial voice are presented as swimming against a homogenising cultural and financial current, which one might assume would mean a resistance to commercial sensibilities. Yet through Parker's steering of the project it became a key ingredient of the film's commercial success. Indeed, interviews promoting the film used this dedication to Dublin as a marketable hook: 'Parker decided to cast his young soul band from as close to the original source as possible, and went to Dublin last year for a mammoth casting session' (Gritten 1991). The phrase 'original source' is noticeable here, portraying Parker as bottling Dublin authenticity for an international market. In the same article, Parker demonstrates awareness between the synergy of American film finance with an authentic Dublin setting and milieu:

> 'At one point (the studio and Beacon backers) came over to Dublin and saw the kids we'd be using. Later in the day, they were out on Grafton Street, and saw some of the same kids busking for beer money.
>
> (Parker, quoted in Gritten 1991)

'I'm not after a bleedin' postcard': Dublin's urban grit

In an interview with RTÉ, Doyle stated that his initial draft of the screenplay was quite removed from the novel, whereas later drafts with input from Parker and the other screenwriters actually returned to the novel: a 'pleasant surprise' ('Roddy Doyle' 1992). Alan Parker's papers further reveal a determination to be true to Doyle's novel's youthful energies and its Dublin setting. In the margins of early drafts of the script, Parker scribbled retorts to screenwriters Dick Clement and Ian La Frenais. A recurrent comment is 'not our language', or next to his edits, that dialogue should go 'snap snap snap' or 'bam bam bam', showing a dedication to authentic 'Dublin-ese' and its spikiness. For a scene mentioning a passing kid, Parker's response was 'kids. It's never just one kid in Dublin' (Clement and La Frenais 1989). This aspect of the film has been remarked upon by Cronin, who notes this recurrent feature of Gale Tattersall's cinematography: 'the rundown streets and flat complexes are presented as teeming with children, the decaying material infrastructure of the city contrasted with the anarchic energies of the predominantly young population' (Cronin 2006: 28). This cinematic Dublin is therefore characterised by 'grit' and 'youth' as bids to authenticity. La Frenais recalls that Parker challenged their choice of the picturesque seaside suburb of Howth for the opening scene in the first draft of the script, asserting that the film needed 'to begin with something gritty and working class', the eventual switch to a marketplace which set the 'grainy, blue-collar texture' tone of the film overall (Clement and La Frenais 2019: 188).

This opening scene was shot on Sheriff Street, a north inner-city residential location with a strong working-class identity, and at first glance a suitably authentic choice for filming; however, the street market is fabricated and no such marketplace ever existed at that location. Yet the choice of Sheriff Street was an interesting one, as a place of significant social engineering and deprivation, the site of a large, run-down, and isolated social housing complex. Statistics from the late 1980s suggest that 41% of the population there was under fifteen, with the local unemployment rate a staggering 80%, with the remaining 20% employed on low incomes (Geoghegan 1989: 56–7). The economic decline of Dublin's docklands had a profound impact upon the area, comparable to the closure of coal mines in Northern England, Scotland, and Wales. Neglect by Dublin Corporation (now Dublin City Council) and a lack of community consultation led to a number of government agencies, including the Custom House Docks Development Authority, under the auspices of the Department of the Environment to implement a strategy of 'detenanting', paving the way for redevelopment. It is therefore ironic that the visual backdrop for the film's opening scene repopulates Sheriff Street with a fabricated street market. In a 1991 interview with *Empire*, Parker states firmly that he captured the city accurately and truthfully:

> Dublin has one of the youngest populations in Europe, a huge working class who live in these places where the book is set. I didn't make anything up. I filmed the film in the place Roddy has written about. That is the Dublin I found.
>
> (Parker, quoted in Lowe 1991: 72)

Parker's statement contains a fascinating mixture of truths and verifiable falsehoods, which provide some insight into the logic of urban space created in the film. In the context of this discussion, a further irony worth noting is that Irish director Jim Sheridan was born and raised on Sheriff Street (Sweeney 2016).

Within the first thirty minutes of *The Commitments*, a strong sense of the urban and social fabric of Dublin is established, with rapid movement through multiple real locations. Yet despite his commitment to the spirit of Doyle's novel, and the energies of shooting on location in Dublin, Parker made the decision to shift the action away from the novel's suburban locations, set in fictitious Barrytown, based on the Northside suburb of Kilbarrack. Apart from a brief early shot of the local DART light rail station (at night and barely recognisable), the low-rise, low-density suburbia of Kilbarrack does not feature. It is the claustrophobia of Darndale and high-rise Ballymun, along with many run-down inner-city locations which instead make up the core visual accents of the film, a type of gritty, faded Victorian grandeur. A note in the margins of Parker's copy of an early draft of the script says 'Boring World is Roddytown', indicating a desire to relocate the action away from Kilbarrack, despite Parker's great many bids to authenticity and fidelity to the novel in other respects (Doyle 1989). Instead, Parker opts for the atmospherics of the inner city to build his own vision of Dublin, emphasising narrow streets and derelict Victorian buildings more reminiscent of the war-damaged Islington of his childhood.

Furthermore, throughout the film, neither Barrytown nor any specific suburbs are named; characters only mention the Northside (most famously in Jimmy's statement that 'the Northside Dubliners are the blacks of Dublin') and the Southside (Dean's assertion that Imelda looks like 'she'd be in one of those Southside cocktail bars sipping drinks with umbrellas in them'). In her essay on Celtic Tiger, Jenny Knell assesses how this trope is articulated in the films of the Barrytown trilogy and beyond:

> The concept of Dublin as materially, socially, and economically halved by the Liffey permeates representations of Dublin. Though this division

is often reduced to a jocular rivalry between North and South (and in fact is the subject of much local satire), these spatial delineations emerge as discourses of class and are a way of referencing social and economic difference indirectly through the cultural vernacular.

(Knell 2010: 214)

The division is inconsistent and elides the wealth of such Northside suburban villages as Malahide, Portmarnock, and parts of Howth (Clement and La Frenais's initial choice of location for the opening shot) or the working-class identity of Southside areas such as Ballyfermot and Crumlin. However, it helps with the engineering on screen of Parker's vision of Dublin for *The Commitments*.

In terms of Dublin's economic and cultural activity, *The Commitments* was arguably an event more than a film, because film was not a priority. Production activity was at a low ebb. The Irish Film Board, set up in 1980 and with an annual budget of just IR£500,000 per annum allocated to Irish film production, was abruptly axed in 1987 and replaced with tax concessions designed to encourage foreign producers from overseas to shoot in Ireland, rather than foster an Irish industry (Pettitt 2000: 110). Government documentation from the period reveals that development plans for Dublin included arts funding, however, film barely registered beyond a small amount for the Irish Film Institute, which had yet to create the public-facing Temple Bar-based Irish Film Centre (set up in 1992). Conn Holohan has argued that Dublin on film lacks the monumentality of cities such as Paris (Holohan 2010: 115; see also Barton 2019: 11–4). However, while this may have been true of *The Commitments* upon its release, its use of locations was prefigurative of the tourist image of the city that emerged from the mid-1990s onwards. Temple Bar is the location of the exterior used for the venue in which the band plays *Take Me to the River* (Parker 2016), and of the pawn shop in which Jimmy and Billy retrieve Billy's drum kit, with these exterior shots revealing the narrow, cobbled streets that seem almost unchanged since the 19th century, and which from the Celtic Tiger years onwards would become the site of countless stag and hen weekends.

However, in 1990, as *The Commitments* was being filmed, the Celtic Tiger had yet to happen. Dublin was still a rather depressed place, its depopulated and derelict inner city lacking a clear tourist image. Even in 1989 officials were still debating whether to implement a long-standing plan to flatten Temple Bar in order to build a new bus station, despite the heritage organisation An Taisce's pleas to save its architectural heritage. Minutes from a government meeting summed up Temple Bar as 'a complex area with a complex problem' and that its 'tourist attraction is debatable' (Department of Taoiseach 1989). Yet the Irish media and Irish audiences warmed to the Dublin on screen in *The Commitments*, despite regarding it as a scene of degradation in need of renewal. A reaction from a teen-ager interviewed for an Irish-language RTÉ magazine programme upon the film's release is typical – while enthusiastic in his enjoyment of it, he says the film depicts Dublin as a 'concrete city' and doesn't think it will do any-thing for tourism ('Tuairimí na nDéagóirí faoi "The Commitments"' 1991, my translation).

This lack of regard for Dublin's inner-city architectural heritage was quite common at the time, and ironic given how renewal of the inner city became a key part of Dublin's surge in tourism from the Celtic Tiger onwards. The decrepit filming locations such as Smithfield and Temple Bar have since been restored and developed as middle-class cultural quar-ters and tourist attractions. And heretically, one of the most heavily fea-tured locations in the film, the pool hall where the band rehearses (then Ricardo's Pool Hall), is actually on Dublin's Southside, albeit the south inner city. In the film, the band's rehearsal space is revealed via a dramatic wide angle shot revealing a smorgasbord of antique bric-a-brac, startled pigeons flying upwards drawing attention to the crumbling yet magnifi-cent ornate plasterwork ceiling. Jimmy's awed reaction and response to the deadpan pool hall manager (Blaise Smith) 'Jaysus that's brilliant' is contrasted with his response: 'Just make sure you leave it in the same shit state you found it'. (In 2020, this location has been restored and repur-posed as a stylish sports bar, the Camden, with a neighbouring pub now named Jimmy Rabbitte's.)

This despairing attitude to the city's former British imperial grandeur and grit was quite typical at the time. Writing a polemical piece on Dublin's architecture in 1991 in the popular *In Dublin* magazine, a commentator articulates the operation of a peculiar Irish cultural cringe and its historical and socioeconomic roots:

> the city's lingering 'charm' was hardly seen as evidence of a former glory. On the contrary, it was seen as a sign of malingering underde-velopment [...] Dublin Corporation's indifference to the conservation of Georgian Dublin was no more motivated by anti-English sentiment than London's own lack of regard for its past. The only difference was that London had the resources to clear its slums and rebuild whereas Dublin did not.
>
> (O'Fearghaill 1991: 7–8)

In the band's shambolic first rehearsal in their crumbling surroundings, when Joey "The Lips" assures his young bandmates that 'Rome wasn't built in a day', Natalie retorts with 'Dublin was' and Bernie adds 'in an hour!'

articulating this cultural cringe. Yet Parker's choices of shooting locations, mainly using decaying Victorian Dublin, has the effect of foregrounding the youth of the cast. This is further compounded by the dated décor of Jimmy's home, his parents' house which he shares with them and his younger siblings, the only purpose-built set in the film. The house is plausibly of the 1991 present day, yet would not look out of place in the 1970s – its old-fashioned look further emphasises his youth and the generational divide between him and his Elvis-obsessed father. He is trying to be an adult, but is unemployed and stuck at home in a liminal state between youth and adulthood, dreams of success with his yet to be formed band providing hope that he might break away.

The youthful human and material fabric of the city of Dublin is a key character in *The Commitments*, and a representational move away from the more rural settings that had been typical of cinematic Ireland on screen. Every daytime exterior scene in the film is crowded, especially with young people and children. Young Jimmy himself might be unemployed, just like around 20% of the Irish workforce at that time, but he is definitely not idle. He seeks the mobility that fame and wealth might make possible, currently constrained by his visibly drab surroundings. A scene in which Jimmy and Dean queue for the dole was filmed in an actual labour exchange, and used its existing queues rather than paid extras (Linehan 2020; Parker 2016). In an almost Neorealist style, while we focus on Jimmy's individual drive, we are very much aware that he is one of many in a country of mass unemployment. At the time, these urban settings challenged past representations and the traditional cultural nationalism of Ireland, particularly expressed in the nationalistic poetry and playwriting of W. B. Yeats, but also in Hollywood representations of the 'old country' exemplified by John Ford's *The Quiet Man* (1952). Beyond filmic representations, Ireland's own understanding of itself, and of its international appeal, was bound up in a fixation with the rural and a negation of the urban. Ireland's tourist image was of a green rural land, rather than the urban grit and crowds of Dublin's inner city.

While *The Commitments'* use of urban settings in 1991 may have been a departure from Irish cinema's earlier rural fixation, as Ruth Barton points out, its urban vision does share the same tradition of Romanticism through its 'aestheticisation of the urban working-class' (Barton 2001: 193). *The Commitments* stills photographer David Appleby's black and white photos of the cast and filming locations similarly aestheticise Dublin's urban decay. While Parker was committed to shooting on location as a bid to authenticity, location manager Martin O'Malley opined that Parker liked to shoot in all the roughest locations in Dublin and make them worse (Pendreigh 1995: 220), and Angeline Ball mentions that he would 'wet down the streets' to give urban exteriors a dreary, rain-soaked aesthetic (Ball 2021). On the Blu-ray commentary, Parker makes particular mention of mud in locations such as Darndale, and that it 'would be nice to film on a tropical island some-where' (Parker 2016). Yet in this context it is another demonstrative fram-ing of the finished film as having derived from his apparently endured and unwavering commitment to a purported type of authenticity.

These types of aesthetic choices play out in the film, during Jimmy Rabbitte's photoshoot of the band (see Figure 1.2). When the photogra-pher suggests choosing a more scenic location instead of the chosen derelict backdrop, Jimmy retorts: 'I'm not after a bleedin' postcard, I'm after urban decay'; hence he has the same attraction to urban grit for his band's aes-thetic as Parker and his team have for the film. Benburb Street, where the scene takes place, was a notorious red-light district, and like many locations used for filming, required the knowledge of local crew to ensure safety and smooth running of the shoot. The location managers and location assistants worked closely with the local community, paying cash in hand for help and cooperation (Linehan 2020; Ball 2021). Rather than bussing in centrally cast extras, additional extras were recruited locally, in a further bid towards authenticity. In spite of this, Parker had a particular aesthetic in mind, which did not always fit the human fabric of the city. Location assistant Hugh Linehan's recollection of Parker's approach is worth quoting at length here as it vividly illustrates these contradictions:

> This is late summer 1990, it's two months after Italia '90, the whole country is still totally football mad, particularly the working-class areas

Figure 1.2 The Commitments photoshoot

that we were shooting in. [...] I remember again and again [...] we would arrive with a truck full of black and brown anoraks and coats, and there would be kids running around in candy-coloured Liverpool and Arsenal and Manchester United jerseys, and we'd be running after them putting these coats on them. Because Parker's aesthetic – it's there in the film and it's the same in *Mississippi Burning*, or *Angel Heart* or a lot of those films he made in the '80s, it's all quite sombre colours, it's browns and blacks, dark colours, lit in a very particular kind of a way. So we were kind of imposing that on this gaudy kaleidoscope of football jerseys.

(Linehan 2020)

While there is a palpable commitment to capturing a Dublin true to locational specificity of the characters and the origins of Doyle's novel, the reality is inevitably filtered through Parker, Tattersall, and Appleby's cinematic eye (see Figure 1.3), and also partly erasing the transnationalism expressed in Ireland's football culture.

Conclusion

In the distant background of the scene on Benburb Street, construction cranes are visible, foreshadowing the coming boom years of the Celtic Tiger. Meanwhile, at Irish government level, plans were being made to regenerate Dublin's depopulated inner city, with a spate of new business

Figure 1.3 Kids on bikes, dressed in greys and browns

development, transport, infrastructure and tourism projects, with the aid of European Community structural funds on course for allocation in 1992. The headline issues of emigration, high youth unemployment, and drug abuse were about to be targeted with a range of initiatives. The film therefore captures a moment where Dublin was on the brink of major change, and none of this change was accidental, but it was dramatic. By 2000, the city would have an entirely different sense of itself. Even only ten years later, with the Celtic Tiger in full swing, a piece by Áine O'Connor in the *Sunday Independent* summed up this change:

> The new decade was an inspiration. *The Commitments* was a new departure in the international depiction of Ireland and it was seen by millions of people worldwide. Urban Ireland existed officially. Cities got facelifts, beautiful old buildings were cleaned and pedestrian streets were paved. Old buildings were modernised rather than replaced; we started thinking of reinvigorating tired and neglected areas, of building roads with more than two lanes and of giving them surfaces that could be driven on by cars as well as farm machinery.
>
> (O'Connor 2000: 6)

It is interesting how the ideas in this piece flow, as though *The Commitments* alone brought Ireland's urban facelift into being. Six years later at the height of the economic boom, Cronin similarly highlighted how the Barrytown Trilogy represented an outward, open, and inclusive shift in Irish culture, from the emigration and economic deprivation of the 1980s into the economic growth, modernisation, and optimism of the Celtic Tiger era, allowing 'a place in that urban, modernising medium *par excellence*, cinema, for the experiences of these modernised others and the spaces they inhabited [...] The real difference now in Ireland was in not being different' (Cronin 2006: 11).

However, O'Connor and Cronin's pieces contrast with Doyle's recollection:

> I wrote the book in 1986. I didn't have the benefit of foresight. A few economists claimed later on that they could see boom time coming. I didn't. I was a teacher at the time and so many of the kids' parents were emigrating, were unemployed. The unemployment rate in the city, in the area of the city where I was working and which I was familiar with because I grew up there, was huge.
>
> (quoted in Giambona 2019: 258)

While Dublin may have changed dramatically in the past thirty years, the extent to which the change benefitted all areas of the city and all communities that cooperated with the shooting of the film is debatable, yet visible signs of gentrification and a booming tourist trade must not be cited as proof of so-called 'trickle down' economic effects. However, as this chapter demonstrates, the film can be considered an inflection point between the depression and decay of the 1980s and the roar of the Celtic Tiger of the 1990s, with Parker capturing and emphasising the city's decay and its youthfulness just prior to the profound economic and cultural change to come.

2 'Say it loud, I'm black an' I'm proud'

Intersections of race, class, gender, and youth on screen and soundtrack

Rejecting the traditionally 'green' rural visions of Ireland, *The Commitments* locates Irish youth within a grittier urban milieu and a specifically working-class identity. As the previous chapter has established, as well as being a distinctly Dublin film, *The Commitments* is also culturally located in Dublin's working-class Northside. This chapter initially hinges upon a famous scene in the film, in which the band's founder and manager Jimmy Rabbitte articulates his choice of black soul music as a form that speaks to a universal urban working-class experience, regardless of race. In a well-known and widely analysed speech, in which saxophonist Dean queries 'maybe we're a little white?', Jimmy answers:

> Do you not get it lads? The Irish are the blacks of Europe, an' Dubliners are the blacks of Ireland, an' Northside Dubliners are the blacks of Dublin. So say it once, an' say it loud, I'm black an' I'm proud

equating experiences of racial discrimination with class discrimination. It also taps into memories of discrimination shared by Irish workers in England with the Windrush generation, often summed up in the 'NO IRISH. NO BLACKS. NO DOGS' signs reported to have been seen by Irish and Afro-Caribbean migrants right up until the 1960s.

But what is remarkable about this scene (and its equivalent moment in Roddy Doyle's novel) is how it has circulated beyond the film to animate an entire interpretative community, manifested in the sheer number of academic studies that have quoted this speech in relation to Irish identity. This chapter will analyse the representational politics of these peculiar collisions of race, class, gender, Irishness, and Catholicism, starting with a meta-analysis of the scene's reception, problematising its reification, and situating it in a wider, musically and generationally specific cultural moment. This generational specificity means that these representational issues are bound up with the cultural politics of youth in 1990s Ireland, as well as the youthful

DOI: 10.4324/9780429296048-3

energies of the film's cast which I argue is inherent to the film's success. Running through the chapter will be an emphasis on the dynamics of screen performance and comedy, areas strikingly neglected in much academic work on *The Commitments*.

Interpreting interpretations of an interpretation

Like much Irish literature, theatre, and cinema, *The Commitments* has been discussed in relation to postcolonial theory, with the Irish affinity with 'blackness' articulated in Jimmy's speech presented as a shared history of British imperial oppression. Lance Pettitt describes the speech as 'an instance of tensions generated by Ireland's ambivalent status as a postcolonial country' (Pettitt 2000: 127), while Timothy D. Taylor similarly offers a postcolonial theory-influenced reading of the novel, asserting that the speech is the novel and film's essential political message (Taylor 1998). Taylor, Pettitt, and others make much of the differences between the speech in the novel and the film, with the novel using the offensive word 'nigger' rather than black, and including the additional line 'the culchies have fuckin' everything'. The omission of 'culchies', Dublin slang for people from 'the country' (i.e. outside Dublin), is deemed by Taylor as placating non-Irish audiences, and by Pettitt as stripping the speech of political commentary given the prioritisation of rural interests by the Irish political establishment. However, in revisiting these readings now during the renewed urgency of the Black Lives Matter movement, these parallels feel uneasy, an unease exacerbated when encountering the novel's use of the n-word. Jimmy and The Commitments are irrefutably white; to describe themselves as 'the blacks of' anywhere is disingenuous.

Much of this writing focusses on the novel, rather than the film. In her class-focussed analysis of the novel, McGlynn situates Jimmy's speech in relation to his wider discussion about the marketability of the band, in which his linking of their economic situation in Dublin with that of black Americans moves 'from audience to profit to politics' and 'shows Jimmy's awareness of their interdependence' (McGlynn 2004: 235). Michael Cronin adopts a more nuanced position, pointing out that Jimmy's speech is met with looks of bewilderment from the rest of the band, a sign of 'hostility to a leaden didacticism' (Cronin 2006: 19), yet that the choice of soul music has the effect of universalising the young Dubliners' class struggle. Similarly, in McGlynn's analysis, the speech is as much about negotiating capitalist economic structures through neoliberal logic as it is about postcolonialism. And yet, these arguments imply that the speech is not fundamentally about race or colour, but instead is about Irish characters drawing attention to the Irish postcolonial condition, and universalising their class politics via music.

By emphasising class politics and the Irish postcolonial condition, these readings elide the specificities of race and racism, and considering these lines thirty years later raises questions, not least because the Irish youth of today have grown up in a much more multicultural, less racially homogenous Ireland. Thirty years later, categories of blackness and Irishness are neither mutually exclusive nor equivalent. As Lauren Onkey argues, the economic boom of the Celtic Tiger years and its resulting immigration dredged up racial prejudice, leading to the 2004 referendum on Irish citizenship and a storm of racist 'debate' about Irish identity, the result of which meant that babies born in Ireland are no longer automatically entitled to Irish citizenship (Onkey 2010: 185–6). The discomfort of re-reading this speech in light of these developments is not merely retrospective or specific to reception within Ireland. Catherine Eagan recalls that:

> when I first saw the film in San Francisco, shortly after its release, the film's audience responded to Jimmy's pronouncement with roars of approval. This dialogue and its enthusiastic reception are so important because they demonstrate the Irish and Irish American tendency to link 'Irishness' to a heritage of oppression that is in many ways very distant from their present-day lives.
>
> (Eagan 2006: 21)

Eagan goes on to problematise these perceived links, demonstrating how, despite Ireland's colonial history, Irish Americans and African Americans have regularly been at odds with each other, and any efforts by political activists to link their struggles have typically been met with a cool reception. The speech downplays the extent that race and colour continue to matter, particularly (though not exclusively) in the US.

Many studies (including this chapter) quote the speech in their opening paragraph (Taylor 1998; McGonigle 2005; Pramaggiore 2007), to the extent that the speech becomes not only a 'way in' to an analysis of the film and/or novel's politics, but a synecdoche for the film's meaning and significance. What is troubling about this repeated quotation and interpretation of Jimmy's speech is that the speech itself is an act of interpretation. As David Bordwell argues, academics and critics employ a particularly institutionalised technique of interpretation, setting up a question about a film, then answering it using a rhetoric that ascribes broader meanings to a film:

> critics apply conceptual structures of a general nature to cues – items, actions, stylistic features – discriminated within the film. Most broadly, the conceptual structures are abstract *semantic fields* [...] On the screen,

a figure is a man; it is the critic who makes an inference and declares that the man is a father figure, or a symbol of masculine authority [...] These are prototypes of interpretative inferences, and some such semantic fields seem necessary if the conclusion is to acquire the generality characteristic of an interpretation.

(Bordwell 1993: 101)

Hence, when Jimmy declares that 'the Irish are the blacks of Europe', in Taylor's interpretation Jimmy delivers a political message in his capacity as a figure of 'the disenfranchised Irish' (Taylor 1998: 291). Taylor then suggests that some critics have found the speech 'mystifying', and by way of explanation points to an illustrious history of linkages between the Irish Renaissance (associated with literary figures such as W. B. Yeats and Seán O'Casey) and the Harlem Renaissance of the 1920s. Taylor's argument is perfectly legitimate, and I do not take issue with his argument *per se*; my issue is that the repeated quotation and interpretation of the speech, more than any other moment in the film, has had the effect of investing the speech with a weightiness that disregards the film's comedic tone and its wider musical contexts. Indeed, as Gerry Smyth points out, by overly emphasising these themes of identity, such readings disregard the core focus of both the book and film – forming a band and making music (Smyth 2009: 65). But it also elides the manner in which Robert Arkins as Jimmy performs this precise type of interpretation, or how the writers foist this act of interpretation upon the character of Jimmy.

Furthermore, the analysis of this speech at the expense of other moments within the film disregards the experience of viewing the film in its entirety and the meanings audiences might ascribe to accumulated scenes and moments, or indeed the broader narrative. In general, the speech becomes the central node upon which to hang an overarching argument concerned with questions of national identity, typically a crucial heuristic of the 'national cinema' tradition. In these interpretations, which take Jimmy's speech at face value, the reflexivity and comedy of the scene is not accounted for. Not only is Jimmy's speech itself an interpretation, it is the culmination in that scene of a series of interpretations by the band of one of James Brown's televised performances of 'Please, Please, Please'. When frontman Deco is asked if he can sing 'that sort of stuff' (as in, James Brown's screams), his response is 'I can sing *anything*', to which Jimmy replies 'It's not the singing, it's how he does it. The showmanship – brilliant [...] It's the *act*, lads – watch!' Jimmy stands up, turns off the TV, and announces to the group: 'That's what you've got to measure up to, lads'.

Here, Jimmy is offering an interpretation of a media text, presenting it as an invitation to the others to emulate soul legend James Brown, contested sceptically by the other members of the band. The gap between the mediated images of Brown and the nascent band is the root of the scene's humour, and Jimmy's earnest 'The Irish are the blacks of' speech is the punchline. Indeed, when Brown drops down onto his knees mid-wail, Deco responds with 'I'm not doin' that, I'll kneecap meself!', humorously undermining his initial show of confidence and further demonstrating to comic effect the gap between The Commitments and Brown's world-class showmanship. It is this incongruous gap between the characters, as Dubliners, and the type of music they wish to perform, that is a crucial element of the comedy of *The Commitments*.

A more nuanced reading by Onkey compares and contrasts the treatment of Jimmy's speech in the film and the book, dissatisfied with the manner in which some have tried to de-race Jimmy's speech. She asserts that in the film

> director Alan Parker ignores the racist history of white appropriation of black music. The film spawned two successful soundtrack albums and even a Commitments tour, essentially a travelling oldies show. Ironically, given the premise of the novel is that the Irish are bankrupt both culturally and economically, the film came to stand for a hipper, youthful Ireland that emerged in the 1990s.
>
> (Onkey 2010: 185)

Onkey's analysis uncovers the contradictions of how a youth film appropriates race in a manner that feels decidedly nostalgic. While the distributor 20th Century Fox initially targeted a young adult audience, 'test screenings demonstrated the picture's appeal to older viewers, due in part to its musical content' (*American Film Institute* n.d.), demonstrating cross-generational appeal in the choice of soul music for the band (explored in more detail in Chapter 3).

In this type of analysis, connections that stress the *musical* context above all seem the least overstretched, and both Onkey and Noel McLaughlin connect the racialised discourses circulating around *The Commitments* with the Irish band U2's output in the late 1980s, which shifted from British post-punk to a more American blues-influenced sound: 'a problematic and flawed attempt by the band to "un-whiten" its sound and to intertwine the two authenticities of blackness and Irishness' (McLaughlin 2014: 181). McLaughlin argues that 'the turn of the 1980s into the 1990s offered up a series of such intertwined yet strained and essentialized "necessary connections" between black and Irish', citing the example of Jimmy's speech (ibid.). These two interpretations situate the film and the speech in a specific period or cultural moment, in which musical 'blackness' was articulated as a 'post-racial' concept. The idea of black and Irish musical connections is further echoed in John O'Flynn's interview-based research carried out between 1999 and 2001 in which he found a repeated articulation by critics and musicians of a rather vague term 'Irish soul', which veered from implying loosely defined Celtic musical heritage to stressing musical linkages between Irishness and blackness forged through waves of migration to the US (O'Flynn 2009).

A more generous view of *The Commitments*'s appropriation of African American music can be applied through the lens of a powerful statement by the New Orleans poet and educator Kalamu ya Salaam, which postulates the global power of African American music to transcend essentialised views of race:

> African American culture has always drawn on everything the world has to offer [...] This is why 'the music' is so revered & so influential worldwide: Everybody can hear themselves in it, find their conditions commented on, feel their dreams aborning. Really, peep this, African Americans are the 20th-century race; [...] We are the world; i.e., the post-colonial world.
>
> (Salaam 1995: 181, punctuation in original)

The power of African American music then is such that it can even resist cultural appropriation, as an expression of the postcolonial condition (i.e. the condition of the majority of the world's population) articulated in Jimmy's speech. For Bronagh Gallagher (Bernie), a Derry native and the only member of the cast who was not from Dublin or its vicinity, the parallels between the postcolonial politics of Ireland in the context of ongoing political struggle, and the struggle articulated in African American soul music, were profound and personal. Underneath the comedy of Jimmy's speech was an acknowledgement of a political and cultural debt to soul music:

> You're looking at a country that was still on its knees economically. Post-colonial, still weeping from church and state collusion. [...] I'm a white working-class girl from Derry. I will never understand that feeling of racism towards the colour of my skin, but we did understand and experience prejudice, and were governed by it. [...] I was born in '72 just four months after Bloody Sunday. [...] The civil rights movement in America triggered the civil rights movement in Northern Ireland. They were an inspiration despite the horror they experienced [......]

We were under British rule. We were British subjects in Northern Ireland deprived of votes, jobs, housing and equality and the British state murdered innocent people marching for change. The struggle in people's hearts was the same, so soul music wasn't our music? It was utterly relatable, so yes it was.

(Gallagher 2021)

Perhaps it is the apparent Irish exceptionalism within the speech which might make it disquieting thirty years on, now that Ireland is ranked one of the wealthiest countries in the world and is a very different place from the 'third world country' described by Jimmy in the dole queue scene. Acknowledging its historical context, pre-Celtic Tiger, and pre-Good Friday Agreement, therefore, allows a more nuanced assessment of Jimmy's speech.

'Stop fucking acting': Performance, social class, and comedy

The above scene can be helpfully situated within the film's overall comedic register of performance and emphasis upon music, which are both in turn bound up in class politics. Just as Robert Arkins's performance of the speech above as Jimmy builds *The Commitments*' own analysis of its significance into itself, much of Jimmy's dialogue provides a critical commentary upon issues around class, identity, music, and authenticity. Early in the film, Jimmy approaches Outspan and Derek, playing pop covers at Imelda's sister's wedding, to form a new band with him. As they return home, walking along the dark grey concrete walkway of Kilbarrack DART station with its gridded backdrop of a high rusted metal fence, the following exchange takes place, a scene which is reproduced in the promotional text 'A Tosser's Glossary' and the press release, highlighting its significance to the film as perceived by Parker:

DEREK: So what kind of music are we gonna be playing, Jimmy?
JIMMY: You're workin' class, right?
OUTSPAN: We would be if there was any work.
JIMMY: So your music should be about where you're from and the sort of people you come from. It should speak the language of the streets. It should be about struggle and sex. An' I don't mean mushy shite love songs about 'I'll hold your hand and love you till the end of time.' I mean riding, fuckin', tongues, gooters, boxes – the works.
OUTSPAN: Jaysis, what music says all that?
JIMMY: Soul.

OUTSPAN/DEREK: Soul?
JIMMY: Soul. We're gonna play Dublin soul.
OUTSPAN: Dublin soul...
DEREK: Fuckin' deadly.

(Beacon Communications 1991c)

As guitarist and bassist, Outspan and Derek form the core of The Commitments band, with each additional member joining in subsequent scenes differentiated slightly from them – Dean with his pretentions to 'art school music', Deco with his ill-mannered arrogance, the two drummers Billy and Mickah's excessive masculine posturing, Joey's age and eccentricity, Steven the medical student's soft-spoken erudition and religious piety, and the three Commitmentettes' strong, assertive femininity. Though Outspan's long curly red hair suggests a hippy sensibility, and physically distinguishes him from the more nondescript Derek, the two characters and their lines are virtually interchangeable. This is exemplified in their chorus of 'soul?' in response to Jimmy in the dialogue above. As the core of the ensemble, they contribute to *The Commitments'* particular dynamics of performance and representation, in which Arkins as Jimmy sounds out his strongly held beliefs about music to the group as a collective, and their responses to him operate almost as a Socratic dialogue. This is demonstrated above, with Jimmy attempting to instil in them his drive and agenda with varying degrees of success. Jimmy's earnestness drives the film and the band's musical ambition, yet it is tempered throughout by both his and the rest of the band's quips and comic interjections. Furthermore, Jimmy is strongly wary of sentimentality ('mushy shite') and pretension (the 'art school'), an outlook situated in the working-class identity he repeatedly affirms.

The above scene articulates an intriguing discourse of authenticity, given that the band will not be performing original material, therefore Jimmy separates out originality from authenticity and suggests that already existing black soul music expresses the collective's working-class struggles more authentically than any other music. Throughout the film, Jimmy continues to reiterate his band and their audience's working-class identity. At the band's first gig in a community centre, he implores the audience to 'please put your working-class hands together', putting class politics front and centre. In her analysis of the novel, Lisa McGonigle points out that: 'as working-class Dubliners, the characters comprise a group traditionally silenced by an imagined Ireland which prioritised and fetishised the rural' (McGonigle 2005: 164), demonstrating the significance of this strategy of representation within Ireland's tradition of cultural nationalism. Parker himself draws parallels between the book, the cast, and his own background (discussed in Chapter 1). This is reiterated throughout the film by Jimmy's earnest pronouncements concerning the band and its career trajectory, and Robert Arkins's serious, intense performance.

Yet we find his earnestness straining at the limits of his class designation and the comedic register of the film. In the regular scenes in which Jimmy imagines himself as famous and interviewed on television by 'Terry', the gap between his aspirations and his circumstances is underlined and sent up by the sight of him sitting in the bath wearing a shower cap, or urinating in a music venue's toilets, while being 'interviewed'. This is one of the key differences between the book and the film which uses Arkins's performance as Jimmy as a visual shorthand to exploit the comic potential of this incongruity. But a more fundamental difference between the film and the book is the act of casting the film from its authentic Dublin milieu, and the notion that with the actors being so close to their characters that they may seem to 'speak' for their generation. Hence, the purpose of the rest of this chapter is to go beyond thinking merely how the various characters that make up The Commitments are represented, and to think about how they are performed.

In the Introduction, I outlined Parker and casting directors Ros and John Hubbard's approach to the casting of *The Commitments*, emphasising their publicised intentions and reiterated discourses of authenticity. The emphasis upon the ensemble as 'unknowns' and musicians more than actors, suggests a closing of the gap between the young actors and the characters they play. Furthermore, the bulk of performance throughout the film is musical performance, not acting. Much academic work on screen performance distinguishes acting as a subset of performance, with acting as 'a dramatic mode of performance that highlights the presence of character' (Drake 2006: 85). Other types of performance, including the musical performances throughout *The Commitments*, are typically 'less committed to character and instead focus upon the display of skills' (ibid.), therefore collapsing the distinction between actor and musician, and between character and performer.

In interviews, Parker frequently emphasised the importance of casting talented musicians with little or no acting experience and then 'turning' them into actors. Yet during a particularly intense night shoot in Dublin's docks, he was heard to shout 'stop fucking acting!' at one of the ensemble (Linehan 2020), and his approach to casting prioritised finding actors who he felt embodied the roles they played, rather than actors who could play a role using their acting skills. Barry King draws a distinction between acting as 'impersonation' and acting as 'personification', such that when assessing performances by professionals, impersonation is regarded as 'good acting' and personification as 'poor acting'. Hence, if a famous actor appears to play themselves, this is considered a sign of a lack of acting ability. Yet paradoxically 'impersonation [...] suppresses what in non-actors would be regarded as the authenticating markers of their personality' (King 1985: 30–1), making acting in this case a barrier to authenticity; hence Parker's peculiar demand to his ensemble.

This idea that the young cast should be 'close' to the characters they play – acting as personification rather in impersonation – was reiterated by the cast. Glen Hansard even mentioned that the casting poster he saw described Outspan as 'someone between 19 and 21 with red hair who plays guitar':

> When they gave me the part to read for I saw it wasn't hard to play because I am a Northside guitarist. That was the whole thing about the film – it was cast so well that everybody in the film is more or less playing themselves.
>
> (Hansard, in interview with Hayes 1991: 18)

It was further reiterated by Parker, who stated that he did not want to feel 'trapped' by the book, and instead 'the character is formed by the personality of the person playing it' (Parker 2016). In terms of casting an ensemble that appear plausible as a group of young Northside musicians, Siegfried Kracauer's concept of 'typage' is relevant: 'the task of portraying wide areas of actual reality, social or otherwise, which calls for "typage" – the recourse to people who are part and parcel of that reality and can be considered typical of it' (Kracauer 1960: 99). Nevertheless, Parker simultaneously relied upon the acting skills of the professionals who played the Commitmentettes (Bronagh Gallagher, Angeline Ball, and Maria Doyle Kennedy) who had previous acting experience, to run the rest of the ensemble's lines for them: 'This was very useful as the girls, in the main, were better actors and it enabled the lads to hear their own lines read with different (and mostly better) intonation than they might employ' (Parker n.d.). There is a paradox at work here – a set of contradictory taste hierarchies – of which Parker was most likely aware. His apparent aversion to 'acting' is directed at individual performers, but not at the ensemble, or at subgroups within the ensemble such as the Commitmentettes, whose acting skills help to power a wider ensemble performance dynamic, supported by plausible 'typage'.

Extratextual knowledge of the actors, especially their lack of acting experience, has the potential to frame interpretation of their performances, which can lead to the assumption that the cast, by virtue of their purported 'closeness' to the characters, are not engaged in *techniques* of performance. Furthermore, attempts to make sense of screen performance – watching it, enjoying it, and talking about it with other viewers – are important too: performance 'is not simply a text; it is a layered social experience, an inter- action between audience and text' (Drake 2003a: 188). Current viewers engage in a process of reading the ensemble screen performance as a set of signifiers, experiencing via screen mediation a performance that occurred thirty or more years ago. This ensemble dynamic is a crucial element, which resists any screen performance analysis associated with academic work on actors and stars which tends to focus on the 'star text' and the 'layering' of an actor or star's screen performance with viewers' knowledge of earlier performances (most famously Dyer 1979), work which is less applicable to the analysis and interpretation of the performance of a cast of unknowns (Straw 2011: 79).

Ernest Mathijs makes a pertinent observation concerning ensemble casts in youth films, and how their non-star dynamic is central to their appeal:

> More often than not, ensemble casts [...] stress a sense of collectivity and community at odds with the structure of protagonism that otherwise characterizes Hollywood cinema. Teen ensemble casts are also exempt from many of the connotations that mark longer careers. Of specific significance here are the so-called 'brat pack' films of debutant actors, such as *American Graffiti* (George Lucas 1973), *The Outsiders* (Francis Ford Coppola 1983) or *Rumble Fish* (Francis Ford Coppola 1983). As expressions of collectivity and marginality, ensembles [...] are at the heart of the sociological appeal of cult films.
>
> (Mathijs 2011: 89)

(Indeed, *The Big Chill*, which Doyle mentioned watching many times as inspiration for adapting the novel for the screen, utilises another ensemble cast in a similar mould.) In this manner, *The Commitments* ensemble can be understood as an expression of collectivity and marginality, and while Jimmy might appear to be the film's protagonist, it is the ensemble dynamic that gives the film its energy, which is expressed in a way that downplays any apparent acting technique as much as possible.

Most scenes in the film involve ensemble performance, which tends to avoid too much scrutiny on any one individual performance, with gig and rehearsal scenes in particular emphasising musical performance. Furthermore, many scenes include substantial numbers of extras, as well as brief appearances by professional actors in supporting roles, while quite a few more banal dialogue exchanges are almost inaudible, either under music, under Jimmy's initial voiceover, or mixed with semi-audible dialogue from extras. The film's overall rhythm and tone is one that repeatedly lay-ers music, overlapping dialogue, sound bridges from one scene to another – a sense of momentum that prevents any individual performances from being scrutinised or assessed for more than a fleeting moment. Moments of privacy for individual characters are rare and regularly undermined by the intrusions of others, providing yet more comic material. For example, Jimmy's moments of introspection, articulated as imagined interviews with his future famous self, are usually interrupted by members of his family, such as his sister or Mr. Rabbitte knocking on the bathroom door, or his younger brother whose head pops up suddenly from under Jimmy's bunk bed after Jimmy says 'and there was that old rock 'n' roll demon, S.E.X. Sex, Jimmy? Sex, Terry', exclaiming 'Sex!'. It is useful then to briefly con-sider a few scenes, including one not burnished by interruptions of extras, minor characters, or musical performance, and which follows on from a musical performance which I will discuss first.

The band's first gig in front of a crowd (which does not occur until nearly one hour into the film), at St Brigid's Community Centre under an initially misspelled 'Heroin Kills' banner, takes up nearly ten minutes of screen time, of which four minutes plays out before the musical performance actu-ally starts. This includes the technical set-up, the band getting changed into their suits, and the arrival of the crowd, all of which not only create a sense of anticipation, but also set up an interplay between the ensemble of the band, and the various supporting characters such as the priest and Jimmy's family, and the crowd at the gig (a mixture of extras, some faces eagle-eyed viewers might recognise from the earlier audition sequence, and the band members' families). This crowd act almost as a surrogate for the viewer, or indeed a cinema audience, which allows for an interplay between them and the band. Mathijs argues that this is crucial to the ensemble performance dynamic in which:

> notions of the audience, or of a strongly implied viewer, inform the acting in profound ways. Ensembles play off each other rather than off reality; or, rather, the members of ensembles play off the received perceptions of themselves held by other cast members and audiences. In other words, it is important for someone in an ensemble cast to act in the way the audience expects, and to make use of that expectation in their playing with (or off) other cast members.
>
> (Mathijs 2011: 90)

Indeed, in this scene, the audience does not even need to be implied, as an audience is there, and forms an additional layer of ensemble performance in itself. Once the band starts to play, there is relatively limited dialogue, with the music carrying the scene. Instead, we see multiple exchanges of glances, reaction shots, and inaudible conversation in the crowd, that play out as a sort of comic dumbshow, between a few interjections of dialogue.

In this scene, the band starts with a stumbling yet enthusiastic performance of 'Mr Pitiful', then 'Bye Bye Baby' with Natalie on vocals and a resentful Deco on tambourine, followed by a rambunctious rendition of 'Show Me' which culminates in Derek getting electrocuted. During the first song, the camera follows the reactions of the crowd as much as the efforts of the band on stage, emphasising the band's nerves, but also showing Mickah's hyperactive efforts to both patrol and work the crowd – an energetically ostensive performance by Dave Finnegan. We see close-ups of a nervous Derek looking like he might throw up, and an anxious Outspan perturbed to see Mickah chatting to Outspan's mother and pointing at the stage, just a few examples amidst an energetic pattern of editing and camera movement. During the first song, Deco addresses the audience with an over the top: 'Hello Dublin! I hope yiz like me group!' to which Imelda reacts loudly with 'fuck off!' This exchange establishes from early on the sense of Deco's ego as both a crucial force of the band's audience appeal and a destabilising source of annoyance to the group, as well as Imelda's no-nonsense assertiveness at odds with patriarchal notions of femininity.

The gig ends abruptly with Deco's mic stand connecting with Derek's bass, causing Derek an electric shock and blowing the building's fuses. The following scene at the hospital plays out in quite a different manner. Unlike the dynamic movement and editing of the gig scene, with its interconnected gestures and reactions, and musical drive, this is a less physical scene with relatively long, uninterrupted shots of some of the group seated in the hospital waiting room (see Figure 2.1), driven by exchanges of humorous dialogue and a more realist than comic mode of performance (Drake 2004: 80). It is notably a Clement and La Frenais scene, with no equivalent in Doyle's novel, in which the characters speculate about whether Derek dying might make them rich and famous, and the various ways that famous musicians have died, in particular choking on their own vomit. In a delicious deadpan, Natalie delivers the punchline, 'Maybe we can get Deco to choke on his own vomit'.

In scenes such as this one, the lines do the work, and often it does not matter who says what line. We remember the exchanges, almost like a joke or routine, rather than which individual said what. After Derek is discharged and The Commitments make their way home, a scene features just Jimmy, Outspan, and Derek – back to the 'core' of the band. Though only a minute long, this scene is a strikingly serious one (of which there are not many), with considerably more scrutiny on individual cast members. Derek and Outspan seem discouraged, and Jimmy moves from trying to muster their

Figure 2.1 Hospital waiting room scene

enthusiasm to an emphatic rant about the importance of 'stand[ing] out from the rest of the tossers'. Here, the focus returns to Jimmy's role as manager, as lead character, and Arkins as lead performer, away from the ensemble dynamic. A focus on individual characters runs into danger of straining the cast's acting capabilities. In his Blu-ray commentary, Parker rather cruelly remarks that Ken McCluskey is 'not the greatest actor in the world. You can see his thought process as he tries to remember the lines' (Parker 2016). This observation suggests an approach that avoided these types of scenes as much as possible, and whenever they were needed, kept them short and punchy.

Parker described the rehearsal process as an intensive one which involved turning his cast into 'an accomplished ensemble theatre group' (Parker n.d.), and which Ball and Gallagher described as feeling especially 'focussed' and 'clinical': 'There was a significant amount of rehearsals before anything was shot [...] rehearsals every morning on set, before we shot anything and before the scene was lit' (Gallagher 2021), with Ball describing 5.30 a.m. starts and twelve-hour working days (Ball 2021). With the music scenes shot later in the day once the group had warmed up, both performers describe a very different dynamic, in which 'no matter how tired you are, because of the music having that drive, that rhythm, every time we gave it 100%' (ibid.). And as Gallagher puts it:

Once that music kicked in, I was in my element. [...] It was shot like a film, but because the music was in the performances, it was like another layer on top of the acting, […] Equally enjoyable and challenging in different ways, but it was kind of a relief, a release to do the singing stuff. […] You were definitely still in character, but you were more relaxed because you were in the zone. The music was so dominant, in the background and over the top, you just plunged into it […] It was such a support, as opposed to the stillness of a quiet room and someone going 'action' and you have to deliver your line.

(Gallagher 2021)

Towards the end of the film, as the band reach their musical peak, relations become strained and the band descend into rows and fights. In his commentary, Parker described the fight scenes as taking place at a point where the cast were all 'very comfortable with their acting' and that the scenes were 'dramatically the most interesting to do' with a lot of improvisation and overlapping dialogue that was difficult to capture and that made for difficult editing and intercutting. He describes how 'the beauty is the spontaneity' and that with the cast all so comfortable at that point, the 'directorial advice is minimal by then; the challenge is covering it all' (Parker 2016). What these descriptions indicate is that the work of rehearsal and reciting lines, rather than restricting the cast, allowed them eventually to have the freedom to improvise as they gained confidence together. The combination of physical fighting with verbal improvisation is particularly challenging, hence by the end of the film the cast's increased accomplishment as improvisers and physical performers parallels the film's narrative of increased musical accomplishment.

A new generation: Youth, gender, sex, and religion

The band is set out from the beginning as a catalyst for upward social mobility and status, not only in terms of social class, but also heteronormative notions of masculinity. Jimmy promises his male recruits that with the band's success they'll be 'fighting women off, they'll be throwing their knickers on the stage'. Despite the male band members' fixation with the Commitmentettes as 'tits' and 'arse', the female characters' assertiveness, and the strength and exuberance of Gallagher's, Doyle's, and Ball's performances, undermines any sense that the film's representational politics around gender are regressive. Though Ball was not entirely comfortable with the sexism articulated in relation to her part as Imelda, exemplified by Outspan's line about 'Imelda Quirke's arse coming down a ladder' (Ball 2021), and the politics of sex and gender in such moments are dubious, they need to be understood within a context in which the old stranglehold of the Catholic Church, and its puritanical attitude to sex, was in the process of loosening. The rest of this chapter will consider Irish youth masculinities and femininities depicted throughout the film, in the context of the unfolding socio-economic change in Ireland, precipitating the emergence of the Celtic Tiger and the decline of church influence.

A key characteristic of how youth is represented and performed in *The Commitments* is not so much in the semantic content of dialogue, but in the prominence of working-class Dublin accents and of frequent swearing. While the script featured many swear words, and the accompanying 'A Tosser's Glossary' booklet explained more obscure Dublin slang to the press, additional swearing was added in improvisation by the cast. Casting efforts were focussed on Dublin, with a view to finding young people with authentic Dublin accents and dialect, rather than potentially unconvincing non-Dublin or non-Irish actors. This focus chimes with what Nicholas O'Riordan identifies as 'an overarching negativity' in the public sphere's 'consideration of accent in Irish film', a longstanding Hollywood heritage of non-Irish actors making unsuccessful attempts at sounding Irish, and unconvincing accents a popular subject of ridicule (O'Riordan 2015: 35). Parker presents a combination of strong Dublin accents, sexualised slang, and swearing as an authentic rendition of contemporary Ireland, and part of a history of colonial oppression, with Parker's opening of the Glossary stating:

> For centuries the Irish were forced to speak English. They got their own back by using it better. From Wilde to Shaw and Beckett to Behan. But the truth is, that the Irish haven't been using English for years. They have their own language. And it isn't Gaelic.
>
> (Beacon Communications 1991a)

Ball considers swearing inherent to her authentic working-class Dublin speech: 'We use it almost like a punctuation. I have to watch myself as well. I live in London and I'm always using the f-word, and I find people looking at me!' (Ball 2021). However, as a native of Derry, Gallagher had to adopt a Dublin accent. As a fan of the book and Parker's earlier films, she was determined to audition, despite concerns from the Hubbards who advised her that Parker would be reluctant to see her because of her strong Derry accent (Gallagher 2021). In her performance as Bernie, she was so nervous about getting the accent right that she kept swearing: ''cos that would help me get into the accent. It wasn't meant to be, I didn't mean to swear so much!'; and as a result, it is believed that Gallagher holds the joint record, with Joe Pesci in *Goodfellas* (1990), for the most uses of the word 'fuck' in a single film ('*The Commitments*' 2007). As the only younger member of the cast with prior acting experience, her performance technique meant that accent and swearing were inextricably connected.

Old fashioned, patriarchal ideas characterise swearing as 'unladylike', and given the preponderance of swearing amongst a young, mostly male cast, the fact that Gallagher holds such a record demonstrates that the Commitmentettes' performance of femininity subverts expectations and resists an older established order. Yet despite the emphasis upon authentic Dublin accents, the band has to adopt a transatlantic voice in order to perform 'Dublin soul'. In their first rehearsal, Jimmy interrupts the band's rendition of 'Mustang Sally' when the Commitmentettes sing 'Roy-ad Sally Roy-ad', with 'Look, don't use your own accents. It's "Ride Sally Ride" not "Roy-ad Sally Roy-ad"'. The voice of *The Commitments* emphasises authenticity, but not originality, given that the band plays cover versions. But the highlighting of language in a moment that emphasises the Commitmentettes' sexuality and the sexual power of the song is defiant (see Figure 2.2). 'Mustang Sally' remains a popular song amongst fans of the film who were young when it was released. Attempting to account for the song's enduring popularity, given that Doyle did not select it in his novel and is not keen on it, he suggested that it gave a 'license to be crude – ROY-AD SALLY ROY-AD [...] to be allowed [to] shout that was a good deal more liberating than it might seem now' (Doyle 2021).

Revisiting TV coverage of the film, the level of fascination with the use of slang and swearwords is striking. The Irish-language current affairs programme *Cúrsaí* featured interviews with teenagers who had just watched the film, with the reporter repeatedly asking what they thought of the 'bad words', largely to the teenagers' amusement ('Tuairimí na nDéagóirí faoi "The Commitments"' 1991, my translation). In the youth magazine *Jo Maxi*'s coverage of *The Commitments*' premiere at the Savoy Cinema in

Figure 2.2 'Roy-ad Sally Roy-ad'

Dublin city centre, the actor Gabriel Byrne praised the film for being free of stereotypes and rebuking apparently widespread criticism of the film's language, asserting that the language is 'real', 'natural, and off the street' (*'The Commitments* Premiere' 1991). These types of reception affirm swearing as a form of youthful rebellion, as authentically Dublin, and as a liberation from stultifying past representations.

Bernie, Natalie, and Imelda are noticeably more confident, including more sexually confident, than the young men in the band, who are rather timid in contrast with Joey "The Lips", an unlikely lothario with whom all three women become romantically entangled. Refreshingly, any attempts to shame them are neutralised by the girls. Bernie corrects the accusation by the men that Joey 'got off with Natalie', retorting that 'Natalie got off with *him*'. Deco's obnoxious response, 'then she's a slut' results in Bernie pushing him off the piano he lies on. And Bernie is not the exception – as illustrated in my discussion of performance above, both Imelda and Natalie are unashamedly caustic in retaliation to the young men in the band, especially Deco's sexism and egotism. While the film does not sanitise the regressive attitude to sexuality which still dominated Ireland at the time (at this point, divorce, homosexuality, and abortion were all illegal), viewed thirty or more years later the strength of the female characters is refreshing, and signals what would be a tectonic shift in social attitudes to come.

The more socially conservative character in the band is Steven, yet even he swears exuberantly as the band's performances improve – 'we were fuckin' deadly!' Injuring his hand at one point, shouting 'Fuck! Fuck Fuck!', Natalie chides him with 'Three Hail Marys for You!' He is differentiated from the others with his more conservative clothing and soft-spoken erudition, but most of all with his involvement with religion. He plays the organ in church, and attends confession, wrestling with a personal battle between pious studiousness and the worldlier fun of playing soul music. In his confession, he states that he has had 'lustful thoughts' about the women in the band, and that 'when I studied, I would sing hymns, but now all I can sing is "When A Man Loves A Woman" by Marvin Gaye'. To his astonishment, the priest corrects him with 'Percy Sledge'. A scene written by Clement and La Frenais, it is one which Doyle dislikes. 'That scene shouldn't have been there because he wouldn't have gone to confession. None of them would have been mass goers. The gag itself is funny. But it was just a gag' (Doyle 2021). For Doyle, the generation he depicted had turned their back on the Catholic Church completely, despite it retaining its stranglehold on the state, and such moments lack authenticity in their depiction of the younger generation.

Nevertheless, the film's references to religion add another layer to the narrative, which Cronin has argued makes the film more sociologically sophisticated than the book (Cronin 2006: 30–4). Steven's reactionary piety was to manifest itself beyond the film. Michael Aherne, who played Steven, is described by Parker as someone who 'still plays organ in his local church and is quite outspoken with his right wing views' (Parker n.d.). Laury Oaks describes a remarkable moment in the year following the film's release in which Aherne, still riding the tide of *The Commitments* fame, made a speech at a march and rally by the notorious traditionalist Catholic anti-abortion Youth Defence on Saturday 6 June 1992, culminating with a rewording of Jimmy's speech: 'Say it now, say it loud, I'm anti-abortion and I'm proud!' (Oaks 1998: 145).

This 'pro-life' rally took place amidst justifiable outrage, protest, and debate concerning the 'X case', in which a fourteen-year-old rape victim was denied permission to travel to England to obtain an abortion (at that time illegal in Ireland). At this point, as Oaks explains, with Ireland having a youthful population in which more than half were under the age of 26, Youth Defence characterised themselves as a 'necessary' backlash against mainstream media that was portraying the youth of Ireland as a new generation with new ideals, and that they were formed to defend against 'attacks on the social fabric of traditional Irish culture and faith' (145). In a vivid ethnographic account of the day, Oaks also describes a moment at the start of the march, in which, following a blessing from a priest, and carrying a large Irish tricolour, the marchers sang a reworded version of Pink Floyd's 'Another Brick in the Wall' (from *Pink Floyd: The Wall* [1982]), another unwitting example of Alan Parker's cultural impact upon that generation of Irish youth: 'We don't need your legislation/We don't need no birth control/ We don't want your referendum/Hey! Taoiseach! Leave our kids alone/All in all you're just another prick in the Dáil' (146). The manner in which Youth Defence incorporated such references to popular culture as a reactionary attack on women's rights to bodily autonomy seems now absurd yet chilling.

The film draws distinct parallels between Ireland's church and religious establishment and soul music, with soul functioning as an alternative religion. For the young band, music, rather than church, offers salvation. As the elder figure, Joey "The Lips" has priest-like qualities, sermonising about the past deeds of deceased musicians, giving the band a name that itself suggests a sort of religious conviction, and describing them as 'the saviours of soul', a line which Jimmy later parrots in an interview with a journalist. Joey's eccentric mother is depicted as religious, singing hymns to a statue of the Virgin Mary, another scene disliked by Doyle: 'I thought that was an outsider's view of Ireland' (Doyle 2021). This brief scene occurs just after Jimmy's 'interview' in his bunk bed, discussed above, referencing sex, and leads into a scene in Joey's bedroom, in which he plays a record of the theme from *Shaft*, recites the lyrics to an unseen presence in his bed, revealed to be Bernie who responds 'will ye stop talking shite Joey' before they kiss.

Despite emphasising that 'the rhythm of soul is the rhythm of ridin'', Jimmy is himself rather chaste and uninterested in sex beyond its potential commercial appeal, rejecting romantic overtures from Natalie, and decrying 'sex, sex, sex, it ruins everything'. After the band's session with a photographer, a shot that starts with a poster being pasted on a graffiti-covered wall featuring the band photo captioned 'THE COMMITMENTS – SAVIOURS OF SOUL' then pans to reveal a bible-clutching priest walking down the street, while young boys on bicycles cycle in the opposite direction, before cutting to a close-up of candles being lit in the church, and Steven sitting in the pews waiting to make a confession. These scenes set the band's adventures in this wider socio-religious context and literalise visually the idea that the younger generation might be moving in the opposite direction of the church. Yet both Steven's piety and the rest of the male members of the band's contrasting mix of bravado and inexperience around sex suggest a more complex picture.

Outspan sums up Joey's peculiarity and difference to others in the group, as 'he talks like a bleedin' priest, and he's wearin' slippers!', and also singles out 'the medical student, he's not like the rest of us', as well as age and class differences which he sees as 'softer' iterations of masculinity. Jimmy's justification for recruiting them, despite having little in common, is their usefulness: Joey for his experience of 'played with all the greats', and Steven's medical knowledge: 'the places we'll be playing, it could be useful to have someone that can bandage heads', articulating the ever-present threat of violence. Throughout the film masculinity is inseparable from social class and economic status. It is also articulated in terms of physicality and aggression, especially for male characters lower on the socio-economic rung such as Billy and Mickah. In contrast, Imelda's fiancé 'dopey Greg', is loathed yet envied by the male members of the band for his hold on Imelda, and for being 'a prick with a job', despite looking 'like he models knitting patterns'.

In her work on masculinity and screen performance, Donna Peberdy emphasises the potential to investigate how masculinity is performed, 'reading such performances in their social and historical contexts', rather than reiterating notions of representation of masculinity ('doing masculinity') (Peberdy 2011: 10). Much of the comedy, especially the physical comedy of *The Commitments*, revolves around the performance of masculinity with strength, violence, and physicality as a compensation for socio-economic disadvantage. Both Billy and Mickah are drummers, a role traditionally considered lower status, lower skilled, lower paid, and barely recognised as truly 'musical' (Brennan 2020). In contrast, the only instrument in the band that requires classical training, the piano, is played by Steven, the only middle-class band member. The drummer is the only replaceable, interchangeable band member, with Billy's departure barely disrupting the band's progress. The disposability of the drummer in The Commitments is reminiscent of the drummer gag in *This is Spinal Tap* (Reiner 1984), in which multiple drummers die in preposterous accidents and are replaced throughout the course of the film.

Mirroring the characters' socio-economic status, drummers are seen as a disposable underclass, and in *The Commitments* assert an aggressive physicality. Billy's reason for departing is his fear that his hatred of Deco will provoke a violent reaction in him which will endanger his probation. Given that Mickah is hired as security despite the band being afraid of him, his almost seamless transition from repeatedly hitting his head with a microphone during a soundcheck, to physically wrestling members of the audience into behaving appropriately during a gig, to enthusiastically playing the drums, fits the notion of the drummer as hyper-masculine, aggressive, and hyper-physical – brawn rather than brains. The physicality of Dave Finnegan's performance as Mickah is particularly striking in the crowd work described earlier, and in a later bravura performance during the band's gig at a roller disco, in which he abandons the drums to run into the crowd and attack the gangster Duffy (Liam Carney), thwarting his attempt to extort money from Jimmy, then returns to the drums to finish 'Take Me to the River'. Parker mentioned that in audition, Finnegan impressed him by swallowing a microphone, and this trick is shown in the final montage at the end

Figure 2.3 Mickah swallows microphone

of the film (see Figure 2.3). Hence, Finnegan's energetic, hyper-masculine physicality in musical performance is later incorporated into the film itself as part of his performance as Mickah.

Conclusion

The Commitments represents and performs ideas concerning race, gender, social class, and religion in complex, interconnected ways, which are perhaps surprising given its light-hearted, comedic tone. Rather than the film holding a mirror to the socio-economic reality facing young people in Dublin in the late 1980s and early 1990s, it uses techniques of adaptation, casting, rehearsal, and performance that contribute to this complexity. Furthermore, the film's narrative builds in its own strategies of interpretation, allowing characters to comment upon race, performance, sexuality, fame, and status, which have later percolated throughout the wider circulation of media and cultural texts before and after the making of the film. What is striking about revisiting the film with close attention to screen performance and comedy is how the comic dynamics of the film are so intrinsically bound up with ideas of authenticity concerning class, dialogue, swearing, and rambunctious performance of gender, further highlighted by the cast's energetic youthfulness. Furthermore, the comedy of the film is an inherent part of its complex engagement with broader sociocultural themes, with ostensive performance and comedic juxtapositions crucial to the film's appeal and wider resonance.

3 Youth culture and music scenes in 1980s and 1990s Dublin

At the heart of *The Commitments* is a concern with popular music and identity, cultural and subcultural, articulated through processes in which a younger generation uses music to define itself in relation to the past. When Jimmy defiantly tells his Elvis-loving father that 'Elvis is not soul', to which Mr. Rabbitte roars 'Elvis is God!', and Jimmy retorts with 'I never pictured God with a fat gut and a corset singing "My Way" at Caesar's Palace', it feels like a real attack upon his father, his father's generation, and that generation's apparent lack of credibility. And yet, this attack feels slightly out of time – while Jimmy might be showing off his musical knowledge and blues-based rock cultural capital, his identification with 1960s soul and his sartorial style (sometimes slightly rockabilly, sometimes slightly Mod) make him a somewhat retro figure of youthful rebellion, disconnected from the music scenes that defined Ireland and the neighbouring UK of the 1980s and early 1990s such as post-punk, indie, or even hip-hop and acid house.

That the Rabbitte family generational conflict is over Elvis is interesting, with the King of Rock 'n' Roll being a pivotal figure of 1950s youth culture and cool, and the 1970s 'sell out' Elvis of sequinned jumpsuits epitomising uncool kitsch. Juxtaposed with other scenes in the film, such as the hospital scene in which members of The Commitments discuss ways in which various rock musicians died young ('choked on his own vomit', 'drowned', 'vomit', 'vomit'), or when Joey "The Lips" recites a list of musical legends he claims he has jammed with, including Sam Cooke ('poor Sam', alluding to his premature death at just thirty-three), it suggests that Elvis's sin in Jimmy's eyes was that he got old (or rather, middle-aged) before he died. Hence, Jimmy reasserts the centrality of youth to popular music over any claims his Elvis-loving father might have over it.

In this chapter, I will explore the vibrant young music scenes of Dublin in the 1980s and 1990s and the influence of US and transnational musical subcultures. This is integral to the film and book's setting; indeed, Roddy Doyle has stated that when he was a schoolteacher in Kilbarrack in the late

DOI: 10.4324/9780429296048-4

1980s: 'every kid in Dublin is or was or will be or wants to be in a band' (Gritten 1991), demonstrating how Dublin's music scene at that time was the city's key youth culture, with music as young people's primary creative outlet. Yet the film's relationship with the reality of 1990s Dublin is hardly straightforward, therefore this chapter will explore the film's relationship with traditions of realism and Hollywood genres such as the musical. The choice of soul music will be interrogated, given the vibrancy and variety of Ireland's live music scene at the time, and the national and international popularity of acts such as U2 and Sinéad O'Connor. Why soul? Why not rock, punk, or electronic music? Doyle has given a fairly glib explanation, that a rock band would have consisted of just four young males, whereas the addition of backing singers allowed him to introduce some female characters and therefore more dramatic possibilities. However, this chapter will argue that Doyle's explanation does not tell the whole story and will provide a broader analysis, considering the transnational dimensions of black popular music and examining debates around music versus industry articulated in the film and beyond.

A partial snapshot of Dublin's 1990s music scenes

It is useful to distinguish between music scenes and music industry, even though the two interact. This section will concentrate on music scenes, with a later section focussing on industry, which can be considered in terms of tensions between subcultural capital and music industry capitalism. Given the lack of much of a soul or funk scene in Dublin at the time, this choice of music has never entirely sat with the youthful premise of the film. A 1991 *LA Times* article states: 'Doyle doesn't claim that there is a host of young soul bands in Dublin performing Stax and Motown covers. "I had them play soul because it allowed the band to be bigger, and I could introduce more characters"' (Gritten 1991). Similarly, the new (in the early 1990s) underground dance music scene took some time to be depicted cinematically, and in Irish cinema it was not until 2018's appropriately named *Dublin Oldschool* (Tynan) that it remotely figured, despite the Mansion House raves of 1990 taking place in the very same year as the Mansion House's auditions for *The Commitments*.[1] An electronic music scene popular with teenagers and twenty-somethings was having its moment, but this moment was underground, niche, and separate from Dublin's wider music scenes which had caught industry attention.

There are multiple possible ways to think this through. Notably, Ireland is also known for Van Morrison and Rory Gallagher, some of the greatest purveyors of soul, R&B, and blues; also pertinent is Ireland's continued devotion to the blues rock of Thin Lizzy and the band's charismatic black

Irish frontman Phil Lynott. It is also worth considering U2 again, and how their albums *The Joshua Tree* (1987) and *Rattle and Hum* (1988) projected a type of transnational Americana. In the same year that *The Commitments* equated black American soul music with the working-class Dublin experience, Sinéad O'Connor had a huge hit with a cover of Prince's 'Nothing Compares 2 U', making a black American song her own. Irish rock therefore had already gained international standing through an embrace of African American music and blues-based rock, if not soul music per se. Taking into consideration these notable cultural and historical moments helps to contextualise *The Commitments*' commercially successful choice of soul for its distinctively Dublin setting.

Furthermore, the narrative device that contains the film's music choices is, in effect, Jimmy Rabbitte's musical tastes, which are repeatedly articulated through dialogue between him and other characters. Early on, Outspan invites Jimmy to manage his and Derek's band by praising his musical tastes, stating 'you know everything about music, Jimmy. You had that Frankie Goes to Hollywood album before anyone else had heard of them, and you were the first to realise they were shite'. Later, with The Commitments formed, a montage sequence soundtracked by the song 'Destination Anywhere' shows the group excitedly discussing and arguing through the night, from pub, to street, to late night café, and finally on the DART. It is here that Jimmy announces to the band 'Listen! From now on I don't want you listening to Guns 'n' Roses and The Soup Dragons. I want you on a strict diet of soul', pronouncing it 'the rhythm of sex, and the rhythm of the factory too – the working man's rhythm'. Comic interjections from the others such as 'you want us to sing as if we're roidin' with someone?' (Bernie) and 'Not in the factory I'm in – there isn't much rhythm in guttin' fish' (Natalie) do nothing to dampen his passion and enthusiasm for 1960s soul above the rock, metal, and dance-influenced indie landscape of the early 1990s. In *Performing Rites*, Simon Frith argues that 'part of the pleasure of popular culture is talking about it', talk which is routinely riddled with 'value judgements':

> To be engaged with popular culture is to be discriminating [...] 'Good' and 'bad' or their vernacular versions ('brilliant' or 'crap') are the most frequent terms in everyday cultural conversation. [However] Value arguments [...] aren't simply rituals of 'I like/you like'; [...] they are based in reason, evidence, persuasion. Every music fan knows that moment of frustration when one can only sit the person down and say (or, rather, shout) despairingly, 'But just listen to her! Isn't she fantastic!'

(Frith 1996: 4)

Substituting Frith's vernacular 'brilliant' and 'crap' with the Dublin vernacular 'deadly' and 'shite' reveals a crucial aspect of *The Commitments'* dramatic drive. Frith goes on to argue that while this type of engagement is the stuff of everyday friendship, for bands the stakes are much higher. It is musicians

> who have to get along well enough to play together, who have to balance the creative/destructive effects of shared and different tastes, and who conduct the delicate business of coming together (and falling apart) almost entirely through stated pop judgements.
>
> (Frith 1996: 5)

The dramatic tension of The Commitments plays out these tensions Frith identifies. While non-musical factors such as class, religious, and sexual tensions contribute to the band's destruction, musical disagreements are arguably more important. Of course, these musical disagreements are not necessarily separate from identity issues, for example, Dean's arguments with Jimmy and Joey about jazz and 'art school bollocks' have a strong subtext concerning class politics.

Jimmy's recruitment ad in the paper reads: 'Have you got soul? If so, the World's Hardest Working Band is looking for you. [...] Rednecks and Southsiders need not apply'. While use of the word 'soul' makes the band's genre reasonably explicit, the phrase 'have you got soul' is more ambiguous. A singer or musician could be described as having soul, despite not playing music classified as soul. The use of the phrase 'the World's Hardest Working Band' references James Brown, 'The Hardest Working Man in Show Business', presupposing some degree of musical knowledge, and signposting Jimmy's later 'say it loud' speech to the rest of the band. The wording of the ad in the film is the same as in the book, and as in the book, Jimmy asks auditioners one question: 'who're your influences?', making snap judgements based on their answers. But obviously, the key difference between the book and the film is that in the film we can hear the auditioners' music. The unsuccessful auditions in the film take up a full six minutes of gloriously energetic music-filled screen time, whereas in the book they are dealt with more concisely, to the point that the section can be quoted in full here:

There were more callers on Monday. Jimmy liked none of them. He took
    phone numbers and threw them in the bin.
He judged on one question: influences.
   – Who're your influences
   – U2.

    – Simple Minds.

    – Led Zeppelin.

    – No one really.

They were the most common answers. They failed.

    –Jethro Tull an' Bachman Turner Overdrive.

Jimmy shut the door on that one without bothering to get the phone number.

    He didn't even open the door to three of them. A look out his parents'
    bedroom window to them was enough.

                                    (Doyle 1987/1998: 17–8)

The brevity of the passage contrasts with the film's long audition sequence, in which we see and hear dozens of young hopefuls in a series of brief yet impassioned appearances. The musical styles performed are diverse, ranging from folk rock, to metal, to indie pop, to Irish trad. According to Parker, everyone who appears had either auditioned at the open call for the musicians or read for the film (Parker 2016). Dublin's actual live music scene was therefore integral to this sequence, and showcases a diverse range of influences, even if none of them are right for Jimmy's purposes. As Michael Cronin argues, 'By incorporating the auditions process into the film, Parker makes explicit the musical sophistication of the culture from which the young performers emerge' (Cronin 2006: 26). Furthermore,

> the specificity of the musical culture is the co-existence and blend of different influences [...] Rather than a notion of the city or indeed the country being the unpolluted reservoir of indigenous musical purity, *The Commitments* in the long auditioning sequence portrays the culture's specific strengths as lying in its porousness.
>
>   (24–5)

Hence, we get a sense of Dublin's music scene as fully integrated into global, transnational musical trends and influences, rather than narrowly 'Irish' in any traditionalist sense.

    The sequence condenses time to comic effect; some auditioners don't get past the front door, a variety of punks, rockers, hippies, and New Romantics. Others are given the opportunity to perform to Jimmy in the house. Detail concerning the royalties for songs enrich our knowledge of the process. Parker wrote a fake Bob Dylan song and a fake heavy metal song with Paul Bushnell to avoid paying excessive royalties. The sequence also features a fake Cajun song, 'Elvis Was a Cajun', which allows an amusing interjection by Jimmy's father – 'That's blasphemy! Elvis wasn't a bleedin' Cajun!' All of the Parker/Bushnell specially composed pastiches cost a fixed fee of US$425/IR£250, regardless of length.

In contrast, Parker includes 'I Dreamed a Dream' from *Les Misérables* as an obscure reference to the fact that he nearly directed a film of *Les Misérables*, adding a hefty US$10,000 for just seventeen seconds (Beacon Communications 1991b).

One song, 'Beauty Queen', is credited to Emily Dawson who is also the performer in the sequence, wearing a striking punk outfit with bleached hair and heavy make-up. With a licensing fee of just US$180/IR£106.80 for ten seconds it was demonstrably cost effective to use compositions by local artists. However, the authorship has been disputed and was the subject of an unsuccessful lawsuit claiming breach of copyright by singer and journalist Aisling Meath. Both Meath and Dawson were members of the long-running (and still active) Dublin punk group Paranoid Visions. Another group member, Peter Jones, also threatened to sue for unlicensed use of the song ('Singer Fails …' 2000). This is an example of how the more DIY elements of music scenes can enter into contested territory when the legal frameworks of the entertainment industry attempt to assign copyright. This conflict between the joy of collaborative creativity and the machinations of capitalism re-emerges within the narrative of the film and beyond, as discussed below.

Jimmy's comically ruthless judgement articulated in the book is transposed amusingly to the film. We do not hear him engage in any conversation with auditioners, beyond 'who're your influences?' and his reaction to all of them, regardless of their musical ability or style is either a door slam or a look of bafflement. While the audition process draws from the city's music scene, it is noticeable that none of the musicians plays soul, or indeed any form of black music. Furthermore, we never actually see the successfully recruited members of the band audition. As in the book, their success is purely on the basis of their stated influences, rather than musical performance; for saxophonist Dean it's 'Clarence Clemons and the guy from Madness', and for Billy the drummer, quite incongruously it's 'Animal from the Muppets'. Ultimately for Jimmy, musical talent matters less than having suitable musical influences, chiming with Frith's assertion that it is musical judgement and values that matter most of all for a band to work collectively. This is paralleled in the pre-production of the film, in which Parker auditioned as much for the ability to argue about music as to play it. An improvisatory exercise in the audition process was instructed by Parker as follows:

I want you to pretend you're really into soul music, and this bloke here, […] he's saying it's shit basically, and you're to *go for it'*. This was no problem for me because I was really into jazz at the time which is even more obscure […] I only had to replace jazz in my mind with soul and it was easy – so off we went […] We got into a big row, all improvised […] There was a lot of cursing. I think he liked the cursing; the passion.

(Smith 2020)

However, as Parker stated at the time: 'we're looking at actors first, and musicians […] but we're open to using people with no experience of film. I'm looking at anybody, anybody who wants to be in the movie, preferably if they are musicians' (Dwyer 1990b: 1–2). Looking at 'actors first' has not usually been emphasised in the publicity around the film, which tended to suggest that musical talent was at the forefront of the casting process. Indeed, the first youth to appear in the audition sequence at the Rabbittes' door, credited as 'Kid with Harmonica', is played by Lance Daly (now a film director). Though of school-going age, Daly was already acting in theatre and advertising, and was invited to audition, rather than queuing up at the Mansion House (Daly 2020). Nevertheless, Daly's account of the audition process still emphasises spontaneity and contingency, to an amusing extent:

I actually had a harmonica in my pocket by chance when I went for the audition. So I auditioned for it, and came out and another guy asked me 'hey, can I borrow your harmonica?' He took it in and auditioned and he never gave it back to me.

(Ibid.)

Under some pressure to cast a star, Parker had a meeting with Van Morrison to discuss a cameo role, however, this was not pursued as a bad-tempered Morrison asserted that The Commitments should be playing his music (Clement and La Frenais 2019: 190). The film had a significant relationship with the Irish music industry, which – in contrast with the struggling Irish film industry – was doing well. Both U2 and Sinéad O'Connor had gained global success, and despite *The Commitments'* rejection of rock in favour of soul, U2's influence is strongly felt throughout the film, with multiple mentions of the band (and O'Connor) throughout the dialogue ('I bet U2 are shitting themselves', to give just one example). In addition, U2's touring sound engineer Joe O'Herlihy is credited as the film's Sound Consultant, and U2's manager Paul McGuinness is thanked in the credits. Kevin Killen, who worked as an engineer on U2's 1984 album *The Unforgettable Fire*, recorded the two Commitments albums at Windmill Lane Studios in Ringsend, Dublin where U2 also recorded. And in an intriguing detail, the 'Shy Skateboard Auditioner', who is too embarrassed to sing on Jimmy Rabbitte's request, is played by Peter Rowan, who was the boy photographed for the covers of U2's albums *Boy* and *War* (see Figure 3.1).

Figure 3.1 Shy Skateboard Auditioner

According to Daly, Rowan had been acting at the time, and was invited to audition. Nevertheless, his brief appearance in no way crowbars his link with U2 into the film; indeed the link is wilfully obscure. Instead, it captures a crucial aspect of his own distinct subcultural identity: 'Peter was there the same day I was. Peter was a skater and they had a skateboard in the script I think, so it was sort of perfect for him' (Daly 2020). Hence, these connections make *The Commitments*' link with the city's scenes, subcultures, and music industry quite apparent – even performative – even if the choice of soul music renders the links less obvious.

From cultural specificity to subcultural capital: Music scenes and discourses of authenticity

Not only do we get to hear the musicians in the film, we also get to see them. Jimmy's judgement of the hopefuls appearing at his door is of their appearance as much as their musicianship, assessing them not only for musical talent but also for cultural and subcultural capital, expressed in what they wear and what they say. The look and style of the auditioners contribute to the sense of capturing a music scene snapshot of Dublin in 1990. Youth culture, music scenes, and subcultures are as much bound up in the visuals of fashions as the sonic qualities of music. Dick Hebdige's seminal work on subcultures discerns meaning in the identifying fashions of particular groups, which start as a deviation against a perceived order or authority: 'the cultivation of a quiff, the acquisition of a scooter or a record or a certain type of suit' and ends in 'the construction of a style, in a gesture of defiance or contempt, in a smile or a sneer. It signals a Refusal' (Hebdige 1979: 3). Subcultural fashions associated with music scenes carry a resistance that is particularly important for working-class youth defying the authority of the older generation.

What is striking about revisiting the film as a thirty-year memory project is how it captures a particular look and feel of the time through clothing and hair which seems authentic to me, based on my own recall. Musicians in the film don't just sound like 'real' musicians, they *look* like musicians in Dublin in 1990. This aspect of the production of the film has not been mentioned in the press, instead there is a sense that the approach to casting was sufficient in laying claim to authenticity, and therefore the labour of costume design has been erased from the film's publicity. Yet what has emerged from my interviews was the importance of costume designer Penny Rose's meticulous efforts to give the cast the right look (see Figure 3.2). With a few exceptions, costume in *The Commitments* was inspired by the auditioners' own clothes, rather than costuming each cast member, major or minor, according to stereotyped ideas of character and fashion. Bronagh Gallagher affirms that Bernie's distinct look was modelled by the wardrobe department on her own:

> That was my look, I had the quiff. That was my own haircut. When it wasn't fixed, I used to wear my Seán O'Casey hat – they were the fashion then, those wee pill box hats. [...] And the earrings [...] I always

Figure 3.2 Publicity still of band, showing clothing styles (photo David Appleby)

wore Levis, heavy thick sailor pants, bomber jackets, denim jackets, red jackets, bandanas. I loved the rockabilly chick look y'know. They'd use pieces I had, or would buy me replicas.

(Gallagher 2021)

Gallagher was eighteen years old during the shoot, and a music-obsessed teenager, devoted to her mother's soul records, and a regular at ska and rockabilly nights in Belfast, which her distinctive quiff reflects (see Figure 1.2). Compared with her native Derry, Dublin was an exciting, vibrant city teeming with musicians, retro clothing shops and cool cafes (ibid.), which the makers of the film tried to capture.

Most of the band and peripheral characters were effectively dressed as versions of their audition selves, with the exception of Michael Aherne (Steven, dressed more conservatively), Johnny Murphy (Joey "The Lips", with his loud waistcoats), and Angeline Ball (Imelda, who was given a glamourous look with 'big' hair) (Gallagher 2021; Ball 2021):

They made it even curlier, bigger. I had heated rollers in every morning. […] I kind of felt slightly less rock 'n' roll than the others as well. Because all the boys were in docs, and the girls, and I was this kind of dolly bird […] Then I really developed a kind of an alternative grunge style. […] Because I just wanted everyone, everyone on the set, everyone in the crew to know *that was not me*!

(Ball 2021)

But these were rare exceptions, and even in his minor role of pool hall manager, Blaise Smith describes Rose's meticulous attention to detail, copying his unusual ensemble of braces, polo-neck and oversized vintage suit trousers:

she basically copied what I was wearing, but they were better. The belt fit beautifully and everything was cut to my size. I remember saying to her, 'can I keep these after filming?' and she said ' no'. […] in case they needed to reshoot anything.

Rose's use of Polaroids for reference meant that

it felt like there was this file on you! *[laughs]* And she showed me all the photos she had of people they'd seen in the street […] That's where I started to think 'they've kind of arrived into this city and they're just absorbing it all'.

(Smith 2020)

The film captures what young, music-obsessed Irish people wore in 1990, and yet what is noticeable throughout the film and cast members' recollections is how, despite this accurate capturing of the 'now' of 1990, the overriding signature of that time was 'retro' or 'vintage', rather than new.

In a 1990 article in *The Face*, a British bastion of subcultural cool, Sean O'Hagan sneeringly portrays Dublin as a music-saturated town with its scene stuck in a dated 1960s hippy sensibility, guitar-centred and 'lacking the beats per minute hedonism of London, Manchester, Ibiza or New York'. He describes the city's soundscape dominated by buskers that sound like the folk rockers Hothouse Flowers or the Waterboys, the overuse of retro slang terms such as 'vibe' and musicians' 'nouveau hippy' look of long hair, colourful shirts, and velvet waistcoats displacing an earlier street uniform of black denim and Doc Martens (O'Hagan 1990: 44–52). The article is reproduced on the website of Irish popular culture archive Brand New Retro, with more recent user comments both relishing and contesting its accuracy. Nevertheless, what the cast of *The Commitments* wear suggests at least a grain of accuracy in O'Hagan's caricature, with Outspan, Dean, and Jimmy's paisley shirts and waistcoats, and Deco's tie-die t-shirt all notable signatures of their style, though Jimmy's Docs and turned-up jeans mark him out as less hippy and more rocker.

Doyle's novel is situated in a slightly earlier 1980s, which would receive nods of recognition in readers with appropriate music knowledge. As well as the presence of rock, punk, and metal, since the 1960s and even now, Dublin is widely known for its traditional Irish music, with groups such as The Dubliners, The Chieftains, and Planxty having an international reach and fame comparable with Van Morrison (Belfast), Rory Gallagher (Cork), and Thin Lizzy (Dublin) mentioned earlier. The presence of so much traditional Irish music in the audition sequence is therefore not surprising, with Dublin in some quarters described as a 'trad city' compared with Belfast or Cork.[2] Academic commentary on music in *The Commitments* is like a Rorschach test of critics' attitudes to music and national identity, and is particularly acute in any kind of 'national cinema' debate. While Lance Pettitt describes the young people in *The Commitments* as 'imbued with American ideas' (Pettitt 2000: 126), Cronin disagrees and argues that not only are such ideas difficult to define, 'members of the band are literate in the popular culture *of their time*, which is predominately but not exclusively American in origin' (Cronin 2006: 37–8; my emphasis). However, Cronin misses the retro aspects of the use of 1960s soul music in *The Commitments*; the music is quite distinctly *not* of the young people's time.

So why do The Commitments play 1960s soul? The most credible context for soul music in Dublin would have been as part of the city's Mod scene. In the book, some of the band's performances are described as attended by 'little mods and modettes, shaking, turning in time together, folding their arms, turning, folding their arms, turning' (Doyle 1987/1998: 82). For Doyle, the fact that so many of the teenagers he taught played music and were in bands was important, but he was also aware of the different kinds of music they liked (metal, ska, punk, rock) through what they *wore*: 'There were the badges on their bags, the badges on their jumpers. Soul wasn't huge' (Doyle 2021). Yet there was a visible Mod scene, of which his job as a teacher gave him an awareness:

> There was one lad I taught [...] he chose to be a Mod because he was spick and span coming out of a house that was *desolate*. I heard about him washing himself in the school gym. And I knew when I saw him out of his uniform, he was a Mod. And it was only a couple of years after *Quadrophenia*. [...] It wasn't just nostalgic or retrospective, it was very much alive. [...] Perhaps if I'd gone into a different job, I'd have waved goodbye to [youth culture]. There was one lad went to a soul night upstairs in a pub in Capel Street. I was aware of things like that.
>
> (Doyle 2021)

Some readers of the novel gravitated to this subcultural aspect, including location assistant Hugh Linehan, then in his twenties:

> I had a very clear idea of what *The Commitments* was. Roddy had written it, Roddy was still a teacher, it was absolutely based on the experiences of young fellas growing up on the Northside and being into Mod culture in the 1980s, they would have worn parkas, skinny trousers and Docs. They had a certain kind of a look and a certain kind of a haircut and that went with a certain kind of a sound. And it was based on a certain notion of class consciousness and geography in Dublin. And I knew at the time that Parker had been a Mod twenty years earlier in London in the sixties, and that was one of the things that appealed to him – that notion of a certain type of working-class culture that looks to African American culture for a way out, for a way to vocalise its concerns and discontents. [...] I thought 'this is great', this meeting of these two generations of Mods coming together.
>
> (Linehan 2020)

However, Linehan was ultimately disappointed that 'there's no sense of this Mod thing in the look or aesthetic of *The Commitments*' (ibid.). No matter what the film does to capture the variety of music scenes in the city, their organic life and their authenticity are contested by the memories of everyone who felt a part of them. Yet none of this is a failure of the film, rather it arises out of the inherent manner in which music scenes and sub-cultures function through the dynamics of shifting discourses of authenticity and conflicting claims to accuracy. In the novel, the songs the Mods respond to are 'Chain Gang', 'Night Train', and 'What Becomes of the Broken-Hearted', with their upbeat, metronomic beats most associated with the British working-class Northern Soul scene. In contrast, the film is better known for the southern-fried bluesy 'Mustang Sally' and 'Dark End of the Street', or the gospel influenced 'Take Me to the River'. Both the novel's and Linehan's mention of Mods emphasise an underplayed cultural link between Dublin and post-industrial English cities, potentially putting Dublin working-class identity at odds with more restricted versions of Irish identity. Perhaps Dublin's Mod scene was simply too niche a cultural reference, or the strain of Anglo-Irish relations at that time, prior to the Good Friday Agreement, meant that Ireland and Irish-America would not have been ready for it.

Nevertheless, Doyle's book came out of a culture of music fandom and fans-turned-musicians which form the basis of local music scenes, and is arguably more about popular music culture rather than music itself. Doyle states that Jimmy was not based on him: 'I would have liked to be more like Jimmy, a bit more self-confident. I met a lot of the Jimmys in teaching, and I admired them' (Doyle 2021). But the decision to make the main character the manager – rather than a musician – was deliberate:

> I didn't play an instrument, and I'd never been in a studio. I didn't have the language [...] Fictional writing about music can be too earnest, and it's earnestness to compensate for the lack of experience. But if I make the manager the main character that's grand, because then he's a fan of the music like myself.
>
> (Doyle 2021)

Doyle insists that 'from the beginning I was going to make it a soul band', rather than any other musical style. His brother had a lot of greatest hits compilations, such as the Four Tops, Marvin Gaye, and Aretha Franklin. 'I didn't have a record player, and I taped a lot of this soul, and I thought yes, this makes sense' (ibid.). Despite the influence of Dublin's live music scenes, Doyle's choice of music was experienced via mediation and recordings, just like the band in the book and the film.

Part of the appeal of *The Commitments* then is musical nostalgia, which the film's distributor Fox identified, noting that the film played better in test screenings with an older generation familiar with the songs. Philip Drake argues that music 'is able to index popular memory and nostalgia' and that this 'offers some advantages for Hollywood cinema, which has been concerned with mobilising the commercial potential of memory' (Drake 2003b: 186). Music allows a film

> to be set visually in the present yet evoke a sense of pastness through its soundtrack. Hollywood cinema has made substantial use of the pop soundtrack to evoke a sense of time past and this is especially the case in the retro film, a cinematic mode that wears stylistic referencing, and pastiche, overtly on its sleeve.
>
> (Ibid.)

Given the commercial success of *The Commitments* soundtrack album and *The Commitments Vol. 2*, any nostalgia attached to soul was clearly exploited to its full commercial potential, and Doyle's choice of soul for his book adapted well to the film as an established 'retro' tendency in popular cinema.

Yet Doyle did not feel that he was making a consciously 'retro' musical choice, given that certain songs from the 1950s and 1960s kept coming back into the charts, such as Jackie Wilson's 'Reet Petite' – 'I wasn't conscious of it being old. Anything self-consciously of the moment becomes dated so quickly' (Doyle 2021). Hence, it was the strength of the songs and their recordings which brought soul to Doyle's mind, rather than Dublin's live music scene. 'It was numbers I was going for. And fun' (ibid.). Layering and juxtaposition are of course crucial to the comedy at the heart of the film:

> superimposing black America onto Dublin. And I'd read Peter Guralnick, *Sweet Soul Music*, and Jerry Hershey, *Nowhere to Run*. Full of energy, full of the personalities. And I liked to think of Jimmy as one of the personalities, making things happen.
>
> (Ibid.)

His choice of songs for the novel was instinctive, choosing ones that were most adaptable:

> I chose songs that I thought had the potential to be good on paper and also to allow the invasion of Dublin into them. So 'Night Train' was an obvious choice. Once it became the DART, it was the right thing to do. [...] I liked the ones particularly where the Dublin accent could get in there [...] But I wasn't methodical. One of the great bores of being the author of *The Commitments* is being cornered by people who know a lot more about soul than I do.
>
> (Doyle 2021)

The notion that types of music belong exclusively to youth cultures and particular generations is perhaps (ironically) a dated one. Musical encounters are not exclusively the preserve of live music scenes, or always of their moment. More important is the role of recordings, books, impassioned conversation, and the sense of music as 'passed down' to younger people, such as Doyle's older brother to him, or Gallagher's mother to her. It is incorporated into the narrative to humorous effect with the trumpet player Joey "The Lips" Fagan. By far the oldest member of the group, he provides a possible live performance link to supplement the band's mediated encounters with the music, claiming to have jammed with the greats including BB King, Screamin' Jay Hawkins, Martha Reeves, and Sam Cooke. His poetic turn of phrase, borrowing from African American jive talk and addressing the other band members as 'brother' and 'sister', marks him out from the other characters' profanities, yet his whiteness and strong Dublin accent undermine the credibility of his claims to fame – another comic juxtaposition.

Nevertheless, Doyle had in mind other senior figures in the British ska movement: 'He'd be the older man, the link with the musical past [...] I was thinking of Rico Rodriguez, the trombone player in the Specials, and Saxa, aka Lionel Augustus Martin, the middle-aged sax player in the Beat' (Doyle 2020). His role in the film is more explicitly patriarchal than the book, naming the band after making a speech about how 'the Lord told me the Irish brothers needed soul' and how a Baptist reverend in Harlem advised him that 'the Irish brothers wouldn't be shooting the arses off each other if they had soul' (the film's only reference to 'The Troubles'), whereas in the book Jimmy (not Joey) names the band with a brief nod to the past ('Good, old-fashioned THE').

Another scene exclusive to the film takes place in Jimmy's house, in which Joey tells Mr. Rabbitte about his time in Graceland with Elvis and his father, a scene laden with patriarchy and exuding a quasi-religious awe, to humorous effect. Framed pictures of Elvis and the Pope are displayed on the wall, underlying Joey's generational affinity with Mr. Rabbitte, hinting that he is a musical father figure to the band, and with American popular music as a religious substitute for Catholicism. Nevertheless, soul is not the opposite of Catholicism's spiritual sensibility, given its sacred gospel influences. Joel Rudinow sees soul music's mixing of the secular and the sacred as a conundrum (2010: 17–8), which suggests another possibility for why soul works for The Commitments. Unlike other forms of black music, such as hip-hop, soul provides a commercially accessible way to articulate Ireland's own social transformation, in which the oppression and social conservatism of the Catholic Church was starting to fracture. Furthermore, its nostalgic yet mythic sensibility prevents it from being too alarming or contentious.

Doyle's explanation elsewhere for choosing soul, that it allowed him to introduce female backing singers and more dramatic possibilities, is frustrating in its implication that women in bands are only capable of singing, not playing instruments. When I put this to him, he provided an interesting explanation:

> I wanted women in the band. Women and music were rare. I mean there was the Bangles, and there were the drummers and bass players, Mo Tucker, and Tina Weymouth, but they were the exception rather than the rule. [...] If one of the women played the bass, that would have become several pages of accounting for it, which would have been valid [...] whereas I preferred the women to be a bit of a unit, and have their own secret world, almost self-contained.
>
> (Doyle 2021)

Like other comparable cities around the world in the late 1980s and early 1990s, the bands of the Dublin music scene were overwhelmingly male-dominated, and any women were typically vocalists, with some vocalists credited as guitarists too. A surprising number of the minority of female musicians who did not sing played fiddle, further confirming the strong role of the trad music scene in Ireland noted above. If The Commitments had a female bass player or drummer, it would have been an interesting story, but a different one, perhaps not reflective of the unacknowledged male dominance of music scenes. Mavis Bayton's interview-based research with female rock musicians in the 1980s paints a vivid picture of the gender-specific obstacles to participation. Growing up in a world in which 'young girls do not see rock musician as a role to which they can aspire', female rock musicians did not go through the processes of practice and identity formation as musicians that male rock musicians had done. Female singers would struggle with imposter syndrome – 'just singing' and therefore expendable – and feel excluded from the instrument-focussed processes of rehearsal. Furthermore, pressures of domestic and caring obligations often prevented commitment to rehearsals (Bayton 1990: 254–6).

There are two scenes in *The Commitments* that demonstrate the gendered dynamic Bayton identifies. In one scene, Jimmy goes to Bernie's flat to reprimand her for not attending rehearsals. The scene shows Bernie in a pressured, chaotic domestic situation, helping her mother look after her younger siblings in their tiny living space, but with Bernie imploring Jimmy that she 'need[s] this band'. Later, her infant sibling's crying disrupts a rehearsal to humorous effect noted in the line 'at least the little bollix is in key'. In another scene, Imelda informs an irate Jimmy that she will not be able to perform at their gig because of her prior commitment to a family holiday;

later we see a grumpy Imelda abandon her family as they board a ferry to the Isle of Man, arriving just in time to play the gig. In these ways, the film both portrays and reinforces a problematic gender dynamic across music scenes, with the female band members resisting domestic obligations as best as they can. Furthermore, the girls sing as a unit in the book, either as backing vocalists or in girl group numbers like 'Walking in the Rain' and 'Stop! In the Name of Love'. In contrast, the film more clearly differentiates them as musicians as well as characters, with Imelda and Natalie each performing bravura solo numbers such as 'I Ain't Never Loved a Man' and 'Too Many Fish in the Sea', and with Parker stressing how talented all three performers were and stating that he wanted them to sing as much as Deco does (Parker 2016).

'*Fame* on the Liffey' – *The Commitments* as 'backstage musical'

As Lynda Myles puts it, *The Commitments* is not 'Loachian realism' (Myles 2020), and in fact shares some features with the most Hollywood of genres, the musical. Alan Parker has a long history of directing musicals, including his debut feature *Bugsy Malone* (1976), Prohibition-era set with an all-child cast; his collaboration with rock band Pink Floyd, *Pink Floyd: The Wall* (1982); and the box office phenomenon *Fame* (1980), following teenagers in New York attending the High School of Performing Arts. During its production, publicity surrounding *The Commitments* drew comparisons with *Fame* more than any other film, as mentioned earlier.

What Parker's musical films have in common is a concern with youth or youth-orientated musical cultures (or both); in contrast, Parker's later 1996 adaptation of Andrew Lloyd Webber's West End hit *Evita* is certainly considered more *a* musical (noun) as opposed to musical (adjective). And yet, according to the film's music supervisor, G. Marq Roswell, '*The Commitments* was absolutely a musical. It had live vocals to playback, great songs, and a brilliant director who created an authentic feel that most musical movies don't have' (Roswell, interviewed by Flattum 2002). But while Roswell is emphatic in his description of *The Commitments* as a musical, he is equally emphatic in his declaration that it has a sensibility not shared by 'most musical movies'. Roswell's comment is quite typical of an ill-defined perception of the musical as lacking authenticity and revelling in artifice, with the dance sequences, immaculate choreography, and elaborate costumes associated with directors such as Busby Berkeley and studios such as MGM representing examples of the quintessential musical. With their urban settings and location shooting, *Fame* and *The Commitments* might be considered too distinct from the Hollywood musical to be part of the genre, apart from the precedent set by *West Side Story* (Wise and Robbins 1961). Like *The Commitments*, as Martha Shearer argues, *West Side Story*'s shifting urban setting differentiates it from Hollywood musicals and is integral to its style and feel, having captured on screen neighbourhoods in which 'material and demographic change was felt and lived, but their representation was also a means of deflecting anxieties about those actual changes' (Shearer 2015: 453).

However, contrary to widely held belief, *West Side Story* was preceded by a swathe of Hollywood musicals with urban settings in the 1940s, such as *Greenwich Village* (Lang 1944) and *It Happened in Brooklyn* (Whorf 1947), functioning as 'informal' backstage musicals: 'in which musical numbers were introduced "naturally"' (Shearer 2015: 452). In much the same way, diegetic songs are performed in *The Commitments* in rehearsal and performance settings, rather than characters spontaneously bursting into song. The point is that this does not prevent *The Commitments* from being a musical. Even its urban setting and nod to social issues associated with 'Loachian realism' – references to drug use, especially heroin, which was an endemic socio-economic problem in Dublin in the late 1980s – are mostly there for purposes of humour and comic punchlines. For example, during the audition scene, a perplexed youth asked by Jimmy 'what do you play?' looks confused and replies that he used to play football at school, then confesses that when he saw the queue, he assumed Jimmy was selling drugs. Similarly, the band's first gig at a community centre, in front of a homemade banner that states 'Heroine kills', with a misplaced 'e', is met with the punchline 'nobody round here can spell'. Rather than offering Loachian critique, these nods to social issues offer dashes of humour and colour as a backdrop for the musical form.

The earlier parts of the film have some songs occur less 'naturally' than in the later rehearsal and gig settings. On the DART, when Jimmy announces that he is putting the band on 'a strict diet of soul', the scene culminates in an *a cappella* rendition of 'Destination Anywhere' initiated by Dean with the rest joining in, synchronising elegantly with the version of 'Destination Anywhere' playing non-diegetically on the soundtrack. This required the band to wear tiny earpieces with the song piped in, so that they could stay in sync and in tune (Parker 2016). 'Nowhere to Run' accompanies a montage sequence, compressing the band members' individual rehearsal time, offering an exploration of the film's urban setting and the world of the characters. Stylistically, this sequence is one of the more conventionally musical-like of all in *The Commitments*, as the song's performance is not confined to a gig or single rehearsal space. Instead, it performs what Richard Dyer describes as the 'utopian' function of song in the Hollywood musical (Dyer 2002: 20) – we see the Commitmentettes singing and practising their dance routines amidst lines of washing suspended in a communal yard; Deco practising singing while working as a bus conductor; Billy practising the drums at his blacksmith's job; Derek practising the guitar in the abattoir, rubbing his hands together in the cold, and so forth.

The uplifting tone of the song contrasts with the grit and mundanity of the everyday urban world of the characters. To quote Dyer:

> Songs in films take up literal but also temporal and sometimes metaphorical space. They impose musical time and length on spoken and acted narration. They allow voices to fill or carry over space and, in dance, permit – even incite – bodies to do the same. This can be lovely, but it may also be disruptive, threatening, subversive. If a song may expand on the narrative moment it may also interrupt its drive.
>
> (Dyer 2011: 30)

The relatively simple, linear plot of the film (and the book), summarised by Doyle as: 'Jimmy forms a band, the band breaks up, it's a straight line from A to B' (Giambona 2019: 261), allows time and space for the songs to fully realise their utopian function. The songs cannot disrupt the narrative, because the band's journey is the narrative.

What *The Commitments* shares even more specifically with early youth musical films of the 1950s is not only a tendency to be dismissed by critics as slight on plot; it also repeatedly restates discourses of authenticity associated with rock culture as well as with soul (those specific to soul will be explored in Chapter 4). Writing about early rock 'n' roll films, Keir Keightley argues that films such as *Jailhouse Rock* (1957), *Expresso Bongo* (1959), and *Wild Guitar* (1962) 'portray the music industry in such critical terms that they effectively "manufacture authenticity" for audiences, by consistently representing the antithesis of authenticity (alienation, fraud, manipulation, phoniness, corruption, etc.) as evils to be avoided', to the extent that they 'contributed to the ideological foundation of rock culture' (Keightley 2003: 166). In this same tradition, *The Commitments* is a story of youthful aspirations tempered by missed opportunities. Despite Jimmy Rabbitte successfully courting press coverage, including one hyperbolic newspaper reviewer naming the band in the same sentence as U2 and Sinéad O'Connor, the band fails to break the big time. His backstage meeting with Dave from Eejit Records (a memorable cameo by comedian Sean Hughes) is in vain as the band break up during the gig (see Figure 3.3). Joey "The Lips" later consoles Jimmy with: 'we could have been famous and made albums and stuff, but that would have been predictable. This way it's poetry'. In this way, the film articulates a tension between art and commerce and a distrust of the commodifying role of the music industry.

Figure 3.3 Dave from Eejit Records introduces himself to Jimmy

In his widely cited and reprinted essay 'The Industrialisation of Popular Music', Simon Frith asserts that this tension and contrast 'between music-as-expression and music-as-commodity defines twentieth-century pop experience and means that however much we may use and enjoy its products, we retain a sense that the music industry is a bad thing – bad for music, bad for us' (Frith 2007: 93). The contradiction is articulated by Dave to Jimmy, in which the lack of financial compensation is presented in implausibly positive rather than negative terms: 'we're a small label but we're good because we care, y'know what I mean? Like, there'll be no money up front but we'll pay for an engineer and studio time for a day'. This happens at a point where the band has become increasingly discontented at their lack of pay despite Jimmy's pleas for 'professionalism'. Jimmy grumbles to Dave: 'First rule of rock 'n' roll, once they get a taste, they become overnight arseholes', to which Dave replies: 'Arseholes? You don't have to tell me, isn't everyone in rock 'n' roll an arsehole? Except for management, that is!' Hence, *The Commitments* simultaneously reiterates and sends up a romanticised conception of youthful sincerity, musical creativity, and authenticity, at odds with the mechanisation, mediation, cynicism, and commercialisation associated with the professionalised realm, even though they are dependent upon each other.

Conclusion

The question of why The Commitments play soul is a complex one to answer. On the one hand, the film went to great lengths to capture the contemporary atmosphere of the city and its youth, yet on the other hand by superimposing a 1960s soul sound, and by emphasising particularly retro clothing styles, it becomes a form of 'retro' film. This chapter has explored the cultural contexts in which soul might have circulated in Dublin at the time, and considered the film's complex transnational relationship with music scenes, film genre, and music industries. Given the diversity of musical sounds and scenes of the 1980s and early 1990s, especially the more synth-driven and sample-based sounds of post-punk, electropop, hip-hop, and acid house, the 'back to basics' of soul perhaps fit with a contemporaneous preoccupation with liveness, musicianship, mediation, and authenticity, which will be explored fully in the following chapter.

Notes

1   The early 1990s Mansion House raves have been alluded to in a variety of anecdotal sources, including the documentary *Notes on Rave in Dublin* (Redmond 2019) and in various blogs, including Braine (2000). When I interviewed Doyle, he was unaware of them: 'I was busying myself with parenthood so raves were far from my mind' (Doyle 2021).
2   These different music scenes are explored in the RTÉ/BBC Northern Ireland documentary *The Irish Rock Story: A Tale of Two Cities* (Connolly, 2015).

4   Songs and sonic authenticity
Mediating musical performance

In an early scene in *The Commitments*, Jimmy recruits bassist Derek and guitarist Outspan from the band And And! And, founded by vocalist and keyboard player Ray who, according to Derek, 'owns the synth'. Jimmy convinces Derek and Outspan to leave Ray's band because 'nobody listens to synths anymore. It's back to basics'. We never get to know Ray, apart from his performance at the wedding gig, singing out of tune and playing the synth, which also supplies an ersatz *bossa nova* drum pattern. His clichéd patter is delivered in the cringe-inducing mid-Atlantic accent associated with middle-of-the-road FM radio DJs. A reaction shot of Jimmy wincing demonstrates his distaste for Ray's performance (see Figure 4.1). It is contrasted later in the scene with our introduction to Deco, an obnoxious drunken 'eejit' of a guest, energetically singing along to The Proclaimers and producing what Jimmy describes, to the initial surprise of Derek and Outspan, as 'something approximating music'. Ray might own the professional-level musical hardware yet is depicted as talentless, his value hinging entirely upon his ownership of the synth to which Derek and Outspan ascribe value but Jimmy dismisses; in contrast, Deco has a vocal talent framed as 'raw', 'pure', minimally mediated, and therefore superior.

This moment is an example of how 'rock authenticity' operates, as described by Philip Auslander, functioning 'as an *ideological* concept and as a discursive effect' (Auslander 2008: 82; original emphasis) in which the 'good'/authentic (i.e. Deco's singing) is contrasted with the 'bad'/inauthentic (i.e. Ray's synth). Hence, synthesisers and their associated musical genres are designated as a technically complex and 'inauthentic Other' to contrast with the sonic authenticity of 'back to basics' 1960s soul singing. According to Auslander (2008), 'the concept of authenticity has always been exclusionary' (p. 79), and depends on 'the nomination of something to serve as the inauthentic Other, whether that thing is current pop music or other rock'; moreover, 'authenticity is often located in current music's relationship to an earlier, "purer" moment in a mythic history of the music'

DOI: 10.4324/9780429296048-5

Figure 4.1 Jimmy's reaction to And And! And

(p. 83). In *The Commitments*, 'rock authenticity' is better understood as 'soul authenticity' which revolves around ideas concerning voice and vocal performance, with the essence of soul as self-expression that is at odds with technical polish or technological mediation. Within the world of the film, it is irrelevant that soul legends James Brown, Stevie Wonder, and Marvin Gaye embraced synthesisers and drum machines throughout the 1970s and 1980s, for example, Gaye's 'Sexual Healing' makes memorable use of the Roland 808 drum machine and its distinctive cowbell sound which became a signature of house and techno. In the context of the early 1990s, we can see Jimmy's distaste for And And! And as a reaction against the polished, synth, sampler, and effects-driven sound of 1980s popular music as a whole, affirming a minimally mediated aesthetic closer to that of 1960s soul.

Furthermore, The Commitments are depicted primarily as a live band, performing in rehearsal and in concert, and the film never features any footage of them in a recording studio (the montage at the end briefly shows Deco in a recording studio pursuing his solo career, almost an extended function of his ego, and a cameo by Alan Parker as the engineer, seated with Paul Bushnell and Sean Hughes) (see Figure 4.2). Unlike And And! And, The Commitments solely feature acoustic instruments (though electrically amplified) which are central to discourses of authenticity surrounding live music. However, the band's initial encounters with soul music take place via records and videotapes, and the young musicians have no truly 'authentic' 'live' link with the music they play or the era in which it was played.[1] Within rock culture generally, recording media are in fact the primary way

Figure 4.2 Alan Parker's cameo appearance as a recording engineer

in which fans encounter bands' music, and live performance typically functions as authentication of the recordings. Within the film's narrative, it is the
elder figure Joey "The Lips" Fagan who offers a potential live performance
link, claiming to have jammed with various soul greats; however, the constant doubts expressed concerning Joey's veracity underline the fragility
inherent in such discourses of authenticity.

This chapter will outline the processes of sonic mediation associated with
The Commitments, as depicted in the narrative, as described in the film's
production and post-production, and employed in the recording and engineering of the two soundtrack albums, *The Commitments* (1991) and *The
Commitments Vol. 2* (1992). It also explores ideas concerning the essence
of soul music, demonstrating the importance of voice and self-expression
to 'soul authenticity'. The choice of soul for *The Commitments* suggests a
nostalgic or retro sensibility, and a distaste for the contested musicianship
of electronic music genres of the 1980s such as synthpop and the sampling
culture of hip-hop. The unusual decision to record vocals live on set during
the shoot rather than use lip-syncing as is typical in film further shares this
sensibility. Philip Auslander's work interrogating the contested and slip-
pery concept of 'liveness' is relevant here, a term used abundantly in relation to the making and promotion of the film. In Alan Parker's words: 'I
had decided that we wouldn't cheat any of the instruments or singing and
that we would attempt to do our music live to remain faithful to the gritty
truth in Roddy's original characters' (Beacon Communications 1991c: 3), a
statement which equates liveness with notions of truth and faith, and with
lip-syncing as a form of 'cheating'. Although Parker's decision to record

the vocals live might seem like a simple and elegant approach, in tune with the 'back to basics' philosophy expressed by Jimmy, it is surprisingly technically complex. By demystifying the process and interrogating some of the discourses surrounding it, one can appreciate what an impressive and relatively unrecognised accomplishment it is. The chapter will also examine the politics of representation of body as it relates to the voice the body produces, paying particular attention to the vocal performance of the film's teenage singer Deco, and relating it to discourses of authenticity concerning soul music.

'Liveness' as ideology

The musical skills of the cast have been repeatedly emphasised, with acting ability regarded as secondary, for the most part. Alongside the publicity concerning the casting of the film via open auditions in Dublin, musical rehearsal was an important part of the extensive auditioning process, with auditioners participating with a team of session musicians (Dwyer 1990b: 1–2). *The Commitments* press kit goes into more detail regarding this process, with Parker noting the 'behind the scenes' contribution of the young session bass player Paul Bushnell whose insider status within the Dublin music scene was invaluable. His initial job during pre-production was to act as an intermediary between the professional session band he had helped assemble, and the auditioners, many of whom lacked music theory knowledge:

> I was very impressed with his musicianship and, more importantly, his patience and kindness as he gently nursed the nervous auditioners through their chosen numbers. Although he'd never worked on a film before, I decided to make him the band musical director and for the next five months he was never far from my side.
>
> (Beacon Communications 1991c: 4)

The Commitments provided the opportunity for Bushnell to work in the US, where he has been based ever since. He has gone on to work with international stars such as Phil Collins, Elton John, Alanis Morissette, Nelly Furtado, and Céline Dion. Though less well known than the cast, Bushnell's career arc exemplifies the articulated ideal of how the production of the film in Dublin provided an internationalised 'big break' career opportunity for young people involved with it.

Bushnell's work in the auditions fostered the musical dynamic of the band, leading on to work in the rehearsal and recording of the songs, writing the arrangements, co-producing the albums, then working with the band during the shoot, and finally providing input into the mixing of the film sound in Los Angeles. Like the young cast, he was in his twenties but established as a session musician in Dublin, performing in multiple band projects as well as gaining some studio experience recording demos. Rather than the 'raw talent' narrative used in the film's marketing, this session scene was integral to the musical success of the film. Angeline Ball stresses her involvement in it too, the camaraderie of seeing the same musicians around, and of having gigged with Bushnell prior to *The Commitments*:

> there was not a lot of money there, you just go where the gigs are. And so I would do that. I'd do session singing, backing vocals. I'd do corporate gigs, in beautiful castles for Mr Budweiser or Mr Coca Cola, with fellow musicians.
>
> (Ball 2021)

In the film, we never see the band in a recording studio, but in reality the recording studio was crucial to the shaping of the band and the film. After several weeks of rehearsals in which the final cast were assembled, then rehearsing the songs alongside the session band (which included Bushnell on bass), the songs were recorded in advance of the film shoot, in an intensive three-week period. The music was recorded at Windmill Lane Studios by Parker, Bushnell, and Kevin Killen, a young engineer and producer from Dublin newly based in New York, who at that point had made his name engineering U2's *The Unforgettable Fire* (1984) and then Peter Gabriel's *So* (1985). Killen has since worked with an impressive roster of artists including Kate Bush, Elvis Costello, and David Bowie. Alongside world-class engineering skills and international experience, Killen had the advantage of being familiar with the music scene in Dublin, and the legal status to be able to work both in Dublin and the US, where the music and sound would be finished in post-production for the film and mixed for the albums.

The session band included Félim Gormley on saxophone, which resulted in Gormley being cast in the film as Dean the saxophonist. This explains a notable oddity of the album credits, which lists Gormley twice, stating: 'The Commitments:', and listing the cast in full, including Gormley; 'plus' Conor Brady, guitar; Fran Breehan, drums; Paul Bushnell, bass; Ronan Dooney, trumpet; Eamonn Flynn, keyboards; Carl Geraghty, Tenor and Baritone Sax; and Félim Gormley, Alto Sax. This double crediting refers to the fact that Gormley plays on the albums as well as in the film. However, the credits are not clear about who plays what where, and in what context. Without stating explicitly, the credits account for the fact that while most of The Commitments play their instruments, Gormley is the only Commitment other than the vocalists who actually plays on the albums. Despite musical ability being an important aspect of casting, what we hear on the albums is not actually the full cast playing.

The recording sessions in Dublin required multiple versions of the songs to be recorded – not only versions for the albums, but also versions for the film, which would be used as backing tracks during the filming of the songs. Where *The Commitments* departs most notably from standard filmmaking practice is in the recording of vocals on set during the shoot. As Parker explained during the promotion of the film:

> We had decided to use a new system for shooting and recording the music which had never been used before on film. Most film music from 'Singing In The Rain' to MTV uses pre-recorded tracks and vocals which are played back as the camera takes up different positions with the artists miming. I wanted to capture the reality of the rehearsals and performing by recording the vocals live on set [...] We used a new system of out-of-phase speakers which enabled us to play the pre-recorded constant backing tracks at maximum volume to give us live performance atmosphere for the vocalists to sing to. Each vocal was then recorded live onto a twenty-four track recorder that was on set with us. Because of the out-of-phase speakers the vocals could be recorded cleanly for re-mixing later. This allowed us the technical precision needed for a complicated cut, but gave us the truth, energy and spirit of a live performance.
>
> (Parker, quoted in Beacon Communications 1991c: 5)

What Parker means by 'out-of-phase speakers' is that the backing tracks were exactly out of phase with the vocals, so that the backing tracks could later be eliminated from the vocal recordings using a process of phase cancellation. For about 95% of the vocals, it worked well, with only a few substitutions from the studio recordings of vocals required in instances where the vocal was too noisy (Killen 2020). This system for recording the vocals on set was devised by Joe O'Herlihy, who manages U2's live sound, and Kevin Killen, who had used this technique with Peter Gabriel on the 'So' album, and is an interesting instance of music industry expertise from live and studio sound engineering influencing film sound practice. Hence, sound recording in *The Commitments* was a major endeavour, given the emphasis on live performance.

The ability of the non-singing cast to be able to play their instruments was considered crucial to the energy of the performances, and musical rehearsal in the afternoons was integrated closely with dramatic rehearsal in the mornings:

By the end of the month [August] we had rehearsed each scene in the film over and over until our ten musicians had become actors and our two actors had become musicians and all of them had become an accomplished ensemble theatre group. By the time we were ready to film, all the songs could be performed by the cast and we could run through the whole script, just like a play.

(Parker, quoted in Beacon Communications 1991c: 5)

Here Parker's comparisons to the process with theatre once again reiterates the concept of liveness as integral to the success of the project. Nevertheless, what we hear for the most part when watching/hearing songs performed in the film is a composite of vocals recorded live on set, and backing tracks recorded in the studio. Furthermore, while the non-singing cast are playing their instruments on set, those are not the performances we actually hear.

Given that the musical instruments were not recorded on set, why go to all the trouble of recording the vocals on set? Why were live vocals considered so important? 1990, as well as being the year in which *The Commitments* was cast and shot and the two Commitments albums were recorded, was also the year of the Milli Vanilli lip-syncing scandal, in which the Grammy award-winning artists were forced to give up their award following revelations that the vocalists had not sung on any of their releases.[2] Hence, the emphasis upon the young unknowns in *The Commitments* actually being able to sing and play their instruments, especially the use of 'live' vocals over 'miming', is perhaps unsurprising.

Michel Chion argues that:

there is no link in a sound film between the filmmaking process and the finished product. One can create the impression of direct sound in a postsynchronized film [...]; conversely, a film can seem postsynchronized [...] when in fact it has been recorded with direct sound.

(Chion 2009: 221)

This impression described by Chion is integral to the aesthetic and technical basis of all post-production sound editing and mixing for film and television, in which the soundtrack is always a composite of recordings from the location shoot, edited sound effects, and Foley work. Moreover, as Mary Anne Doane describes it, the soundtrack and image track are inherently 'materially heterogenous', and there is no 'natural' unity of sound and image (Doane 1985: 54). Nevertheless, in contradistinction to Chion's argument there is a sense, even in professional circles, that the use of direct or live sound is distinctive, with Parker, Bushnell, and Killen all stressing how integral the live vocals were to the success of *The Commitments*:

That's what made the Commitments really connect with the audience. As you watched them sing, they were singing, that was *the* take. Every song, every frame that they sung on was something that they had recorded on set. There was no disconnect between the visual, the sound and the performance.

(Killen 2020)

Similarly, Bushnell reiterated the importance of live sound:

We needed to use the recorded music but the live vocals. It was a brilliant set up and almost 100% of the movie vocals were literally shot on location as they were shooting those scenes. And I think that translates. I've seen so many movies where you know they're not playing; they're miming and it's fake.

(Bushnell 2020)

For *The Commitments* albums, the versions of the songs heard in the film provided the basis of the album versions, but they adhered to the rule that no instrument not visible on screen could be utilised in the film mix. Through collaboration with Parker, Killen and Bushnell realised that these album versions therefore needed to be subtly fleshed out, adding additional percussion and keyboards by session players Alex Acuña and Mitchell Froom: 'we did a great job of representing the music for the film […] [but] if you're buying the soundtrack, and you're just listening to it in isolation, it may not hold up' (Killen 2020). While both *The Commitments* soundtrack album and *The Commitments Vol. 2* were recorded in Dublin, the former was mixed in Los Angeles during the same period, and *Vol. 2* was mixed at a later period (prompted by the commercial success of the first album) at Skyline Studios in New York by Killen, and mastered by Bob Ludwig at Masterdisk, New York.

The achievement of the film's sound and music recording did not go unrecognised in industry. Along with *Dances with Wolves* and *The Silence of the Lambs*, *The Commitments* was nominated for a BAFTA for Best Sound, losing out to *Terminator 2: Judgement Day*. Nevertheless, the technical accomplishment and creative labour of the film's sound, and the film's music, have been downplayed. This is not untypical as film sound practice has traditionally been marginalised and underrecognised. Moreover, the rhetoric of 'back to basics' and a distrust of technology permeates both the rock authenticity that dominates music criticism as outlined by Auslander, as well as within the narrative of the film itself.

Despite this apparent distrust of music and recording technology and its arguable capacity for 'fakery', musicians revere recording studios associated with soul, such as Muscle Shoals in Alabama, where many of the great southern soul songs of *The Commitments* were originally recorded. However, musicians tend to use strikingly non-technological vocabulary, for example, in his description of the Muscle Shoals sound, U2 frontman Bono has stated: 'That sound made it through to even Ireland and Britain. And we felt the blood in that, we felt the sort of pulse of it, and we wanted some, y'know'. Similarly, American songwriter Candi Staton describes the Muscle Shoals sound as 'deep down in your stomach, coming up out of your gut, coming up out of your heart, that's that Muscle Shoals sound' ('Storyville' 2014). Instead of technology, the musicians describe Muscle Shoals in human, emotional, and very bodily terms.

While the mediation of sound and recorded music necessitates a split or separation of the sound from its instrument, and in the case of vocals, a separation of the voice from the body of the performer, musicians and fans typically reconcile this split through a belief in the ideology of liveness and the centrality of live performance, and the reunion of the voice and body on stage. Hence the importance of The Commitments' vocals being recorded live on set, as well as their live performance at the Waterfront in Dublin after the premiere of the film at the Savoy, and their promotional performances in the US alongside Wilson Pickett. The band was a combination of members of the cast and session musicians, under Bushnell's musical directorship:

> Wilson Pickett jammed with us three times [...] In the China Club in New York City and the Park West in Chicago and the Palace here in Los Angeles. After everyone's seen the movie and nobody knows he's going to show up and then boom! He's on stage. It was mind-blowing.
>
> (Bushnell 2020)

Despite what is essentially a fabrication of the band on record, with only the vocalists and Gormley actually playing on the albums, the band The Commitments had to seem to be able to play live on stage in order to exist in the critical and popular imagination as a band. While the narrative of the film denies the young musicians the chance to jam live with Pickett, keeping the soul great firmly in the mediated realm, the promotional performances allowed an ephemeral moment of spatially and temporally united live performance with Pickett.

Musicianship and screen representations of liveness

A key distinction between the film and the book is that the film allows us to actually hear The Commitments, whereas in the book we rely on Roddy Doyle's sparse yet evocative descriptions, which describe what the band aspires to sound like as much as what they sound like in the reader's imagination. Doyle eschews any musical terminology to rely upon onomatopoeic verbal descriptions of songs based on the recordings which are The Commitments' reference point, for example: '-THU –CUDADUNG CUDADUNG CUDADUNG – Billy blammed out the "Reach Out – I'll Be There" beat, then stopped' (Doyle 1987/1998: 96). The pleasure of Doyle's descriptions is enhanced by the reader's own knowledge of the music; without that knowledge, the descriptions are bare. Timothy Taylor suggests that being able to hear the music in the film

> mitigates the book's political message [...] The Commitments are good musicians. In the book they never get very good at all, but since they're together for community and the articulation of their viewpoint as much as for the music, it doesn't matter. But a movie about a bad soul band with as much music as Parker's would be excruciating. He has made a film that is primarily about a band, not music and politics.
>
> (Taylor 1998: 298)

For Taylor, this inherent aspect of the film makes the book's politics challenging to translate. In contrast, with the film we can hear the band playing, albeit mediated via the film's production, post-production, and exhibition. The politics of representation apply just as much to sound as they do to image. I will now explore these issues in relation to discourses of authenticity concerning musicianship.

As Kevin Killen observes, time passes rather ambiguously in *The Commitments*:

> The funny thing about the story as I recall [...] from the beginning of the film to the end, you are unaware of how long that time period is. It doesn't say 'six months later' or 'a year later'. So we were tasked with trying to figure out, how bad were they in the beginning and how much better do this band get?
>
> (Killen 2020)

Similarly, Hugh Linehan describes the level of improvement of the band over the course of the film as 'preposterous' (Linehan 2020). Bushnell and Killen therefore had to devise ways to make the cast sound less skilled in the earliest musical sequences and more skilled in the later ones, while the parallel project of the albums required the band to sound as they do at the peak of their abilities in the film. Parker picks out 'Try a Little Tenderness' in their final gig as his favourite musical moment and 'probably as good as the band gets' (Parker 2016) with the dramatic irony that the band reach an interpersonal nadir by then, fighting and breaking up immediately afterwards.

This moment is signposted by a performance in the film of 'Dark End of the Street' (discussed again below), in which the band finish up on a high, then in a café afterwards have their first really big row over money, sex, and 'professionalism'. In order to demonstrate The Commitments' improvement, the cast's varying musical abilities had to be tempered in different ways. According to Killen:

> we had to establish how bad they were in the beginning [...] And because they were all musicians, to make that transition believable we asked them to swap their instruments, so if you were a bass player we put you on drums and vice versa. The musicians had some kind of familiarity with the instrument but didn't know it well enough, so they were fumbling. And that's the kind of thing you see when bands are starting off. We started to capture those performances [...] to establish what that threshold was.
>
> (Killen 2020)

Similarly, Bushnell described arranging the songs in the band's first rehearsal scene in the room above the pool hall to incorporate musical errors:

> Glen [Hansard] [...] is a brilliant musician who I literally had to teach wrong chords to and insist that he play them. Glen said to me 'jaysus Bushy this doesn't sound right' and I was like 'you are correct my friend, you are correct. But it's to make you guys sound like you don't know what you're doing!'
>
> (Bushnell 2020)

Parker's discussion of the cast's musicianship tends to emphasise it as a collective effort: 'ten of them were musicians, only Bronagh Gallagher (Bernie) and Johnny Murphy (Joey) had ever acted before' (Parker n.d.). This avoids drawing attention to the delicious irony that Johnny Murphy, as Joey "The Lips" Murphy, cannot actually play the trumpet, despite Joey's role as musical mentor to the rest of the group. Instead, his trumpet parts in the film and on record were played by session trumpet player Ronan Dooney. Furthermore, a scene with Joey and Dean shows Joey coaching Dean as he tentatively learns the saxophone, advising him to imagine the reed as 'a woman's nipple' (see Figure 4.3). In contrast, Félim Gormley, who played Dean, is a skilled saxophone player and (as mentioned earlier) the only non-singing member of the cast who played on the albums.

Figure 4.3 Joey coaches Dean's sax playing

In a real-life mirror image of the 'woman's nipple' scene, a scene in which we first hear Joey play the trumpet ('Moon River', his favourite 'lip loosener'), Gormley coached Murphy in rehearsal of the take in how to appear to play the trumpet convincingly (Bushnell 2020). Robert Arkins (Jimmy), also a skilled trumpet player, was in contention for multiple roles besides Jimmy, including that of Deco. In the DVD director's commentary, Alan Parker expresses a certain degree of regret that Arkins does not play music in the film: 'Robert Arkins is such a confident musician and performer, comfortable on stage, but we never get to see him. His primary instrument is the trumpet, which he never gets to play much', then later: 'it must be frustrating for Robert Arkins seeing Joey "The Lips" play the trumpet, when he's such a good trumpet player himself' (Parker 2016). The song that plays over the opening credits, 'Treat Her Right', is sung by Arkins, not Strong; perhaps some consolation for the actor.

As the film enters its second hour, The Commitments perform in a pub venue, playing 'Take Me to The River', then 'Dark End of the Street'. In the Blu-ray commentary, Parker reiterates that all the vocals are live, but also emphasises this scene as a turning point in the sound of the band, with the backing tracks getting better and closer to the sound people expect (Parker 2016). What he alludes to, without actually stating, is that this is the moment in the film in which the backing track switches, from The Commitments themselves, to the session band (Killen 2020; Bushnell 2020; Gallagher 2021). Both songs feature the live vocals, and the brass players are the same (Gormley and Dooney). But the rest of the band, in the transition between these two songs, is invisibly replaced, the 'raw' talent of The Commitments on the soundtrack becomes the more professional sound of the session band, and from that moment on, The Commitments, other than the vocalists and Gormley, are miming to other musicians' performances. The transition is not noticeable, unless the spectator is made aware of it and becomes conscious of it. On repeated listens, the rhythm section in particular sounds a lot tighter on 'Dark End of the Street' than 'Take Me to the River', and the guitar sound switches from quite crunchy and quite low in the mix, to a more mellifluous sound more prominent in the mix.

The emphasis upon the live vocals is reinforced visually in the shot composition and editing. Parker explains that the performances were shot with two cameras simultaneously, with a close-up of Strong singing functioning as a master shot, a filming process which was 'backwards' from what one would usually do (Parker 2016). It is noticeable that the shots in 'Dark End of the Street' are longer in duration, emphasising the faces of the band, and feature more close-ups of vocalists Strong and the Commitmentettes; whereas in 'Take Me to the River' the editing flits from one musician to the other, making more of the band and their bodies visible, and including quite a few close-ups of hands and fingers plucking and strumming. This illustrates further how the emphasis on capturing live vocals influences the visual grammar of the film, and how a shift from the rest of the band playing on the soundtrack means a de-emphasis on showing them play. Yet the slower tempo of 'Dark End of the Street' appears to be what motivates the shift in visual style, allowing a seamless transition to take place on the soundtrack. In the film's narrative, this point of musical transition is also the start of the fracturing of the band, with the next two scenes featuring arguments about sex and money, and Billy the drummer's departure from the band because of his hatred of Deco.

Parker has described how a desire to capture the vocals live influenced the film's visual style, with he and cinematographer Gale Tattersall striving for 'a very gritty realistic look […] you learn to do things in an elegant way, and you have to forget what you've learned. You don't want the cinematography to be too pleased with itself' (Parker 2016). His emphasis is on capturing live performance, rather than carefully blocking out specific shots and camera angles, and 'keep it as rough and as real as possible […] avoid doing anything too elegant, even left in a few zooms' (ibid.). However, live performance still required continuity, with the band having to try to interpret the song as similarly as possible in each take. The requirements of live sound recording even shaped the cinematic space of the film. In order to record the live vocals and play the backing tracks, the crew had to use two very bulky twenty-four track machines, one for playback and one for recording. For the gig at the community hall, its location, Archbishop Byrne Hall in Synge Street, had to have a false back and a false side built into it by the art department. The false wall hid 'an army of people' required to record and monitor the live vocals and backing tracks (ibid.).

Furthermore, live performance was important for the promotion of the film, and the Waterfront café was an important venue in this respect. It was a real music venue, located by the Liffey on Sir John Rogerson's Quay, and used for some of the auditions for *The Commitments* (in addition to the Mansion House). It was also the shooting location for the band's final gig in the film (referred to as 'Gallaghers'), and it was the location of promotional press screenings and parties. In the rock music magazine *Spin*, Jim Greer recounts that at the cast party at the Waterfront after the premiere,

> director Parker performs as master of ceremonies, introducing each of the cast member's real life bands [...] Each group knocks off a couple of songs, then the Commitments themselves take the stage and rip into 'Mustang Sally'. I don't know, maybe it was all the free Guinness, but I thought the band was magnificent. Strange that a made-up band can sound so much more convincing than a dozen 'real' ones.
>
> (Greer 1991: 13).

Richard Lowe of *Empire* magazine describes the cast party in similar terms, with Parker having the manner of a 'kindly youth club leader compering the annual talent show' (Lowe 1991: 70). Thus, the live energy and collective efforts of the band are emphasised at all times, and for promotional purposes they exist as a fully live band, even though the processes of recording and mediation described above paint a more complex picture.

Voice, body, and soul

When Jimmy puts The Commitments on a 'strict diet of soul', he prescribes 'James Brown for the growls, Otis Redding for the moans, Smokey Robinson for the whines, and Arethra Franklin for the whole lot put together'. He emphasises voice, and moreover, vocal sounds that do not fit with Western classical definitions of 'good' or 'correct' singing – all involuntary, bodily sounds. This emphasis chimes with what commentators elsewhere have articulated in debates on what constitutes the essence of soul, that is, self-expression, a person's essence, at odds with technological mediation and the regulatory aspects of Western classical notation. Soul music, according to Peter Guralnick, is music that keeps 'straining at the boundaries [...] that it has imposed upon itself', rather than a music of entirely uninhibited emotional release. Yet he contrasts this with 'the cultural refinements of Motown' which despite sharing soul music's church influence 'rarely uncorks a full-blooded scream' and 'only occasionally will reveal a flash of raw emotion' (Guralnick 2002: 7). However, Rudinow takes issue with Guralnick's exclusion of Motown and of northern soul, exposing the flaws of such essentialism (with Aretha Franklin, more Detroit than southern, incorporated into Guralnick's rather strained definition), instead defining soul as a truly national musical movement (Rudinow 2010: 13–4).

Guralnick and Rudinow emphasise soul's popular and universal appeal, whereas Portia Maultsby locates the music within African American blues tradition in her 'Map of the Music', and situates it historically and politically as evolving from the 1960s Civil Rights and Black Power Movements, promoting black pride, class consciousness, and African heritage, as a vehicle for social change (Maultsby 1995, 1983). For Maultsby, soul can be defined as 'black nationalism' – in relation to music. It allowed black performers to reassert their music's identity in the face of a deeply segregated music industry in which black performers were hitherto boycotted by white consumers, and white performers appropriated black musical and performance styles for commercial gain. In the 1940s, black music recordings were marketed as 'race records', which gave way to the term 'rhythm and blues' in the 1950s. Following the assimilation and appropriation of r 'n' b and rock 'n' roll styles by white performers considered more palatable to white consumers, soul provided a label which proudly reasserted the music's blackness (Maultsby 1995). Maultsby's analysis thus situates the history of soul within a history of racism and political activism.

Popular music from the 1950s onwards represented a shift from the written score and concert performance as the primary work of music, to the recording as the primary work. With this shift came a switch in emphasis from melody to timbre:

> With recording one is able to experience, revisit, and analyse nuances of particular sounds and voices […] Recording thus encouraged a paradigm shift from an emphasis on the composer and the written score – and by extension the relative unimportance of timbre – to emphasis on performers and the experience of timbre.
>
> (Smith 2008: 121)

Referring to the work of Evan Eisenberg, Jacob Smith points out the importance of the phonograph in spreading styles of blues singing which previously would only have been encountered in live performance contexts in local scenes in the southern states of the US, also allowing many white musicians to draw upon previously inaccessible musical innovations, in particular the throaty rasp associated with the singing voice of Louis Armstrong (133–4). In the US, the rasp became strongly associated with African American musical culture, but its reach went far beyond:

the rasp became increasingly freighted with cultural meaning for male singers over the course of the century; it indicated blackness, class conflict, masculinity, and catharsis. That so much meaning could be carried by the rough edge of a singer's voice demonstrates the importance of sound technology's ability to preserve specific timbres, as well as the power of the voice as a conveyor of cultural meaning and identity.

(Smith 2008, p. 117)

Smith further argues that through its contrast with the *bel canto* mode of classical singing the vocal technique of the rasp gained heightened significance for white musical culture, employing techniques strictly proscribed in classical singing instruction, yet denoting a particular energy and authenticity.

In *The Commitments* and the two soundtrack albums, Andrew Strong's voice is characterised by a throaty rasp, striking for a youngster of sixteen years of age. As Smith points out, the rasp is also associated with the condition leukoplakia (precancerous lesions of the mouth and throat) which is

exacerbated by overindulgence in activities such as smoking and drinking and [...] in addition to being associated with black performance, the rasp is also an index of 'bad living' which perhaps adds to its status as a sign of outlaw authenticity.

(Smith 2008: 146)

A post-rehearsal scene in *The Commitments* has Deco confrontationally ask the Commitmentettes 'are youse choir girls? [...] because you're not putting much of *that* into it', grabbing his crotch. Here Deco crudely sexualises his vocal and physical performance style and contrasts it with a more hegemonic classical mode associated with religious singing, typically encountered in Ireland's Catholic educational system.

The centrality of vocal techniques outside of classical Western tradition is also manifested in Jimmy's use of James Brown's performance of 'Please, Please, Please' as a yardstick by which the band must 'measure up' – the video they watch emphasises Brown's bodily movement, facial contortions, and screams. Similarly, when the soft-spoken religious piano player Steven enters a confessional booth, he admits to having 'lustful thoughts' about the girls in the band and humming soul songs instead of hymns. Repeatedly, *The Commitments* sets soul music, with its emphasis on sensibility and sexuality, against the refinement and repression of classical religious music.

The gender dynamic extends beyond physical sensibility to singing style. In contrast with Deco, the Commitmentettes use a sweeter, more rounded tone, reinforcing Smith's arguments around the rasp being associated with masculinity, despite female singers also being able to access the same range of vocal techniques (Smith 2008: 149). Nevertheless, Angeline Ball's performance of 'I Can't Stand the Rain' (heard nondiegetically early in the film) stands apart from her other vocal performances as using a lower pitched, throatier singing style closer to Andrew Strong's rasp yet still unmistakeably feminine. When compared with her less raspy and overall higher pitched vocal on 'Too Many Fish in the Sea', a listener might assume the two performances were by two different singers. But as backing singers, the three Commitmentettes' sweeter, softer style provides contrasting accompaniment to Strong's rough rasp.

In the early stages of rehearsal, Paul Bushnell worked with the singer Rob Strong, Andrew Strong's father, and provides a particularly evocative description of the process in which Andrew Strong was cast as Deco:

> I think at the end of the second day we got a phonecall that Rob was sick. He's lost his voice or something, these were pretty intense days. And he was going to send his son, who kind of knew all these songs. His son was 15 years old, long hair, y'know, and in walks Andrew Strong. [...] And he starts singing and we're like 'holy shit! Wow! What the hell is going on? This kid is amazing!' And it seems to be not only can he vibe on the songs, but he goes off into that other world, that Joe Cocker abandoning your body, like your body becomes this thing that just kind of flails along [...] You could just hear the clunk of jaws on the floor, when Parker saw Andrew perform. Parker had actually already in his mind cast Robert Arkins as the lead character in the movie, and he immediately changed his mind when he saw Andrew, he's like 'oh my god, this is the guy'.
>
> (Bushnell 2020)

Ian La Frenais similarly emphasises that Parker's decision to cast Andrew Strong was based on his impressive audition, despite him mismatching the part in the working draft of the script, and he

> felt strongly that for an audience to believe our kids could actually make it, then that belief had to spring from the singer. Not the lead guitarist, or the drummer, or the bass player – it had to be the frontman.
>
> (Clement and La Frenais 2019: 190)

The mismatch of Strong's physical appearance with the character described in the book leads to a unique dynamic in which Strong's voice and body are a striking signature of the film and its albums. According to Killen:

In the original book [...] that character Roddy had painted as debonair. Andrew did not quite physically match up to that description but there was no mistaking the power and conviction of his voice. He was so magnetic that you could not take your eyes off of him.

(Killen 2020)

Killen similarly describes a mismatch between Strong's voice and his body, and his age mismatching his physical appearance. Later, MCA released Andrew Strong's debut album, *Strong*, advertised with the strapline, 'The Voice of The Commitments', and placed as an insert in *The Commitments* CD.

On release of the film, critics noted this gap between Strong's voice and his appearance, for instance, Barry Egan describing him as 'thirty-something-voiced wunderkid' (Egan 1991: 2). In his work on the bodies of popular singers, Mark Duffett points out the regularly noted gap between singers' spoken voices and singing voices. Using the example of Scottish talent show phenomenon Susan Boyle, he describes Boyle's classically trained singing voice as 'exquisitely feminine', in contrast with the 'broad Scottish twang' of her spoken voice and her unconventional and widely mocked appearance, hence her voice is not one singular thing. Duffett argues that Boyle's singing voice 'did *not* recall her body, even though listeners were conditioned to recall it, creating a kind of "Boyle shock" as a result' (Duffett 2011: 181). As is typical in blues-based popular music, Strong's singing voice bears little trace of the Dublin accent of his spoken voice; like Boyle, Strong's singing voice and spoken voice sound distinctly different to each other. Yet the remarkable power of Andrew Strong's voice arguably created a similar type of shock that Duffett describes upon the release of *The Commitments* and its associated albums, given the additional layer of foreknowledge that Strong was just sixteen years old. The voice mismatches the body, the singing voice mismatches the spoken voice, and both body and voice mismatch the singer's age (see Figure 4.4).

And yet, throughout the film, Deco's body is regularly presented as excessive, almost grotesque. He is presented as not in control of his body, with the Commitmentettes describing him as eating 'like a pig', or when he exclaims 'I have to fart!' before audibly farting in the band's recently commandeered Mr Chippy van; yet in contrast with his excessive body, he has a voice that Joey says 'belongs to God'. His loss of control of his body is bound up in his performance style to an extreme degree, such as when he gets so swept up with singing 'Show Me', raising the microphone stand as he drives the calls and response of the chorus home, electrocuting Derek the bass player. In a later altercation with Deco after Billy the drummer

Figure 4.4 Deco singing 'Show Me'

knocks a drum over at the end of a song and Deco calls him a 'fucking eejit', an enraged Billy threatens to stick a drumstick 'up your hole. The one you don't sing out of [...] So keep your Vaseline handy'. The spectacle of Deco's excessive body elicits a mixture of fascination and disgust, yet rather than his voice being presented as his one redeeming feature, its power and beauty is grotesquely associated with his bodily excesses.

Conclusion

The reception and circulation of *The Commitments* is as an entity that is more than a film, or a fictitious band. To further comprehend this idea, it is worth considering the afterlife of the film on TV and VHS. In the rentals section of British film magazine *Empire*, the lack of suitability of the film to the small screen was pointed out:

> On the big screen it is no doubt possible to buy the idea that Rabbitte's band is briefly kissed by the same muse that once inspired Otis Redding and Percy Sledge. In our living rooms, however, we are unlikely to be similarly intoxicated.
>
> (Hepworth 1992: 21)

Hence, although the film circulated widely on home video throughout the 1990s and was broadcast many times on television, it could be argued that the energetic sonic afterlife of the film's youthful musical performances was more successful via the two albums. Kevin Killen was sensitive to these contexts of reception, suggesting the albums could sonically replicate the 'big screen' impact at home:

> If people walked out of the theatre excited about the film and this music, they would most likely want to go and buy the soundtrack, but it still had to have the same kind of power coming out of small speakers as it had coming out of big movie theatre speakers. Because the playback environments are different, you have the sheer weight of volume of air being pushed at you in a movie theatre, then to get that same impact on a small car stereo or your home stereo, there were certain tricks we do as mixers to make sure that that is as impactful.
>
> (Killen 2020)

Beyond the film, several acts have emerged which tour the live music circuit, including Dave Finnegan's Commitments, and The Stars From the Commitments, which included Ken McCluskey (Derek, bass), Michael Aherne (Steven, piano), and Ronan Dooney, who played Joey's mimed trumpet parts. A third touring band called 'The Commitments' also featured Ken McCluskey alongside Dick Massey (Billy, drums). A commercially successful 2011 Commitments tour, dubbed the 20th anniversary reunion, featured most of the cast engaged in musical performance, including Robert Arkins, but not Maria Doyle Kennedy or Johnny Murphy, with Paul Bushnell as musical director. Notably, Roddy Doyle expressed bemusement regarding the tour: 'It's called a reunion but they were never actually a band. One or two of them forgot that' (quoted in Gaffney 2011). The book, the film, the albums, and a suite of live performances have therefore become an expanding and contracting entity, or an example of cross-platform adaptation and remediation, with Doyle's observation reasserting his authorship of The Commitments as fundamentally a product of his imagination. The less told story then is of how the band's musical performances have been sonically represented on film, on record, and beyond, through the processes outlined in this chapter, such that the sound transcends the film.

Notes

1   On this question of live versus mediated encounters, I asked Doyle if he had ever heard any of the songs in the novel performed live prior to writing the novel: 'The chances are I never saw those songs performed by the original people [...] The only regular visitor from black America in my memory was BB King'. Doyle did see James Brown perform in concert in Ireland, but sometime

after the novel was published and the film was released. 'It's not impossible that Elvis Costello might have done one or two of [the songs] [...] but hand to heart I can't say I actually did [hear any of the songs performed live]' (Doyle 2021). Like the cast, Doyle's encounter with the songs had been through recordings first and foremost.

2 See Auslander (2008: 73–127) for detailed discussion of this moment.

5 Conclusion

The legacy of *The Commitments*

Since its release, *The Commitments* has been increasingly celebrated as an Irish film, despite its British and American production history, and in this concluding chapter, I will consider its anointing as such by critics, audiences, and Irish officialdom in the context of a new-found cultural confidence amid the economic change of the 1990s. I will also outline its influence on later Irish youth music films, demonstrating how its preoccupations provide a blueprint that is regularly refreshed in tandem with wider changes in Irish society. What this will show is that films as events are amenable to the shifting ways in which they are understood as time passes, permeating a wider culture. The film's popular reach has meant the expansion of *The Commitments* as an evolving musical entity beyond the film, as well as a regular revisiting of the cast's careers as a metatextual echo of the film's own narrative of youthful promise.

'Where are they now?': Quaint encounters with capitalism, and *The Commitments* as metatext

Given *The Commitments*'s narrative of youth seeking fame and fortune, it is perhaps unsurprising that press coverage of the cast has reiterated a fascination with the trajectories of the film's young performers. Of the cast, the three Commitmentettes have had the most consistently successful careers as actors, and continued to work as musicians. Angeline Ball (Imelda), Maria Doyle Kennedy, (Natalie), and Bronagh Gallagher (Bernie) have appeared prolifically in British and Irish film, television, and theatre over the past thirty years. Gallagher made a brief but memorable appearance in *Pulp Fiction* (1994), wearing an official The Frames t-shirt during the famous scene in which Mia Wallace (Uma Thurman) is given an adrenaline shot to revive her from a drug overdose. As Gallagher later explained, this was not accidental and needed to be cleared with Island Records and approved by Quentin Tarantino ('Bronagh Gallagher …' 2013), demonstrating a

DOI: 10.4324/9780429296048-6

notable loyalty to her fellow Commitment Glen Hansard and a desire to help promote his musical career, continuing the fame and fortune narrative as a metatext. A consistent theme in press coverage is the cast's youth, their 'overnight' stardom, and the difficulty of choosing between music and acting, and even within mere months of the film's release newspapers were running 'Where are they now?' reports.

What is striking is how there is a slight sense of unease around the extent that they were financially compensated. For instance, the *Irish Independent* stated that:

> Although each of the twelve was given a contract worth £18,000 each at the start of eight weeks of filming, none will receive any royalties. The only royalties due are for work on the soundtrack album, and of the 12 only Félim Gormley will earn any credits for his sax blowing
>
> ('And Some of the Band ...' 1991: 19)

failing to acknowledge that the singers on the albums received royalties too. It then assures the reader that 'all of the Commitments are content with their payoff' and quotes from Dick Massey (Billy), Dave Finnegan (Mickah), and Michael Aherne (Steven), all stating that they did not mind and knew what they were signing. Furthermore, Massey agreed to split his money with the other two members of his band, who also went for auditions (ibid.). However, the unease grows with later coverage. While later articles stress some of the cast's successes, others quote more negative assessments, including for instance Glen Hansard stating that he was 'burned' by his experience on the film and Finnegan complaining he did not receive royalties whereas other members did (Milton 2016).

Hansard and Doyle Kennedy already had record deals with their bands The Frames and The Black Velvet Band respectively, and the credits of the film reflect this, describing their appearances as courtesy of their labels Island Records (the same label that signed U2) and Elektra. Signed by MCA, Andrew Strong released a debut album, *Strong*, in 1993, but was then quietly dropped by the label (Milton 2016). He has had a solid music career, continuing to tour and release music, most notably enjoying a number 1 hit in Denmark in 2000. Coverage in the early 1990s describes an overnight glamourous success, a home in Hollywood, and a multi-album deal (Egan 1991), though this early success does not appear to have been sustained, and his discography demonstrates a continued reliance upon his association with *The Commitments*, with a 2012 album entitled *Live: The Commitments Years and Beyond*.

The journey of Robert Arkins is notable, given that much of the press tipped him for stardom as an actor, with journalist Lise Hand betting on him to be the biggest star (Hand 1991: 3). As well as continuing their musical careers, in 1992 Arkins and Gormley went on to front an RTÉ programme showcasing new Irish bands called *On the Waterfront* (Lynch 1992: 14), filmed in the Waterfront venue used in *The Commitments*, and one of the new bands showcased was The Cranberries, prior to their global success. As a result of his appearance on the film and his contribution to the soundtrack, Arkins's band Housebroken was signed to MCA, the same label that released *The Commitments* soundtrack album and *Vol. 2* ('Robert Arkins Being Jimmy Rabbitte' 1992). However, the record deal collapsed before the album was finished, and in later years Arkins stated that he resented having to choose between acting and music, feeling that his indecision led to a lack of success in either career (Milton 2016).

Much coverage of the cast's promotional tour of the US describes it in positive, albeit naïve terms, recalling stretch limos and meeting Hollywood stars, though years later Arkins reflected on it as a difficult experience for him: 'I wasn't prepared, I was too young. There was no one holding me up, no one looking after me. And I couldn't take to people [in LA], I found them fake' (Milton 2016). Despite some forays into acting, many of the band members have later toured their own soul covers bands, with Dick Massey and Ken McCluskey touring as The Stars of the Commitments, and Dave Finnegan with Dave Finnegan's Commitments. The marked exception was Michael Aherne, who went straight back to his job as a civil engineer with Roadstone after the film wrapped ('And Some of the Band …' 1991a: 19; Milton 2016).

The Commitments is briefly mentioned by Ruth Barton as an example of 1990s Irish commercial cinema, in a romantic tradition, concerned with 'quaint encounters with capitalism' (Barton 2001: 193). These press narratives play this quaintness out as a metatext concerning the young cast's encounters beyond the narrative of the film with the capitalism of the movie and music business. While the film's narrative builds to greater competence and missed opportunities – failing to jam onstage with Wilson Pickett and failing to sign a record deal – the narrative of the film's promotional success allowed these opportunities to happen, with Pickett jamming live on stage with some of the young musicians at promotional parties at premieres in New York, Chicago, and Los Angeles. Doyle's first draft of the screenplay includes an appearance by James Brown, rather than Wilson Pickett, jamming on stage with The Commitments, and as in the book they play quite a few James Brown songs; however, despite the efforts of the music supervisor G. Marq Roswell, none of these songs could be cleared for recording (Doyle 2021). But in 1992, James Brown played in Ireland for the first time, with The Stars of the Commitments (Dick Massey and Ken McCluskey) and Andrew Strong's father Rob Strong playing support, allowing some of The Commitments to share the same bill with the Godfather of Soul, if not actually jamming on stage together. And twenty years after the film's release, The Commitments performed live in a 20th anniversary reunion tour, again with Paul Bushnell's involvement, and the co-operation of much of the cast, even Hansard. A clip from RTÉ news coverage includes a contribution from Bronagh Gallagher in which she frames the uplifting spirit of the tour as a way to help Irish people overcome hopelessness of the post-Celtic Tiger economic crash: 'We've got through this before, we're gonna get through this again' ('The Commitments Reunite' 2010).

In part, the positivity and exuberance of the film can be understood as a youth-led Irish rejection of British cultural domination and embrace of the American dream. Both Pettitt (2000: 114–37) and Taylor (1998) have read this somewhat ambivalently, positing *The Commitments* as an example of Irish culture moving from British to American subjugation. However, Michael Cronin contests this, pointing out that '[t]he one character, Deco, who most ostensibly embraces the cult of success and stardom, is in fact almost universally reviled' (2006: 38), suggesting the possibility of more open interpretations. Again, this plays out as a metatext of the band members' own discussion of their careers. Of all the cast, with his band The Frames and their distinct folk-influenced indie-rock sound, Hansard has managed to carve out a musical identity that is the most distinct from The Commitments. He quickly distanced himself from *The Commitments* album given his lack of royalties, and further distanced himself from *The Commitments*:

> The film has gone from the film people's hands to MCA and MCA are promoting the album. The album is basically Andrew Strong's. I don't mind but I don't want to be wasting my time going around doing promotion for Andrew Strong. Nothing against Andrew but I'd much rather be doing it for myself.
>
> (quoted in Hayes 1991: 18)

Despite the 'I don't mind', Hansard's criticism of MCA is laced with implicit criticism of Strong, another metatextual moment. Parker was even more pointed in his assessment:

> Andrew Strong was given the best opportunity for the future with an instant contract from MCA after we finished the film. Perhaps Andrew's personality was too similar to Deco's: echoing the scene I put at the end of the movie where he throws a glass of Guinness at the long suffering record producer, played by myself. Whatever the reasons, Andrew's incredible voice never lived up to its potential.
>
> (Parker n.d.)

Beyond the core cast, it is remarkable how many young people in minor roles, in front of and behind the camera, went on to further their careers in media, film, and music. After narrowly missing being cast as a Commitmentette, singer Niamh Kavanagh, who sings two songs on the soundtrack including 'Destination Anywhere', went on to win the Eurovision Song Contest for Ireland in 1993, and still earns royalties from singing on The Commitments albums (Sweeney 2020). The film's music coordinator John Hughes was introduced by Bushnell to (a then unknown) Jim Corr, and indeed, all members of The Corrs appear briefly in *The Commitments* with Andrea Corr playing Jimmy's younger sister Sharon. Hughes then became The Corrs' manager. A 1991 article in local newspaper the *Dundalk Democrat* reports on the Corr family appearing in *The Commitments* before they became a global pop phenomenon, merely as a local human-interest story ('*The Commitments* and the Corr ...' 1991: 5).

The casting directors Ros and John Hubbard's daughter Amy worked as a production assistant on the film, and has since gone on to have a successful casting career herself. Lance Daly, who played the Kid with Harmonica in the audition sequence, is now an acclaimed film director, whose credits include *Black '47* (2018), a striking revenge thriller set during the Great Famine and huge box office success in Ireland ('Famine Film...' 2018). In yet another connection, the Hubbards' son Daniel was casting director for *Black '47*. In the 2010 Screen Directors Guild of Ireland AGM, with Parker as guest of honour and Daly in attendance, the clip from *The Commitments* of Daly playing his harmonica and being admonished by Mr. Rabbitte was screened (Daly 2020), providing a snapshot of young film talent in the making, and perhaps an acknowledgement of the film's and of Parker's role in launching Irish creative careers.

The Commitments as an evolving musical entity

Though rumoured, a sequel to *The Commitments* never materialised, although at one point the now disgraced film producer Harvey Weinstein had acquired the rights (Fleming 2000). However, Doyle's stage adaptation in 2013 constitutes a reboot of sorts, with an entirely new cast. Doyle retained the rights to stage adaptation of his novel and turned down multiple offers to do so, before deciding to do it himself (BBC 2013). A notable difference between the musical and the film is the music choices, which like Doyle's novel and first screenplay draft are much more orientated towards funk and Motown than the southern soul that dominates the film. What is clear in any comparison between the novel, the different versions of the screenplay, the film, and the musical, is the very different musical interpretations that Doyle and Parker had in relation to the story. Parker's papers demonstrate how as an adaptation, the film shifted Doyle's emphasis upon James Brown and Motown to the Southern Soul associated particularly with the label Stax (Memphis, Tennessee) and the recording studio Muscle Shoals (Sheffield, Alabama).

Given that the musical makes no reference to the film, for legal reasons (Parker n.d.), and that Doyle was so protective of the rights to it, it might be interpreted that there is disagreement or animosity between the two men concerning the musical interpretation of the film. Some press has over-emphasised an idea that Doyle had a 'bumpy' relationship with the film, as opposed to merely a desire to move on to new creative projects (Cummins 2013; Brown 2013). It is true that Doyle had little involvement in music choices in pre-production, the film shoot, or post-production. Doyle only visited the shoot twice. Yet he is positive about Parker's efforts to keep him in the loop, sending him a C120 cassette of the songs they had cleared for use: 'and it was brilliant. There was no James Brown there, and there were other absences, but he hoovered it up, it was brilliant' (Doyle 2021). Doyle was aware of the fundamental difference between writing music and film-ing music.

> In the novel, you can have 'Chain Gang,' and other pop hits, with something that Otis Redding might have sung, and it didn't really mat-ter. But when it comes to the sound, that extra ingredient a film would have, that's different, the choices must be different'.
>
> (Ibid.)

Parker also sent him a tape of the rushes during the early stages of post, and discussed with him the idea of selling affordable tickets for the Dublin premiere: 'He was great, very gracious', singling out Parker for individual praise. Nevertheless, 'I think, when it's in the machine, it's a bit differ-ent' and Doyle was not invited to the film's premiere in Los Angeles. 'I didn't even know when the world premiere was. Nobody told me. [...] That shouldn't happen really, that was rude' (ibid.).

Doyle states that he has only seen the film twice, at the cast and crew screening, and the premiere in Dublin, and not since, but insists that both times he thought it was 'tremendous'. Despite it replacing 'Night Train' in the novel and first draft, Doyle singles out the choice of 'Treat Her Right' as the opening song for particular praise: 'I thought it was actually clever in that it wasn't actually Andrew Strong singing the opening song, that was great storytelling'. Overall, Doyle doesn't recall objecting to any song choices in the film, although, when pressed, he recalls not being so keen on 'Mustang Sally': 'I think because it became *the song*', indicating both its strong asso-ciation with The Commitments, and its ubiquity. To illustrate this point, he describes several years later performing a reading at an event promoting his sombre domestic violence novel, *The Woman Who Walked Into Doors*, and being introduced with a wildly inappropriate blast of 'Mustang Sally' and its strutting male machismo.

> And yet people love the song. It's in the musical. It's in the encore, the little gig at the end, and people go mad for it, and that's grand. I'm happy enough for it to be there [but] its popularity baffles me I have to say.

Yet he is charitable about the music choices throughout the film: 'there's so much more that's important than my taste in music to the film - there's Andrew's face, and what he does with his face' (ibid.). Putting the music choices in Doyle's musical and novel into dialogue with the film's music choices demonstrates a difference of opinion, certainly, but not outright conflict. However, what is striking about much of this discussion is the sense of The Commitments persisting as a musical idea or entity beyond the film or novel.

The Irish youth musical

The film has provided a template for a recurring Irish youth musical. *The Last Bus Home* (Gogan 1997), is arguably a punk Commitments, depicting a Dublin suburban ennui. Along with a wave of 1990s Celtic Tiger films it consolidated urban and suburban Ireland as legitimate settings that are not incompatible with Irish identity. It further shares with *The Commitments* a youthfulness and a wariness of the commercial aspects of music. The punk music played by the film's fictitious band The Dead Patriots was written by cult Irish rocker Cathal Coughlan, of Fatima Mansions. Sadly, this film was not widely seen beyond a limited cinema release. In contrast, the international box office phenomenon and Oscars success of *Once* (Carney 2007) has particularly overt links with *The Commitments* given that it stars Glen Hansard as a Dublin busker, and again capitalises on his musicianship and status as a musician-actor rather than a professional actor. Like its predecessor, it explores the classic art versus commerce debate, yet its setting fifteen years later reveals a radically changed Dublin with newly found wealth, youth employment, and immigration rather than the mass emigration of the past. The music at the heart of the film is particularly white folk rock, yet the unnamed young female musician character who plays opposite Hansard, Markéta Irglová, though white, is designated an outsider through her eastern European immigrant identity. Though a Dubliner, Hansard's character appears estranged from the wealth of the city and his affinities with Irglová's character is through their precarious economic status. In a premonition of *Once*, Hansard's final appearance in *The Commitments* is of him busking in Grafton Street, back to the musician's musical roots (see Figures 5.1 and 5.2).

Killing Bono (Hamm 2011) shares *The Commitments'* links with U2, and a script by Clement and La Frenais, and is similarly a film that explores young male hubris, but with added middle-class Dublin swagger. Two young brothers from the Northside attempt to make the big time with their band Shook Up!, but end up watching from the side-lines as their irritating classmate Bono and his band U2 achieve rock mega-stardom. The film's key bid to authenticity is its basis on the true-life events of Irish musician turned journalist Neil McCormick, adapted from his 2003 memoir; and though the music was written for the film, it is a convincing pastiche of 1980s post-punk with some New Romantic sensibilities. What is especially poignant about the trajectory of Shook Up! is McCormick's bizarre synchronicity of choosing dates for the band's pivotal gigs that clash with major cultural events, such as Pope John Paul II's 1979 rally in Phoenix Park, Dublin, and Live Aid in Wembley Stadium in 1985. Meanwhile, the band's litany of failure is paralleled by the seemingly irresistible rise of their former school friends U2.

The more recent Dublin-set films *Sing Street* (Carney 2016) and *Dublin Oldschool* (Tynan 2018) have a peculiar relationship with pre-Celtic Tiger era Dublin. *Sing Street* is set in the 1980s and is about a group of school-going teenagers forming a band, but unlike *The Commitments* it is quite unapologetically a middle-class film with very different class politics. Maria Doyle Kennedy appears in *Sing Street* as the main character's mother, a

Figure 5.1 Jimmy meets Derek and Outspan busking in Grafton Street

Figure 5.2 Glen Hansard busking in Grafton Street in *Once* (Carney, 2007)

generational shift for fans of *The Commitments*. Although *Dublin Oldschool* is ostensibly set in the present day, the youthful drug-fuelled techno music scene it depicts, of underground clubs and illegal raves, seems very much of the mid-1990s and could be seen as another iteration of the 'retro' film of *The Commitments*, but twenty-five years later and with a very different set of musical taste frameworks and subcultural capital. In the film's climactic outdoor rave scene, its comedically chemically addled character Dave 'the Rave' turns down the music and addresses the crowd with 'Young people of Ireland... WRECK THE FUCKIN' GAFF!' parodying the address of Pope John Paul II at Phoenix Park in 1979. Nearly thirty years on, the Irish youth musical continues to posit music and its associated subcultures as resistant to Ireland's Catholic hegemony, even as it recedes into the past and Ireland has entered into a more secular present.

Becoming an Irish film: *The Commitments,* the Celtic Tiger, and cultural legitimacy

At the start of this book, I outlined *The Commitments*' status as simultaneously Irish, British, and American. The paradox at the heart of this exploration of *The Commitments* is that Ireland's most culturally significant and commercially successful film of the early 1990s was – in material and economic terms – a British film financed with American money. Shot in Ireland, and with an Irish cast, it is textually Irish, even if its financing and its 'above the line' (director, producer) credits categorically were not. However, using

Rick Altman's concept of 'cinema as event', with the film serving as a 'point of interchange between [...] the work of production [and] the process of reception' (Altman 1992: 3) as opposed to 'film as text' or 'autonomous aesthetic entity most closely related to other autonomous textual entities' (2), helps to account for the film's status as Irish, while acknowledging the importance of its transnational production contexts. It recognises the pivotal role of the cast and the younger members of the crew in bringing to the film aspects of themselves that can be understood as 'a subset of culture at large' (3), and the hype, publicity, and box office success of its release in Ireland, the circulation of the soundtrack albums and associated songs, and the endur-ing popularity of the film and its fictitious band, which 'broadens out again, eventually reaching the point where it is indistinguishable from the culture in general' (4). Thinking about *The Commitments* as an event, in terms of the participation of young Irish people in its making, reception, and celebration, and the cultural circulation of an evolving Commitments metatext, helps to understand how it became legitimised and memorialised as an Irish film.

The film's legitimation as Irish is detectable very early on, in a submis-sion from the lobby group Film Makers Ireland to the Irish Department of Finance (dated 19 December 1990), describing 1990 as a 'watershed year' and referring directly to *My Left Foot* and *The Commitments* (Gilsenan 1990). These films, alongside Neil Jordan's 1992 success with *The Crying Game*, built momentum and political will to renew investment in Irish film-making and to re-establish the Irish Film Board in 1993, which still exists today (renamed Screen Ireland). *The Commitments'* status as an *Irish* cul-tural product was further cemented by its use in a collection of four com-memorative stamps celebrating a century of Irish cinema in 1996, alongside Robert O'Flaherty's *Man of Aran* (1934), *My Left Foot* (1989), and *The Field* (1990), both directed by Jim Sheridan (see Figure 5.3). (In yet another connection, Jim Sheridan went on to direct a BBC radio adaptation of *The Commitments* in 2013.) Notably, of the four films chosen, the two Irish-directed ones were directed by the same person, and of the other two, one was directed by an American (O'Flaherty), and the other was directed by a Brit (Parker) – the triumvirate of nationalities so regularly discussed in this book in relation to *The Commitments'* financing and production. It is unclear whether the Stamp Design Committee of An Post, the Irish post office, were aware that their choices mirrored the regular British and American influences on Irish cinema. In addition, a still from *The Commitments* was requested for use in a CD-ROM to illustrate a section on Irish cinema, pro-duced by the Irish Department of Foreign Affairs for visiting delegations and press, in aid of the 1996 Irish presidency of the European Union, further legitimating the film as an Irish cultural product in the contexts of Irish-European diplomacy (Mellerick 1996).

Figure 5.3 The Commitments stamp (top right), Ireland, Centenary of Cinema, 1996

Overall, what is striking about *The Commitments* now, given the extent of social change in Ireland since its release, is its exuberant disregard for authority, as well as its sincerity of aspiration, laced with caution, which prefigure the cultural shifts of the 1990s. In 1992, Sinéad O'Connor tore up a photograph of Pope John Paul II on live television, signalling the beginnings of a rapid decline in the Catholic Church's authority in Ireland throughout the decade, brought about in part by the shockwaves of clerical sexual abuse scandals. In 1993 homosexuality was finally decriminalised in Ireland, and divorce legalised in 1996 after a 1995 referendum (but rejected in a 1986 referendum). Dublin went on to experience the boom of the Celtic Tiger years most strongly, with the increased foothold of global corporate tech capital established in parallel with the rise of cultures of consumption and leisure, the superpub, and the rise of Temple Bar as a stag and hen weekend destination rather than a hip cultural quarter; in other words, the marketisation of 'the craic', which remains Dublin's main tourist draw.

Taken together, all the films discussed in this Conclusion demonstrate the economic, social, cultural, and musical shifts that Ireland, particularly Dublin, has experienced; yet overall *The Commitments* has generated a resilient blueprint which all the films follow to varying, and intriguing, extents. As I have argued throughout this book, *The Commitments* was more than just a film. The scale of its audition process took the blueprint laid down by Doyle's novel to create the film out of its interactions with the youth of the city, promoting it back to them, and beyond. Yet it was the 'above the line' personnel and financiers that profited most from the film's success, and took much of the profits out of Ireland. Nevertheless, revisiting *The Commitments* thirty years on, I have been left with the palpable sense, spurious or otherwise, that the fate of the young Dubliners echoes the plot of the film. Arguably, as an event or as an organising principle, the film *The Commitments* was to Dublin what Jimmy Rabbitte was to The Commitments, succeeding in raising the city's spirits and expanding its horizons, whether it meant to or not.

Bibliography

Altman, R. (1992) 'Introduction: Cinema as Event', in R. Altman (ed) *Sound Theory, Sound Practice*, New York: Routledge, pp. 1–14.

American Film Institute (n.d.) 'The Commitments', *AFI Catalog*, online, https://catalog.afi.com/Catalog/MovieDetails/58833.

'And Some of the Band Played On' (1991) *Irish Independent*, 9 November, p. 19.

Auslander, P. (2008) *Liveness: Performance in a Mediatized Culture*, 2nd edition, New York: Routledge.

Ball, A. (2021) *Zoom Interview with the Author*, 16 April.

Barton, R. (2001) 'Kitsch as Authenticity: Irish Cinema and the Challenge to Romanticism', *Irish Studies Review*, Vol. 9, No. 2, pp. 193–202.

Barton, R. (2004) *Irish National Cinema*, Abingdon: Routledge.

Barton, R. (2019) *Irish Cinema in the Twenty-First Century*, Manchester: Manchester University Press.

Barton, R. and O'Brien, H. (eds) (2004) *Keeping it Real: Irish Film and Television*, London: Wallflower.

Bayton, M. (1990) 'How Women Become Musicians', in S. Frith and A. Goodwin (eds) *On Record: Rock, Pop and the Written Word*, London: Routledge, pp. 238–57.

BBC (2013) 'Roddy Doyle's *The Commitments* Becomes West End Musical', *BBC*, online, 24 April, https://www.bbc.co.uk/news/world-europe-22270533.

Beacon Communications (1991a) 'A Tosser's Glossary', *The Commitments* (1991) Documentation, Press Kit – 1991, Folder PRK – 1 – 18 – 6 – 2, Alan Parker Papers, British Film Institute.

Beacon Communications (1991b) 'Music Cue Sheet with License Fees', 6 June, *The Commitments* (1991) Documentation, Post Production Music 1991 –1992, Folder PRK – 1 – 18 – 5 – 1, Alan Parker Papers, British Film Institute.

Beacon Communications (1991c) 'Some Notes on the Making of the Film', *The Commitments* (1991) Documentation, Press Kit – 1991, Folder PRK – 1 – 18 – 6 –2 Alan Parker Papers, British Film Institute.

'Best 100 British Films – Full List' (1999) *BBC News*, online, 23 September, available at: http://news.bbc.co.uk/1/hi/entertainment/455170.stm.

'Billboard 200: Week of January 25, 1992' (n.d.) *Billboard*, online, https://www.billboard.com/charts/billboard-200/1992-01-25.

Bordwell, D. (1993) 'Film Interpretation Revisited', *Film Criticism*, Vol. 27 No. 3, pp. 1–28.

BPI (n.d.) 'BRIT Certified: Certified Awards Search', *BPI*, online, https://www.bpi.co.uk/brit-certified/.

Braine, J. (2000) 'My Personal Experience of the Early Days of Dublin Raving and Clubbing', *John Braine: Stuff Wotsits and Thingies*, online, https://www.johnbraine.com/music/words/history-of-dublin-clubbing.html.

Brennan, M. (2020) *Kick It: A Social History of the Drum Kit*, Oxford: Oxford University Press.

'Bronagh Gallagher and that Frames T-Shirt in *Pulp Fiction*' (2013) *Saturday Night Show*, [television programme clip], online, RTÉ, Ireland, uploaded to YouTube 24th November 2013, https://youtu.be/R8k6siLmtA4.

Brown, M. (2013) 'The Commitments to Be Turned into West End Musical', *Guardian*, online, 23 April, https://www.theguardian.com/stage/2013/apr/23/the-commitments-west-end-musical.

Bushnell, P. (2020) *Skype Interview with the Author*, 9 July.

Chion, M. (2009) *Film: A Sound Art*, New York: Columbia University Press.

Clement, D. and La Frenais, I. (1989) 'The Commitments' script, 2nd draft, Dec 1989', *The Commitments* (1991) Documentation, Draft Scripts, Folder 1 of 2, Folder PKR – 1 – 18 – 1 – 2, Alan Parker Papers, British Film Institute.

Clement, D. and La Frenais, I. (2019) *More Than Likely: A Memoir*, London: Weidenfeld & Nicholson.

'Commitments' (n.d.) *Official Charts*, online, officialcharts.com/artist/27280/commitments.

Cronin, M. (2006) *The Barrytown Trilogy*, Cork: Cork University Press.

Cummins, S. (2013) 'Interview: Roddy Doyle on *The Commitments* Musical', *Irish Post*, online, 24 April, https://www.irishpost.com/entertainment/interview-roddy-doyle-on-the-commitments-musical-6043.

Daly, L. (2020) *Skype Interview with the Author*, 4 March.

David, M. (2015) 'Alan Parker Lists Just Above the Sunset Strip', *Variety*, online, 13 May, https://variety.com/2015/dirt/real-estalker/alan-parker-lists-just-above-the-sunset-strip-1201494670/.

Department of Taoiseach (1989) 'Minutes of Working Group Sub-Region No. 1 Dublin City and County (20/3/1989)', from file *Dept of Taoiseach, National Programme of Community Interest for the Greater Dublin Area 2019/30/473*, Bishop Street, Dublin: National Archives of Ireland.

Doane, M.A. (1985) 'Ideology and the Practice of Sound Editing and Mixing', in E. Weis and J. Belton (eds) *Film Sound: Theory and Practice*, New York: Columbia University Press, pp. 54–62.

Doyle, R. (1987/1998) *The Commitments*, London: Vintage.

Doyle, R. (1989) 'The Commitments' script, 1st draft, Feb 1989 (copyright Roger Randall-Cutler and Lynda Myles)', *The Commitments* (1991) Documentation, Draft Scripts, Folder 1 of 2, Folder PKR – 1 – 18 – 1 – 2, Alan Parker Papers, British Film Institute.

Doyle, R. (2020) 'Roddy Doyle on Writing *The Commitments*: 'Whenever I Needed a Name, I Used the Phonebook', *Guardian*, online, 12 December, https://www

.theguardian.com/books/2020/dec/12/roddy-doyle-on-writing-the-commitments
-whenever-i-needed-a-name-i-used-the-phonebook.

Doyle, R. (2021) *Zoom Interview with the Author*, 15 February.

Drake, P. (2003a) 'Low Blows? Theorizing Performance in Post-Classical Comedian Comedy', in F. Krutnik (ed) *Hollywood Comedians: The Film Reader*, London: Routledge, pp. 187–98.

Drake, P. (2003b) '"Mortgaged to Music": New Retro Movies in 1990s Hollywood Cinema', in P. Grainge (ed) *Memory and Popular Film*, Manchester: Manchester University Press, pp. 183–201.

Drake, P. (2004) 'Jim Carrey: The Cultural Politics of Dumbing Down' in A. Willis (ed) *Film Stars: Hollywood and Beyond*, Manchester: Manchester University Press, pp. 71–88.

Drake, P. (2006) 'Reconceptualizing Screen Performance', *Journal of Film and Video*, Vol. 58, Nos. 1–2, Spring/Summer, pp. 84–94.

Duffett, M. (2011) 'Elvis Presley and Susan Boyle: Bodies of Controversy', *Journal of Popular Music Studies*, Vol. 23, No. 2, pp. 166–89.

Dwyer, M. (1990a) 'Alan Parker Goes Casting', *Irish Times*, 15 June, p. 3.

Dwyer, M. (1990b) 'Parker's Chosen Few', *Irish Times - Weekend*, 11 August, pp. 1–2.

Dwyer, M. (1991) 'The New Soul Rebels', *Irish Times*, 14 September, p. 26.

Dyer, R. (1979) *Stars*, London: BFI.

Dyer, R. (2002) 'Entertainment and Utopia', in *Only Entertainment*, 2nd edition, London: Routledge, pp. 19–35.

Dyer, R. (2011) *In the Space of a Song*, London: Routledge.

Eagan, C.M. (2006) 'Still "Black" and "Proud": Irish America and the Racial Politics of Hibernophilia', in D. Negra, (ed.) *The Irish in Us: Irishness, Performativity, and Popular Culture*, London/Durham, NC: Duke University Press, pp. 20–63.

Egan, B. (1991) 'Sound Man with Soul', *Sunday Independent*, 29 December, p. 2.

'Famine Film *Black 47* Has Made Over €1 Million at the Irish Box Office' (2018) *TheJournal.ie*, online, 20 September, http://jrnl.ie/4246331.

Flattum, J. (2002) 'The Story Leads the Dance: An Interview with Music Supervisor G. Marq Roswell', *Muse's Muse*, online, http://www.musesmuse.com/00000398.html.

Fleming, M. (2000) '"Commitments" Encore Gets Leight Touch', *Variety*, online, 3 January, https://variety.com/2000/voices/columns/commitments-encore-gets
-leight-touch-1117760417/.

Foote, J. (1992) ''Made in Ireland' Doesn't Mean Irish', *Newsweek*, 13 July, p. 46.

Frith, S. (1996) *Performing Rites: On the Value of Popular Music*, Cambridge MA: Harvard University Press.

Frith, S. (2007) 'The Industrialisation of Popular Music', in *Taking Popular Music Seriously: Selected Essays*, Aldershot: Ashgate, pp. 93–118.

Gaffney, C. (2011) 'They Shouldn't Be Calling Themselves The Commitments Roddy Doyle's Surprise Blast: "They're not a Band, That Was All Just Acting"', *Daily Mail*, online, 27 February, https://www.dailymail.co.uk/tvshowbiz/article
-1361067/They-shouldnt-calling-The-Commitments-Roddy-Doyle-s-suprise
-blast-Theyre-band-just-acting.html.

Gallagher, B. (2021) *Zoom Interview with the Author*, 21 January.

Geoghegan, D. (1989) 'Who Shot the Sheriff?', *In Dublin*, 3 August, pp. 56–7.

Giambona, G. (2019) 'The Rhythm of the City: Roddy Doyle on Dublin, the Past, Identity and the Healing Power of the City', *Irish Studies Review*, Vol. 27, No. 2, pp. 253–64.

Gilsenan, A. (1990) 'Letter to Albert Reynolds, Re: Film Makers Ireland – Pre Budget Submission, 19 December 1990', Irish Film Board: General Financial Affairs, 1982–1987, Department of Finance, Folder: 2017/7/218, Irish National Archives.

Gray, M. (1999) 'The Commitments', in *Stills, Reels and Rushes: Ireland and the Irish in 20th Century Cinema*, Dublin: Blackhall Publishing, pp. 196–9.

Greer, J. (1991) 'Total Commitment', *Spin*, October, p. 13.

Gritten, D. (1991) 'MOVIES : Irish Soul : How Alan Parker Drew upon the Working-Class Kids of Dublin to Power His Movie 'The Commitments,' about a Fictional Irish Band', *Los Angeles Times*, online, 11 August, https://www.latimes.com/archives/la-xpm-1991-08-11-ca-800-story.html.

Guralnick, P. (2002) *Sweet Soul Music: Rhythm and Blues and the Southern Dream of Freedom*, Edinburgh: Mojo Books/Canongate.

Hand, L. (1991) 'Reel Dubs Set to Paint Film World 'Scarleh'', *Sunday Independent*, 23 June, p. 3.

Hayes, D. (1991) 'Film star Glen's True Commitment Is His Band', *Irish Press*, 28 November, p. 18.

Hebdige, D. (1979) *Subculture: The Meaning of Style*, London/New York: Routledge.

Hepworth, D. (1992) 'The Commitments', *Empire*, May, p. 21.

Holohan, C. (2010) *Cinema on the Periphery: Contemporary Irish and Spanish Film*, Dublin: Irish Academic Press.

Keightley, K. (2003) 'Manufacturing Authenticity: Imagining the Music Industry in Anglo-American Cinema, 1956–62' in K. Dickinson (ed.) *Movie Music: The Film Reader*, London/New York: Routledge, pp. 165–80.

Killen, K. (2020) *Skype Interview with the Author*, 15 July.

King, B. (1985) 'Articulating Stardom', *Screen*, Vol. 26, No. 5, pp. 27–51.

Knell, J. (2010) 'North and South of the River: Demythologizing Dublin in Contemporary Irish Film', *Éire-Ireland*, Vol. 45, No. 1, pp. 213–41.

Kracauer, S. (1960) *Theory of Film: The Redemption of Physical Reality* (Reprint, 1997), Princeton, NJ: Princeton University Press.

Linehan, H. (2020) *Skype Interview with the Author*, 9 March.

Lowe, R. (1991) 'A Director from Over Here Who's Doing Rather Well Over There…', *Empire*, October, pp. 70–4.

Lynch, C. (1992) 'New TV Series to Help Music Talent', *Irish Press*, 7 January, p. 14.

Martin, A. (1991) 'The Commitments', *Film Critic: Adrian Martin*, online, October, http://www.filmcritic.com.au/reviews/c/commitments.html.

Mathijs, E. (2011) 'Referential Acting and the Ensemble Cast', *Screen*, Vol. 52, No. 1, pp. 89–96.

Maultsby, P.K. (1983) 'Soul Music: Its Sociological and Political Significance in American Popular Culture', *Journal of Popular Culture*, Vol. 17, No. 2, pp. 51–60.

Maultsby, P.K. (1995) 'A Map of the Music', *African American Review*, Vol. 9 No. 22, pp. 183–4.

McGlynn, M. (2004) 'Why Jimmy Wears a Suit: White, Black, and Working Class in "The Commitments"', *Studies in the Novel*, Vol, 36, No. 2, pp. 232–50.

McGonigle, L. (2005) 'Rednecks and Southsiders Need not Apply: Subalternity and Soul in Roddy Doyle's *The Commitments*', *Irish Studies Review*, Vol. 13, No. 2, pp. 163–73.

McLaughlin, N. (2014) 'Post-punk Industrial Cyber Opera? The Ambivalent and Disruptive Hybridity of early 1990s U2', in M. Fitzgerald and J. O'Flynn (eds) *Music and Identity in Ireland and Beyond*, London: Routledge, pp. 179–202.

McLoone, M. (2000) *Irish Film: The Emergence of a Contemporary Cinema*, London: BFI.

McLoone, M. (with McLaughlin, N.) (2008) 'Irish Soundscapes: Hybridity and National Musics', in M. McLoone (ed) *Film, Media and Popular Culture in Ireland: Cityscapes, Landscapes, Soundscapes*, Dublin/Portland OR: Irish Academic Press, pp. 143–64.

Mellerick, J. (1996) *Mellerick to Lisa Moran, 30 July 1996. [Fax] Held at: PKR – 1 – 18 – 8 – 3 (Film – The Commitments – Use of Images – 1994–1996)*, BFI Special Collections.

Milton, S. (2016) 'He Said It Once and Said It Loud... So what Became of Jimmy Rabbitte?', *Independent*, 2 October, online, https://www.independent .ie/entertainment/he-said-it-once-and-said-it-loud-so-what-became-of-jimmy -rabbitte-35086004.html.

Myles, L. (2020) *Telephone Interview with the Author*, 22 April.

O'Connor, Á. (2000) 'Sexing the Shamrock', *Sunday Independent ('Living' supplement)*, 19 March, p. 6.

O'Fearghaill, S. (1991) 'Fair City', *In Dublin*, 29 March, pp. 6–8.

O'Flynn, J. (2009) *The Irishness of Irish Music*, Kent: Ashgate.

O'Hagan, S. (1990) 'The City That Time Forgot', *Face*, June, pp. 44–52.

O'Sullivan, P. (1992) '"Tell Me a Story": Ireland and the Movie Moguls', *Irish Studies Review*, Vol. 1, No. 1, pp. 2–4.

Oaks, L. (1998) 'Irishness, Eurocitizens and Reproductive Rights' in S. Franklin and H. Ragone (eds) *Reproducing Reproduction: Kinship, Power, and Technological Innovation*, Philadelphia, PA: Pennsylvania University Press, pp. 132–55.

Onkey, L. (2010) *Blackness and Translatlantic Irish identity: Celtic Soul Brothers*, New York: Routledge.

O'Riordan, N. (2015) '"Don't Use Your Own Accents!": Representations of Dublin's Accents in Contemporary Film', in B. Monihan (ed) *Ireland and Cinema: Culture and Contexts*, New York/Basingstoke: Palgrave Macmillan, pp. 35–46.

Parker, A. (n.d.) 'The Commitments: The Making of the Film', online: http:// alanparker.com/film/the-commitments/making/.

Parker, A. (1986) 'A Turnip Head's Guide to British Cinema', *Thames Television*, online, https://youtu.be/yAdE5MXBhwo.

Parker, A. (1991) *Film: The Commitments* (1991), Congratulatory Letters – Previews and Premieres, May–Nov 1991, Folder: PKR – 1 – 18 – 7 – 1, Alan Parker Papers, British Film Institute.

Parker, A. (2016) 'Director's Commentary', *The Commitments: 25ᵗʰ Anniversary Edition* [Blu-ray], USA, 1991, 118mins [RLJ Entertainment].

Peberdy, D. (2011) *Masculinity and Film Performance: Male Angst in Contemporary American Cinema*, Basingstoke: Palgrave Macmillan.

Pendreigh, B. (1995) 'The Commitments', in *On Location' The Film Fan's Guide to Britain and Ireland*, London/Edinburgh: Mainstream Publishing, pp. 220–4.

Pettitt, L. (2000) *Screening Ireland: Film and Television Representation*, Manchester: Manchester University Press.

Pramaggiore, M. (2007) *Irish and African American Cinema: Identifying Others and Performing Identities 1980–2000*, Albany NY: State University of New York Press.

'Robert Arkins Being Jimmy Rabbitte' (1992) *Nighthawks*, [television programme clip, online] pres. Shay Healy, RTÉ, Ireland, broadcast 14 January, 2 minutes 26 seconds, online, https://www.rte.ie/archives/2017/0110/843992-commitments-star-robert-arkins/.

'Roddy Doyle' (1992) *Writer in Profile* [television programme clip, online], Pres. David Hanly, RTÉ, Ireland, 10 June, 5mins 59secs, online, https://www.rte.ie/archives/2013/0610/455655-roddy-doyle-and-the-commitments/.

Rudinow, J. (2010) *Soul Music: Tracking the Spiritual Roots of Pop from Plato to Motown*, Ann Arbor, MI: Michigan University Press.

Ryan, R. (1991) 'Aidan Thankful for Chance Meeting', *Irish Examiner*, 2 October, p. 9.

Salaam, K.Y. (1995) 'How We Sound Is How We Are', *African American Review*, Vol. 29, No. 2, pp. 181–2.

Shail, R. (2007) *British Film Directors: A Critical Guide*, Edinburgh: Edinburgh University Press.

Shearer, M. (2015) 'A New Way of Living: *West Side Story*, Street Dance and the New York Musical', *Screen*, Vol. 56, No. 4, pp. 450–70.

'Singer Fails in £30,000 Film Claim' (2000) *Independent.ie*, online, 9 May, https://www.independent.ie/irish-news/singer-fails-in-30000-film-claim-26117647.html.

Smith, B. (2020) *Skype Interview with the Author*, 5 February.

Smith, J. (2008) *Vocal Tracks: Performance and Sound Media*, Berkeley, CA: University of California Press.

Smyth, G. (2009) 'Bringing it All Back Home? The Dynamics of Local Music Making in *The Commitments*', in *Music in Irish Cultural History*, Dublin: Irish Academic Press, pp. 65–83.

Speed, L. (1998) 'Tuesday's Gone: The Nostalgic Teen Film', *Journal of Popular Film and Television*, Vol. 26, No. 1, pp. 24–32.

'Storyville: Muscle Shoals – The Greatest Recording Studio in the World' (2014) dir. Greg Camalier Greg, broadcast on BBC4, Sunday 29 June, https://learningonscreen.ac.uk/ondemand/index.php/prog/06AADB4A?bcast=111954029.

Straw, W. (2011) 'Introduction: The Small Parts, Small Players Dossier', *Screen*, Vol. 52, No. 1, Spring, pp. 78–81.

Sweeney, K. (2016) 'Movie Director Jim Sheridan: "I Think It's Sad the Area I Grew Up in Has Been Infiltrated by Drug Gangs"', *Irish Sun*, online, 21 June, https://www.thesun.ie/archives/bizarre/182888/movie-director-jim-sheridan-i -think-its-sad-the-area-i-grew-up-in-has-been-infiltrated-by-drug-gangs/.

Sweeney, K. (2020) 'IN YOUR AISLES: Eurovision Champ Niamh Kavanagh Tells How Bosses who Hired Her to Work in Tesco Are Too Young to Remember Her Victory', *Irish Sun*, online, 19 May, https://www.thesun.ie/tvandshowbiz/music /5443038/coronavirus-eurovision-niamh-kavanagh-bosses-hired-tesco-victory/.

Sweeney, T. (2006) 'The Commitments: Where are they now?', *Sunday Tribune*, 30 April, pp. 16–17.

Taylor, T.D. (1998) 'Living in a Postcolonial World: Class and Soul in *The Commitments*', *Irish Studies Review*, Vo. 6, No. 3, pp. 291–302.

'The Commitments' (2007) *Movie Connections* [television programme], narr. Ashley Jensen, BBC, UK, 22.35, 17 September, BBC1, 40 minutes.

'*The Commitments* and the Corr Connection' (1991) *Dundalk Democrat*, 12 October, p. 5.

'*The Commitments* Premiere' (1991) *Jo Maxi* [television programme clip, online], Pres. Shauna Lowry, RTÉ, Ireland, 4 April, 6mins 0secs, https://www.rte.ie/ archives/2013/0920/475397-the-commitments/.

'The Commitments Reunite' (2010) *RTÉ News*, [television programme clip], online, RTÉ, Ireland, uploaded to YouTube 7 October, https://youtu.be/_Lx0GD71El8.

'The Last Real Showman' (2000) *Irish Times*, online, 23 December, available at: https://www.irishtimes.com/news/the-last-real-showman-1.1122565.

The Numbers (n.d.) 'The Commitments: Box Office', *The Numbers*, online, https:// www.the-numbers.com/movie/Commitments-The#tab=box-office.

Tracy, T. and Flynn, R. (2017) 'Contemporary Irish Film: From the National to the Transnational', *Éire-Ireland*, Vol. 52, No. 1, pp. 169–97.

'Tuairimí na nDéagóirí faoi 'The Commitments'' (1991) *Cúrsaí*, [television programme clip], online, Pres. Neasa Ní Chinnéide, RTÉ, Ireland, 27 September, RTÉ 1, 2mins 46secs, https://www.rte.ie/archives/category/arts-and-culture /2015/0401/691297-the-barrytown-trilogy-by-roddy-doyle/.

Valenti, J. (1991) 'Letter to Alan Parker, 23 September 1991', *Film: The Commitments* (1991), Congratulatory Letters – Previews and Premieres, May-Nov 1991, Folder: PKR – 1 – 18 – 7 – 1, Alan Parker Papers, British Film Institute.

Weinraub, B. (1991) 'Hollywood Agent to Create A Film Unit at Universal', *New York Times*, online, 7 October, https://www.nytimes.com/1991/10/07/movies/ hollywood-agent-to-create-a-film-unit-at-universal.html.

Wollen, P. (2006) 'The Last New Wave: Modernism in the British Films of the Thatcher Era', in L.D. Friedman (ed) *Fires Were Started: British Cinema and Thatcherism*, 2nd edition, London: Wallflower, pp. 30–44.

Index

For Product Safety Concerns and Information please contact our EU
representative GPSR@taylorandfrancis.com
Taylor & Francis Verlag GmbH, Kaufingerstraße 24, 80331 München, Germany

Markets vs Public Health Systems

Problems related to the functioning of public healthcare systems encourage the search for alternative solutions, for example to ensure improved access to medical services. However, these proposals also require appropriate theoretical support to better present and apply them. This book draws on Austrian Economics to provide a theoretical framework to support greater involvement of the private sector to improve inefficiencies in public healthcare.

The Austrian School of Economics has a solid theoretical output describing and explaining the functioning of many aspects of the market economy (e.g. money, prices, interest rate, or capital). This work applies those principles to a market-based healthcare system and its individual elements, including health insurance. The study in these chapters is divided into two parts. The first part contains the theoretical aspects of the functioning of a complete market system. Particular importance is placed on presenting health insurance as a market institution and exploring its role in the market system. This examination also includes an analysis of alternative forms of financing access to medical services, such as direct payments, medical savings accounts, medical subscriptions, and charity. Additionally, solid counterarguments are provided for so-called market failures: asymmetric information, public goods, and monopolies. The second part of the book explores the theoretical aspects of interventionism and the functioning of public systems, and aims to better highlight the sources of the associated problems.

This work provides an important contribution to the literature on health economics, healthcare management and policy, and Austrian Economics more broadly. It is essential reading for health economists and those holding key public positions related to healthcare.

Łukasz Jasiński is an economist and researcher at the Faculty of Economics of the Maria Curie-Sklodowska University (Poland, Lublin).

"Łukasz Jasiński explains flawed public health systems and presents the merits of a genuine market approach. A major innovation is his elaboration of health insurance from an Austrian School perspective."
– **Robert P. Murphy**, economist and co-author of *The Primal Prescription: Surviving the "Sick Care" Sinkhole*

Routledge Focus on Economics and Finance

The fields of economics are constantly expanding and evolving. This growth presents challenges for readers trying to keep up with the latest important insights. Routledge Focus on Economics and Finance presents short books on the latest big topics, linking in with the most cutting-edge economics research.

Individually, each title in the series provides coverage of a key academic topic, whilst collectively the series forms a comprehensive collection across the whole spectrum of economics.

Islamic Economics and COVID-19
The Economic, Social and Scientific Consequences of a Global Pandemic
Masudul Alam Choudhury

The Economics of Intellectual Property and Openness
The Tragedy of Intangible Abundance
Bartłomiej Biga

Economics, Education and Youth Entrepreneurship
International Perspectives
Marian Noga and Andrzej Brzeziński

Markets vs Public Health Systems
Perspectives from the Austrian School of Economics
Łukasz Jasiński

For more information about this series, please visit: www.routledge.com/Routledge-Focus-on-Economics-and-Finance/book-series/RFEF

Markets vs Public Health Systems

Perspectives from the Austrian School of Economics

Łukasz Jasiński

Routledge
Taylor & Francis Group

LONDON AND NEW YORK

First published 2022
by Routledge
4 Park Square, Milton Park, Abingdon, Oxon OX14 4RN

and by Routledge
605 Third Avenue, New York, NY 10158

Routledge is an imprint of the Taylor & Francis Group, an informa business

British Library Cataloguing-in-Publication Data
A catalogue record for this book is available from the British Library

Library of Congress Cataloging-in-Publication Data
Names: Jasiński, Łukasz, author.
Title: Markets vs public health systems : perspectives from the Austrian School of Economics / Łukasz Jasiński.
Description: Milton Park, Abingdon, Oxon ; New York, NY : Routledge, 2022. |
Series: Routledge focus on economics and finance |
Includes bibliographical references and index.
Identifiers: LCCN 2021041215 (print) |
LCCN 2021041216 (ebook) | ISBN 9781032193939 (hardback) |
ISBN 9781032193946 (paperback) | ISBN 9781003258957 (ebook)
Subjects: LCSH: Public health--Austria. | Health care reform--Economic aspects. | Health insurance--Economic aspects.
Classification: LCC RA493 .J37 2022 (print) |
LCC RA493 (ebook) | DDC 368.38/2009436--dc23/eng/20211007
LC record available at https://lccn.loc.gov/2021041215
LC ebook record available at https://lccn.loc.gov/2021041216

ISBN: 978-1-032-19393-9 (hbk)
ISBN: 978-1-032-19394-6 (pbk)
ISBN: 978-1-003-25895-7 (ebk)

DOI: 10.4324/9781003258957

Typeset in Times New Roman
by Taylor & Francis Books

To Epaminondas: First Among the Greeks

Contents

About the author

Łukasz Jasiński is an economist and researcher at the Faculty of Economics of the Maria Curie-Sklodowska University (Poland, Lublin). In 2021, he completed his doctoral dissertation entitled 'Market processes and interventionism in the health system of the United States of America from the view of the Austrian School of Economics'.

He is also a regular collaborator and lecturer at the Mises Institute (Poland, Wroclaw), where he publishes his original series of essays entitled: 'On the way to the market health system'.

In 2016, he won the fourth edition of the 'Ethics in Finance: The Robin Cosgrove Award' (2016 – Polish edition). His essay, titled 'Ethics in life insurance', earned first place in the competition, which is organized annually by the Polish Bank Association and Banking Ethics Committee. More information is available here: https://www.researchga te.net/publication/327498403_Ethics_in_Life_Insurance.

Introduction

This book is a theoretical introduction to my future publications on healthcare, especially the relationships between interventionism and market processes and their impact on access to medical services (e.g. in the US). These issues were presented in terms of the Austrian School of Economics, which has considerable theoretical achievements devoted to the analysis of the market economy and interventionism.

The two parts of this book deal with the theoretical aspects of market and interventionist solutions in the area of health systems, which aims to create appropriate arguments for the former. At the same time, creating a theoretical framework for the functioning of the market health system and constructive criticism of the so-called market failures are the main goals of this book. This is to help promote stronger market solutions in this area.

Nowadays, the provision and financing of rare medical goods and services takes place mainly through public systems, and the share of the market or private initiatives in this area is quite limited – both in financial and regulatory terms.

However, after many decades of experience in the development of public health systems, there are still no uniform solutions in this area, and the problems encountered by public systems existing in different countries are the reason for seeking alternative forms of organizing healthcare systems. The negative effects related to the domination of the public healthcare system (e.g. rising costs and expenses or lengthening queues for benefits) in many countries contribute to the fact that widely discussed ideas in this area include, among others: increasing the role of private health insurance as forms of financing access to medical services, decentralization of the institutional structure responsible for financing access, and the provision of medical services, giving more freedom to the consumer in choosing suppliers of such services or adding elements limiting the moral hazard and increasing costs to a given system (e.g. co-payment).

DOI: 10.4324/9781003258957-1

The above changes are also intended to help better adapt public systems to increasingly important challenges or problems: negative demographic trends, the increasing number of chronic diseases, or costly technological changes.

From the perspective of the Austrian School, however, it can be said that these systems are part of a hampered market economy where the government interferes with the economy (including the health system) through commands and prohibitions. In this context, the problem of interventionism, according to representatives of this school, is not the difficulty of determining 'natural', 'fair', or 'appropriate' tasks of the state and government, as these may change over time depending on conditions. From an economic point of view, this problem boils down to the question of how the interventionist system works. Can it achieve the goals that its adherents have set for themselves? This question has its own specific connotation in terms of the organization of health systems.

However, public health systems do not have to be one solution. An alternative to them may be a system entirely based on market solutions. In this case, however, theoretical arguments in its favour should be properly presented – which is one of the goals of this study.

Contrary to public solutions, the market system does not have a 'rigid' or formalized structure. It is also subject to certain dynamic changes caused, among others, by the processes of competition between suppliers or insurers, etc. Very often there are also accusations that the poor or the sick would not be financially able to afford treatment with the simultaneous inability to take advantage of health insurance. At the same time, it is supposed to prove that market solutions are faulty.

In order to adequately counter these objections, first of all, one should look at individual (main) elements of the market system, namely private sources of financing access to medical services: medical insurance, medical subscriptions, direct payments, and charity support. This will allow a better understanding of how it works.

Particular attention was paid in particular to insurance institution. In the spirit of the Austrian School, insurance is a market institution that arises and evolves thanks to unrestricted market processes, such as, for example, money. Insurance does not have to be the most popular option for such a system to function efficiently. At the same time, the institution has certain limitations (but which should not be seen as disadvantages) that make alternative solutions necessary. Interestingly, the subject of insurance or insurance markets was not particularly developed in this paradigm. The subject of insurance (economic and social) appears, for example, in L. von Mises (1998, pp. 833–834) or M. N. Rothbard (2006, pp. 74–77, 127–133), but these are only short fragments that can be further elaborated.

In the context of the discussed issues, it will be particularly helpful to use the achievements of the Austrian School of Economics. Thanks to the appropriate reference to the issue of probability, risk, or the role of economic calculation, it will be possible to adequately and exhaustively reflect the essence of health insurance and (in a broader context) of the market health system. In this case, an appropriate (i.e. rational) structure of financing access to medical services without the imposed domination of insurance is of particular importance.

Appropriate arguments showing the superiority of market solutions must also refer to the most frequently raised market failures: asymmetric information, the possibility of providing public goods, and the issue of monopolies. The above issues constitute the first part of the work.

The second part presents theoretical aspects of interventionism and its impact on the processes forming the market health system. It will also be important to present the principles of operation of the public system. As a result, they will be easier to compare with the market system. The use of the term 'health system' instead of the commonly used term 'healthcare system' is also adequately justified.

References

Mises L., 1998, *Human action. A treatise on economics*, Auburn: Ludwig von Mises Institute.
Rothbard M. N., 2006, *Making economic sense*, Auburn: Ludwig von Mises Institute.

Part I

Market processes in the health system

Introduction

Arguments in favour of market solutions in the health system of any country in the first place must be based on correct theoretical inference, which will be able to adequately show the specificity of these processes and the characteristics of their individual elements.

This issue concerns especially the institution of health insurance, which has been losing its market character more and more over many decades. However, in order to be able to properly interpret these changes and their effects, it is first necessary to present the conditions necessary for the establishment and proper functioning of this institution. Insurance has certain limitations which prevent comprehensive financing of access to medical services for the whole society. However, it would be a mistake to perceive these limitations as a disadvantage of insurance – it is a more specific specificity of this institution. Therefore, it must be supported by other solutions, such as direct payments or charity.

It will also have a positive impact on the competition process and will allow us to avoid many problems present in universal (public systems), e.g. the lack of negative selection or moral hazard. Better understanding of the functioning of market solutions boils down to the appropriate presentation of the relationship between the various forms of financing access to medical services. The process of their free shaping allows for the emergence of a rational financing structure that does not exclude the most needy.

It is also important to present the so-called market failures, which are to be a fundamental obstacle preventing the application of market solutions in the indicated area.

DOI: 10.4324/9781003258957-2

1 Insurance as a market institution

Uncertainty as the main reason for the emergence of insurance

Uncertainty is inextricably linked to the future[1] and human action. Uncertainty, understood as the lack of complete certainty of a person as to the occurrence of future events in the real world, causes that they take action (engages appropriate resources) to satisfy their needs (remove discomfort), which is tantamount to the elimination or reduction of this uncertainty. The existence of uncertainty thus gives human action a speculative dimension.[2] The future may bring about events that improve or deteriorate an individual's situation. Humans show determination to learn about future conditions (recognizing opportunities and threats) as well as they possibly can, thanks to which they will be able to better meet their needs. Two main sources (spheres) of uncertainty can be identified: sufficiently unknown natural phenomena and human activities involving the selection of individual goals and means for their implementation (Mises, 1998, p. 105).

Thus, the mere existence of uncertainty does not limit human action. When trying to meet the challenges of the future, people use their knowledge, experience, and creativity in a unique way. As Huerta De Soto (2010, p. 15) points out: 'In a broad or general sense, entrepreneurship actually coincides with human action. In this respect, it could be said that any person who acts to modify the present and achieve his objectives in the future exercises entrepreneurship.'

Entrepreneurship can be considered as a key human skill for reducing or eliminating uncertainty. What can be considered a paradox, on the one hand, is that thanks to entrepreneurship, it is possible to eliminate a certain amount of uncertainty. On the other hand, entrepreneurship itself, especially at the stage of vision and creating new plans, widens this uncertainty. However, this kind of uncertainty is not pejorative, but gives hope for a better tomorrow.[3] For example, societies experiencing

DOI: 10.4324/9781003258957-3

constant improvement of their material conditions as a result of the industrial revolution were unable to indicate the exact direction of technological changes or specific inventions that would arise in the future, but they intuitively realized that these processes had already started and that positive results would occur in the near or distant future.

Uncertainty is so closely related to human existence that it is difficult to even imagine a reality in which the future is known exactly. There would be no room for human action in this kind of world. Entrepreneurship and economic calculation would not occur, as all possible activities and their effects would be known (discovered) in advance. In such a reality there would also be no space for the creation and development of an insurance institution. Certainty can be understood in two ways: that certain events may or may not happen. There is no third possibility, no option: the event may occur. In the first case, it is known, for example, who will set fire to the house and who will not, so people who have suffered the damage would receive compensation not so much from the insurance, but from predetermined (as to the time and amount of compensation) capital transfers from the rest of the society.[4] The insurer would not employ staff responsible for the identification, selection, or qualification of the risk. Professions such as underwriter or actuary would simply not exist. In a world of certainty, they would be an unnecessary expense. A similar situation would occur if certain events did not occur at all. If a given (negative) event does not occur, then there cannot be its cause that could cause adverse consequences for the individual. For example, in a world of complete certainty, car accidents or crashes would not happen, as they could be prevented in advance. The inability of a given event to occur in the future will not cause a feeling of uncertainty (discomfort) in an individual, which they will want to counteract by purchasing insurance.

Therefore, uncertainty should be considered the first, necessary factor, a kind of sphere in which, thanks to human entrepreneurship, the institution of insurance was established and evolved. At this point, however, it should be emphasized that the mere existence of uncertainty is not enough to create insurance, which is rightly associated with concepts such as probability and (especially) risk. Other essential conditions must therefore be met.

It is also worth mentioning that although the future and uncertainty are terms that are intuitively understood in the same way by most people, at the same time they are perceived differently by each person. In this sense, they are not homogeneous. Each person creates their own vision of the future (sets goals) and strives to implement it on the basis of their own actions. By implementing the previously assumed goals, the individual realizes their plans, but does not feel that their actions constitute a certain contribution to the overall future. Of course, people are aware of their similar needs. Most people dream of their own apartment or house, and in a world of scarcity of goods, entrepreneurs (producers) try to satisfy their needs in the best possible way. Recognition of the convergence of needs (and costs that consumers are able to incur) is therefore an important element of entrepreneurial activity and gives a chance to make a profit. The better entrepreneurs recognize the greater the convergence of needs and costs, the greater the chances for profits. This observation is also true and particularly relevant to the insurance market.

Probability and risk

Although the concepts of probability, risk, and uncertainty are inter-related, skilfully distinguishing them is an important step in under-standing the origins of an insurance institution. The very concept of probability is quite general and assumes the possibility of a given event occurring in the future. However, some events, and more specifically the probability of their future occurrence, can be represented in terms, symbols, or mathematical models, which can facilitate decision-making in a world of uncertainty. The issue of the possibility of using numbers allows for two types of probability to be distinguished: the class probability and the case probability (Mises, 1998, p. 107).

Mises (1998, p. 107), who is the creator of the probability classification presented in this way, points out that:

> Class probability means: We know or assume to know, with regard to the problem concerned, everything about the behavior of a whole class of events or phenomena; but about the actual singular events or phenomena we know nothing but that they are elements of this class.

Let us assume that we have statistical data from the last several dozen years, which show that, for example, out of 10,000 houses, five catch fire each year. This information forms a class (group) of specific, homogeneous events. It is not known exactly which house will catch fire (we do not have any information on this), but it is assumed that in the following year their number will be the same, if there are no other factors increasing or reducing the likelihood of such an event. Similar conclusions can be drawn based, for example, on the average life expectancy of a given population. Although the average age of the members of a certain community is known and amounts to e.g. 78

years, on this basis it is not possible to estimate the life expectancy of its individual members. We have knowledge of the entire class of events, but we know nothing about its individual elements.

The situation is completely different in the case of case probability. Mises (1998, p. 110) states that:

> Case probability means: We know, with regard to a particular event, some of the factors which determine its outcome; but there are other determining factors about which we know nothing.
>
> Case probability has nothing in common with class probability but the incompleteness of our knowledge. In every other regard the two are entirely different.[5]

This type of probability has particular application in economics or more broadly in praxeology. Each act of human action is unique, in part because of the subjectivity of the value judgements of the acting individual. As Huerta De Soto (2010, p. 31) points out:

> Therefore, each time man acts and exercises entrepreneurship, he does so in a characteristic, personal, and unrepeatable manner all his own, a manner which arises from his attempt to gain certain objectives or arrive at a particular vision of the world, all of which act as incentives and which, in their particular form and circumstances, only he possesses. The above enables each human being to obtain certain knowledge or information which he discovers only depending on his ends and circumstances and which no other person can possess in an identical form.

This type of probability cannot be assigned to any class precisely due to the fact that these events are not homogeneous, but unique. In this approach, we cannot talk about the frequency (repeatability) of events as in the case of class probability. An example is a match between two football teams, such as Real Madrid and UD Levante. Real Madrid has a much bigger budget and better players. Every year it fights to get as many trophies as possible. In turn, Levante is a club with much lower aspirations, for which staying in the league is a satisfactory result. Simply put, it can be assumed that, taking into account the results of the past, in ten matches played between these teams, nine will end with a victory for Real, and in one the team from the Valencia suburbs will be able to draw or win. However, these data, in the perspective of the next match, do not allow for a completely certain conclusion that this will happen. When assessing these chances, the data from the past does not say anything about the next match; it only contains information about the course of events (match results) in the past, taking into account specific past conditions. It is not known whether the next game will be the one in which the team from Madrid will not be victorious. Of course, an objective observer will easily be able to tell that Real's chances of winning are definitely greater (due to the better soccer skills of its players) based on some of the information it has at its disposal. However, you can as well imagine that someone, after a thorough analysis, will 'risk' the statement that Levante will not lose the next match. What both have in common is that the final outcome predictions are based on incomplete data. If it were otherwise, the result would be known in advance.

A similar line of reasoning can also be applied to other cases where there is human action, such as decisions made by consumers (e.g. buying blue or black trousers), actions of entrepreneurs (uncertainty about making a profit), or presidential elections. All these cases are unique due to the fact that when making decisions, people are guided by reason – they do not react passively to external stimuli.[6]

Although the two types of probability are very different, it is possible to confuse the probability of individual events with that of classes. This error was described by Mises as the so-called gambler's fallacy. After diagnosing a specific disease in a patient, the doctor informs the patient that 5 out of 100 cases end in death during the treatment process. If the patient asks the doctor if these five people have already died, it means that they has succumbed to this delusion. Forecasting based on only part of the information covering one specific case is unreliable; therefore in such cases knowledge about the behaviour of the whole class is used. Therefore, if the prognosis of the patient's chances of survival is to be more reliable, it should be compared to other, similar cases (e.g. survival among men up to 30 years of age, etc.). Better examination of the patient will allow for obtaining more information and assigning them to a different class (determined on the basis of more criteria), but the prognosis for their health will still be based on the behaviour of the whole class (Mises, 1998, pp. 110–111).

Although the concept of risk does not appear in the quoted fragments on probability, the definition of class probability suits it well. In the literature, the term risk is usually associated with F. H. Knight, who is credited with distinguishing between risk and uncertainty (Knight, 1921, p. 233). We talk about risk when a given event can be classified into a sufficiently large class of the same events, and the frequency of occurrence of events belonging to this class can be determined with great certainty in a mathematical form, that is, presented by means of the probability calculus.[7] In the absence of such a possibility, according to Knight, we are dealing with uncertainty, i.e. events that cannot be represented by numbers. In other words, the difference between risk and uncertainty boils down to the possibility of presenting (expressing) the probability of these events occurring in the form of mathematical symbols. Interestingly, for Knight himself, this distinction only served to create his own probability classification. As Foss and Klein (2012, p. 84) point out:

> this particular distinction is only invoked in passing (1921: 21, 233). His fundamental argument, developed in chapter 7 of Knight (1921), involves a tripartite classification of the notion of probability into 'apriori probability,' 'statistical probability,' and 'estimated probability.' Situations that can be described epistemically in terms of the two first categories represent risk, while the third condition describes situations involving uncertainty.

Comparing the two classifications to each other, it can be concluded that the Misesian class probability corresponds to Knight's risk, and the case probability to uncertainty.[8] Obviously, this is not the only economic interpretation and classification of risk, probability, or uncertainty, but it introduces more clarity to the argument in question. In this aspect, it is also worth getting acquainted with, inter alia, the works of K. J. Arrow, who did not introduce a detailed distinction between risk and uncertainty and used both terms interchangeably (Klimczak, 2008, p. 65).[9]

For the creation and development of an insurance institution, the issue of the application of the probability theory is of key importance. The present state of the modern insurance market is inextricably linked with the evolution of insurance mathematics. It is thanks to the use of probability calculus and mathematical statistics that it is possible to calculate the amount of insurance premiums or the level of provisions. Without these mathematical 'tools', the possibilities of calculating insurance (actuarial) risk would be very limited, and the insurance activity itself would be reduced to standardizing the level of premiums and limiting rather than extending the scope of insurance. With insurance mathematics, some uncertainty becomes 'measurable', making it much easier for insurers and consumers to make decisions. Professor N. Ferguson (2008, p. 190), an expert in economic and political history, even argues that: 'In short, it was not merchants but mathematicians who were the true progenitors of modern insurance.'

Both the contracts between merchants agreeing to jointly cover losses resulting from the failure of trade expeditions and social institutions supporting their members financially as a result of unfavourable events in the future (e.g. death, accident, or disease) functioned more as a form of protection against an uncertain future as insurance.[10] However, it should be emphasized that before the development of mathematics brought about the creation of insurance,[11] these institutions were, considering the conditions of that time, particularly important for certain social groups, and even entire nations. It is difficult to imagine the development of trade between individual regions if merchants undertaking a long and dangerous journey would not have any security as a result of unfavourable events (e.g. sinking of ships carrying goods during a storm at sea). In the absence of a willingness to participate in losses, trade (and thus economic development) would develop much slower.

For insurers, the use of mathematical achievements is an indispensable element of economic calculation. This is one of the features that distinguishes insurers from 'ordinary' companies for which costing has a different dimension. If 'ordinary' entrepreneurs anticipate consumers' needs well, revenues will exceed costs and thus a profit will be generated. Costs incurred in the past (prices of production factors) do not have to be the same in the future; therefore the entrepreneurial function consists, among other things, in noticing factors that may influence these changes. However, the costs incurred in the past do not change; they are data and constant. The situation is slightly different in the case of insurers for whom some of the costs resulting from the insurance contract (e.g. future compensation payments due to fires) are not costs already incurred, e.g. purchase of raw materials in the case of 'traditional' activities, but planned (hypothetical) costs that will have to be incurred in the future. In this case, the insurer is not entirely sure about their amount. This part of the economic calculation relates to class probability, therefore an insurer needs skilled workers (especially actuaries and underwriters)[12] to specialize in the economic calculation process based on this probability, in other words, in the process of identifying, selecting, and classifying actuarial risks. Of course, decisions regarding for example the strategy and directions of development of a given insurance company, marketing campaigns, or the creation of new insurance products are an example of the probability of individual events and they concern all entrepreneurs. Rothbard (2009, p. 555) put it this way: 'Estimates of future costs, demands, etc., on the part of entrepreneurs are all unique cases of uncertainty, where methods of specific understanding and individual judgment of the situation must apply, rather than objectively measurable or insurable "risk".'

However, in addition, insurance companies, which is their special feature, also make extensive use of a particular type of economic calculation based on class probability. Insurers compete for customers with other enterprises not only in terms of the price and quality of insurance products, but also through a different type and quality of economic calculation. Examples include an insurer that offers private health insurance and a medical network that sells medical subscriptions. Although these products may have a similar range of medical services and prices, the process of their production and calculation was completely different. The insurer is looking for a competitive advantage also in the area of the form of economic calculation; other enterprises also use it, but it is not so much based on class probability.[13]

One important feature of risk is that it is a component of complex economic phenomena and so does this over time. In this respect, the risk can be described as successive phases, which makes it more dynamic than static. Therefore, the concept of risk should not be reduced only to the theory of probability. The following stages can be mentioned that constitute risk understood as a process taking place in time: threat, danger, realization of danger, loss, mental reaction, emotional reaction, behavioural reaction. In the case of the first four stages, one can speak of objective risk, i.e. the risk where the calculus of probability applies. The other three, on the other hand, qualify for the so-called subjective risk, subject to human value judgements (Kowalewski, 2001, p. 35). In the latter case, however, the use of the term 'risk' may be misleading because, as discussed earlier, the subjective human evaluations are unique and cannot be represented in terms of classes.[14]

The threat as a potential source of risk may come from the action of natural forces or human activity. For example, driving a car, despite the undoubted benefits this brings to its owners, may lead to a road accident. The sources of danger and risk may be, for example, unfavourable weather conditions or careless driving by the driver. As a result of such an event, property and often personal damage may occur. The resulting damage would undoubtedly result in financial losses and the loss of a part of the victim's property. The existence of a person's awareness of a possible unfavourable development of events (mental reaction) can lead to anxiety (emotional reaction) while driving a car. As a result, such a person may be more inclined to purchase life insurance or motor insurance (behavioural reaction). From the economic perspective, the last three stages are not so important because the act of acting itself is more important, i.e. making an informed decision as to whether or not to purchase insurance. Identifying these specific incentives can be useful to some extent in economics if risk is to be shown as a process over time. The second stage is more important for the marketing activities of insurance companies trying to attract the attention of potential customers, which undoubtedly contributes to the development of the insurance market.

At this point, another important feature of the insurance institution should be mentioned. The primary purpose of insurance is to compensate the insured for losses resulting from certain unfavourable future events (random events). Therefore, the amount of the sum insured (and thus the insurance premium) is adjusted to the material and financial situation of the insured. Any deviation from the optimal sum insured may be considered underinsurance or overinsurance. In his work on insurance and risk, Mowbray indicates a significant risk division: pure risk and speculative risk (Mowbray & Blanchard, 1961, pp. 6–7).

In the case of pure risk, characteristic of the insurance market, there is no loss (non-realization of risk) or loss (realization of risk resulting in loss). The insured allocates appropriate funds in the form of insurance premiums; however, according to the exchange theory, it is a favourable situation for them – he gains insurance protection in an uncertain future for them. Importantly, the insured cannot make a profit in the event of a loss. It is completely different in the case of speculative risk. Here, in addition to loss or no loss, it is possible to make a profit. The action taken is because there is hope for profit. Examples of such activities include participation in gambling (e.g. roulette) or the purchase of certain assets (e.g. real estate, shares, etc.) with the hope of selling them at a higher price in the near or distant future (Outerville, 1998, p. 3). The difference between these two types of risk is that none of the insured want to take the pure risk, while the realization of speculative risk is not pejorative for the player. It can be concluded that the chance of making a profit means that a person can, through their conscious actions, strive to increase the chances of its implementation. Thus, a person tries to create a speculative risk and at the same time reduce the probability of pure risk (e.g. healthier eating as a method to reduce the risk of a heart attack). Therefore, common underwriting risks are assigned pure risk traits where class probability applies. In turn, speculative risk can be equated with both the case probability and the class probability.

At this point, it is worth mentioning that another important feature that distinguishes an insurance institution is its group character. The use of insurance mathematics is used by insurers to create, based on separate criteria, specific risk classes (groups) that differ from each other, e.g. in the amount of premium or the scope of insurance. Although individual classes differ in the level of risk, i.e. they are not homogeneous, the common feature of all of them is the group character created by individual units belonging to specific classes.[15]

Therefore, insurance companies strive to acquire new insured as soon as possible and create real (numerous, mass) risk groups. If the insurer enters into an insurance contract with only one person, it will not be considered insurance, but gambling.[16] While in the described situation the probability calculation applies, the lack of other insured persons means that in the event of an insured event, the insurer has to cover the resulting losses from equity (and thus maintain a higher level of provisions). That is why it is so important to create a large group as soon as possible when introducing new insurance products to the market. The larger the group (the more insured), the greater the predictability of events (the law of large numbers), i.e. the greater the stability of the insurance company. Of course, there are situations when the insurer has to wait until a certain (longer) period has passed and a sufficiently large group of insured persons has been formed. Such cases include, for example, 'insurance' of the vocal cords of individual singers, or even 'insurance' of certain parts of the body of sports stars. However, the actions of insurers consisting in creating sufficiently numerous risk groups as soon as possible should be considered an economically justified rule.

On the basis of the content presented above, it can be concluded that insurance is a market institution that uses advanced economic calculation (based in particular on the probability calculation) in order to compensate (according to predetermined rules) losses resulting from certain adverse events to one insured with funds from the invested premiums of all insured persons included in a given risk group (class), in particular those who were not covered by the given events.

Health as a subject of insurance

One of the types of adverse event resulting in losses for the insured person is loss of health (e.g. as a result of an accident or illness). The related discomfort causes a person to want to recover as soon as possible, and insurance should be considered one of the measures to achieve this goal. However, in order for an appropriate insurance product of this type to be created, first of all, it is necessary to define what health is and how its loss may result in the consumption of insurance.

One of the most frequently quoted definitions of health is the one introduced by the World Health Organization (WHO, no date) in 1948. According to this: 'Health is a state of complete physical, mental and social well-being and not merely the absence of disease or infirmity.' This definition draws attention to the fact that health can be understood as active human activities aimed at maintaining its current state or even improving (even better quality), and not only considering health as a certain lost value and the desire to restore it from the moment of the onset of the disease. However, this approach has its limitations and problems. The use of the word 'complete' in the cited definition is particularly critical. 'Full' means that any deviations are treated as a non-health condition, which may result in excessive focus on the development and use of technology or drugs in situations that often do not require it. As a result, specific medical procedures apply to entire groups rather than individual members. Therefore, these are not economic solutions. Another problem is that as a result of, inter alia, the development of medicine, it has become possible to live with chronic diseases or, to put it another way, to develop a chronic disease; although it is a personal drama for many people, it does not have the same serious consequences as it used to be. Thanks to the progress of medicine, it is possible for many people to pursue their professional career despite the presence of chronic diseases. Therefore, these people contribute to creating added value in the economy and treating them as sick or unfit for work is not appropriate due to their adaptability (Huber et al., 2011, p. D4163).

The border between health and disease does not have to be sharp and unambiguous, but reflections on the definition of health, possible thanks to the development of medical knowledge, should increasingly take into account the factors contributing to the health–disease dichotomy and the possible consequences of this state of affairs.

For insurance companies, the problem of recognizing health comes down to, inter alia, defining the conditions justifying the use of medical services by the insured or receiving a cash benefit. As the insurance is intended to compensate for the loss (loss of health), the incident causing it cannot, by definition, occur before the insurance period. That is why the assessment of the health condition of people applying for insurance is so important. It is also important how the loss is to be compensated. On this basis, sickness and accident insurance can be distinguished as a special type of health insurance, which involves the payment of predefined cash benefits to the insured in connection with the occurrence of specific events. However, with so-called medical insurance,[17] the insured receives access to medical services, financed by the insurance company, instead of cash. Medical services are usually provided by specific medical facilities that cooperate with the insurance company (Osak, 2008, p. 163). Both types of insurance can be offered in parallel. Sickness and accident insurance compensate the insured for financial losses resulting, for example, from loss of earnings during treatment, while medical insurance covers the costs of medical services. Medical insurance is beneficial in this respect, as it is the insurance company that is responsible for organizing the structure responsible for treating the insured, which undoubtedly shortens the initial process and improves the quality of the insurance product.

Economic calculation based on probability plays an extremely important role in the process of creating health insurance (especially medical insurance). It is applied in two stages. The first stage concerns the calculation of the very probability of a given event (e.g. disease) occurring in the future. In turn, in the second stage, it is extremely important to estimate the costs of using specific medical procedures (and their effectiveness) in the treatment process. Medical insurance differs in this respect, for example, from life insurance in that the insurance risk, and more specifically the process of its calculation, is more complex and the mere use of insurance mathematics to determine only the quantitative probability of a given event is not sufficient. Even if the risk of developing a given disease in a particular group (class) of people is determined with high probability, the sphere of calculation, including the impact of individual treatment methods (and their costs) on the improvement of the insured's health, is equally important.

It is possible that the risk of a given disease can be determined, but at the same time the current state of medical knowledge does not allow for a rational calculation of treatment costs. It can therefore be concluded that for a given disease it is not possible to make a rational economic calculation in the second stage. Therefore, it cannot be determined whether the initially estimated level of the contribution is appropriate, too high, or too low. As a result, a given risk is considered, in the present circumstances, as insurable. Guzel (2013b, p. 125)[18] claims that:

> an example of such a disease is discopathy, which can take many years to develop and cause complaints of varying severity. The scope of potential changes found in the spine in people with discopathy and their impact on the risk of incapacity for work are so extensive that it is practically impossible to rationally estimate the level of the necessary increase in the insurance premium (e.g. due to the lack of appropriate clinical trials). Therefore, it seems that the best solution is to apply an appropriate exclusion.

In the case of life insurance, it is much easier to estimate the potential costs resulting from the death of the insured person and thus the sum insured on the basis of the insured's income or the amount of financial liabilities (e.g. a loan). The economic calculation taking into account the calculation of probability in life insurance concerns mainly the first stage.

In the case of health insurance, both stages of the calculation are preceded by a thorough scientific analysis, especially the research carried out on the appropriate group of people.[19] It can be concluded that the process of obtaining data, analysing them and using the knowledge thus acquired in order to determine risk is the initial stage of economic calculation. The successively growing medical knowledge allows insurers to better and better calculate risk and thus to compete by creating more 'advanced' risk groups (classes). The processes based on the appropriate use of medical knowledge in the development of health insurance are called Evidence Based Underwriting (EBU) and are derived from medicine based on reliable (i.e. scientifically supported) data (Evidence Based Medicine – EBM) (Lipka, 2013a, pp. 94–98). Properly verified medical knowledge allows, among other things, the development of more effective procedures that can be used in the treatment of specific diseases and, ultimately, to include them in the scope of medical insurance. Thus, it can be concluded that developing medicine affects the quality of economic calculation.[20] Therefore, insurers are interested in the latest results of research concerning, for example, the effectiveness of the use of new medical procedures in the treatment of selected diseases, as well as scientific studies focusing on forecasting specific trends, e.g. concerning the eating habits of the population. It should be emphasized that the constantly growing number of scientific publications is a great challenge for insurers and requires the involvement of more and more human resources and their proper management.

The health insurance market as an effect of entrepreneurial processes

The core of insurers' business is risk calculation. Its purpose is to adjust the amount of the net insurance premium[21] to the risk group (class) represented by the insured person. Each insurance company creates its own risk groups based on appropriate criteria, thanks to which it is possible to define rules for the appropriate calculation and assessment of insurance risk, including health risk. Often the activity of insurance companies is equated with collecting premiums from the insured and activities consisting in fulfilling the insurance contract to a limited extent, which is to be a source of their profit. This is a misconception. The basic assumption of the insurer is the payment of compensation or benefits due to the occurrence of a given event. Risk is inherent in the real world and its implementation results in a loss. One of the ways to eliminate or reduce the negative effects of risk implementation is insurance. Insurance companies, using an advanced economic calculation taking into account probability, are able to determine with increasing accuracy what factors cause a higher (or lower) probability of a given event. Thanks to this, they can distinguish further groups (classes) of risk from one general group. These groups differ in terms of risk and, as a result, the amount of insurance premiums. The higher the likelihood of a given event (e.g. a serious illness) occurring, the higher the likelihood of consuming the necessary medical services and, consequently, the insurance itself. Therefore, young and (in the opinion of the insurer) healthy people pay relatively lower premiums than the elderly and those who are already sick. An insurer that, in the conditions of an unfettered market economy, restricts access to certain benefits denies the sense of having insurance and is replaced by competitors that are more enterprising, i.e. better at calculating risk.

Although there may be a lot of individual risk groups,[22] each insurance company uses a basic division into the so-called standard risk and substandard risk. The first type means a risk that is accepted by the insurer without premium increases, while the substandard risk means admission to insurance, but after taking into account the premium increases (Lipka, 2013b, p. 117). Subsequently, the insurer may create further subgroups for standard risk (e.g. S1, S2, S3, etc.) and for substandard risk (e.g. Sb1, Sb2, Sb3, etc.). The ability to properly calculate risk and create appropriate risk groups (classes) based on it is the main tool for creating a competitive advantage on the market. Therefore, the insurer does not strive to limit substandard risk only to its appropriate calculation. The rule according to which the premium paid is proportional to the risk represented by the insured person is called the 'principle of fairness' (Guzel, 2013a, p. 99) and constitutes the basis for the stability of the functioning of insurance companies.[23]

Appropriate risk assessment[24] is of particular importance in the case of health insurance. Unlike, for example, life insurance, health insurance may be consumed many times. Moreover, the frequency of using medical services may result not only from the deterioration of the insured's health, but also from certain habits. This is a big challenge for insurance companies due to the fact that it is very difficult to identify people who use health insurance without valid reasons, and it is even more difficult to change this state (Kostrzewski, 2013, pp. 140–141). Moreover, the insurer cannot change the rules of using the insurance during its term, which makes the risk assessment process[25] so important.

An error in the form of wrong premium estimation or inadequate risk classification may result in losses for the insurance company and, as a result, deterioration of access to medical services. Obtaining information about the health of the insured person is of particular importance for the insurer, as it is mainly on this basis that decisions are made whether and on what terms a given person may be covered by insurance. If the risk assessment did not take into account the factors that could affect the terms of the insurance, the so-called anti-selection occurred.[26] This phenomenon has two causes. The first is the low quality of the risk assessment by the insurer itself, which leads to an incorrect determination of the amount of premiums or the scope of insurance. Usually, the insurer is quick to understand the situation and improves the quality of the risk assessment. On the other hand, the second reason is more difficult to eliminate, because its source is deliberate concealment of information by the person applying for insurance protection. It can therefore be concluded that the source of anti-selection is the asymmetry of information between the insurer and the insured. The insurer, wishing to counteract such practices, undertakes a number of actions aimed at eliminating or at least limiting anti-selection. These include, in particular, the establishment of an appropriate level of co-payment,[27] i.e. the costs incurred by the insured when using the insurance. Other possible actions include, for example, the introduction of limits on the use of medical services or the application of exclusions of certain risks from insurance protection. Such activities, although they may be misunderstood by part of the public, are essential to the creation of solid insurance products. An emotional approach to insurers' practices (e.g. foreclosure) may obscure the fact that risks would otherwise be uneconomically grouped. For example, persons with a sub-standard risk would be admitted to insurance on a standardized basis and, as a result, would pay a premium that is inadequate to the risk contributed. This would result in over-consumption of medical services and increase costs. Subsequently, the insurer would have to increase premiums to cover the rising costs, but some insured persons could then opt out of insurance.

Therefore, in order to avoid such situations, the insurer must be able to limit or completely eliminate intentional actions of some insured persons, otherwise known as moral hazard. Moral hazard can be defined as the insured's deliberate action aimed at bringing them tangible benefits (e.g. concealing information about their health in order to be accepted for insurance or pay a lower premium), but without incurring the costs of such actions. Such attitudes are not any form of restoring greater social justice and, it is worth emphasizing, they do not hit only insurers, but most of all other insured people (which is too rarely mentioned). It is on them, as a last resort, that the additional costs of such activities are passed on – honest customers of insurance companies subsidize those who are tempted to abuse.[28] If someone claims that paying higher premiums by sick people is unethical, then one should consider whether a young and relatively healthy person should incur higher costs with a low probability of using insurance. It can be concluded from this that insurance companies also care about the interests of their clients who have trusted them. Anti-selection or moral hazard, which is not dealt with, may cause financial problems for insurers and, ultimately, loss of the trust of the insured. It is not a win-win situation.

In the health insurance market, the laws of the economy work the same as in other markets. Purchasing insurance is an act of exchange that benefits both parties. The insured person receives a guarantee that in the event of a given event (e.g. an accident), they will be able to count on the insurance to obtain access to specific medical services. Their belief is not unfounded. The insurer, thanks to the appropriate risk assessment and the ability to reduce the moral hazard, is able to create a stable insurance programme, thanks to which it can achieve profit from the invested premiums. The greater freedom of action the insurer has, the greater the stability of insurance programmes, and thus the more secure access to medical services for the insured. The insured person who pays the insurance premium covers not only the administrative costs borne by the insurer, the costs constituting the commission for financial intermediaries, or the costs constituting the remuneration of entities providing medical services, but they also finance access to these services for those insured who have been affected by certain events (e.g. accident or illness). For example, if a person with a good health condition has been correctly classified to a given risk group, e.g. to the standard risk group S1, and other insured persons in this group will also represent the same risk, then such insurance will be able to adequately meet their needs. On the other hand, if the S1 risk group includes a certain number of people representing the Sb1 substandard risk (e.g. due to concealing information about their health condition), the insurer will have to allocate more funds to finance medical services and increase the premium. For some of the insured with standard risk S1, it may turn out to be too high and they will not be interested in further insurance coverage. Hence, specific actions of the insurer are fully understandable, because by creating appropriate risk groups, differentiating premiums, or applying exclusions, they care for the interests of their clients. On this basis, it can be concluded that, in economic terms, it is not so much the insurer excludes its clients as its clients exclude themselves. If an insurer does not meet their expectations, its competitors will. Nobody who is relatively healthy wants to overpay for an extensive health insurance package that they do not use, but that only pays extra money to people who frequently use medical services.

This is in line with the theory of price imputation, which says that productive goods have value because they can produce the consumer (end) goods and services that consumers desire. Entrepreneurs (including insurance companies) bear certain costs, because they assume that the price they offer for their products will be accepted by customers (insured) and will allow them to cover the costs and achieve the assumed profit. The prices of consumer goods and services are therefore a derivative of the preferences of consumers who are ready to buy them (Machaj, 2013, p. 109). Therefore, the consumer pays attention to the benefits of consuming the final product. They do not think about the costs of the factors of production that were involved in the production of a given good or service. It is similar in the case of insurance, where the insured expects an appropriate price and quality of insurance and does not reflect on the risk group they are in. They compare the given insurance to the competition's offer and selects the best option for themselves, or they do not purchase the insurance at all, if they are not satisfied with any offer.

Importantly, while the use of exclusions in health insurance excludes this form of access to medical services (or may limit the choice between individual offers of insurers), it does not prohibit such access at all. Health insurance should therefore not be seen as a form of access to such services, but rather as a form of financing that access. Insurance in itself does not increase the supply of doctors, drugs, or new medical devices. Thanks to insurance, it is possible to transfer funds from people who were not affected by a given event to those to whom it happened to cover the costs of treatment. If, for some reason, the number of doctors, medical facilities, or medical equipment remains constant, but the number of insured consumers who consume medical services is growing, costs will increase or even visit limits will be introduced. The benefits of health insurance should not obscure the fact that it is only one form of financing access to specific medical services. Therefore, it should be remembered that in the conditions of the market economy, people who, for various reasons, cannot be covered by insurance are not deprived of it at all, only the form of (financing) access to these services changes. The more developed individual market institutions are, the easier these processes occur.

Exclusions in the health insurance market are nothing special, as they are in the rest of the economy. Owing to exclusions, it is possible to establish property rights enabling a rational calculation of the factors of production. The price system also reflects the economic nature of goods and services. High prices reflect the relationship between supply and demand – they inform about the unavailability of certain goods and, in a way, force their economical use. Exclusions and limitations are one of the foundations of civilization and the economy (Rockwell, 2012). A car manufacturer negotiating a new contract with its suppliers has the right to withdraw from the contract if it deems that it does not meet its expectations. If this is not done, the final product may turn out to be worse than the competition and the producer will suffer losses. Likewise, the consumer has the right not to buy a given product if they deem it not worth the price. What seems to be a paradox, it is thanks to exclusions that it becomes possible to maintain a certain unity and solidarity between members of particular groups. It is of particular importance for the health insurance market, because due to the correct risk assessment and a number of other activities of insurance companies, the insured will be convinced that their interests are looked after. Thanks to this, they will continue to pay contributions. Insurance companies will gain their recognition and reputation of stable institutions that can be relied on in difficult situations. Departure from this principle will not result in greater social justice, but only in favouring certain social groups at the expense of others and the disappearance of the insurance institution. The question of the trust of members who make up particular social groups, although he did not directly mean insurance, was well expressed by Sinek (2009, pp. 114, 122):

> only when individuals can trust the culture or organization will they take personal risks in order to advance that culture or organization as a whole. [...] When we believe someone has our best interest in mind because it is in their benefit to do so, the whole group benefits.

This is especially important as the loss of even a small number of customers can result in losses for insurers. Usually, people who are already ill, who try to access certain medical services at a low cost, are more interested in joining health insurance. Insurance is a more economical option for them than, for example, direct payments. They may also be more determined to continue insurance, even in the case of constantly increasing premiums. On the other hand, relatively healthy people do not show that much interest in purchasing insurance, as they relatively rarely use medical services. The difficult role of the insurer is to rationally evaluate the health risk for these particular groups. The higher frequency of using health insurance by the insured means that even a small loss of some insured (e.g. persons representing standard risk) may result in losses for the insurer. For example, it is indicated that in the United States of America, which has several types of private health insurance and public programmes, 10% of the population consumes about 72% of healthcare expenditure, and 2% of the population consumes 41% of healthcare expenditure (Light, 2000, pp. 969–974). The situation is similar in Poland, where, according to the data of the National Health Fund for 2009, only 5% of the insured in the public system generated 60% of all costs. In turn, treatment of 75% of the insured accounted for about 10% of expenses (Dziełak et al., 2010, p. 4). These data show that a relatively small proportion of the insured are able to generate most of the expenses.[29] Therefore, in commercial insurance, where contracts are voluntarily concluded, risk assessment is of such special importance. Therefore, the insurer's risk is not that a given event will take place, but whether the frequency of such events (e.g. diseases or the intensity of using medical services by the insured) falls within the framework assumed by the insurer. The insurer assumes that a given event will take place and monitors the level of deviations that occur at the same time. In other words, for the insurer, the risk will be, for example, that during the insurance period a greater number of people fall ill than assumed, which will affect the level of treatment costs.

However, in the health insurance market, a situation is possible where the insurer's portfolio is dominated by sub-standard risks, if the insured classified to particular sub-standard risk groups accept an increased premium for the insurance. Insurance coverage may even apply to events taking place in the past, if special conditions allow it, e.g. in group insurance concluded at the workplace, all employees usually form one risk group with one, average premium. It also often happens that the employer pays part or even all of the premium. However, this does not change the nature of the insurance, as the insurer continues to use advanced risk assessment and constantly monitors the use of medical services by the insured. Even if a certain group of employees who were ill before uses insurance, it is possible thanks to contributions paid by other employees and the employer. If the insurer has not made a mistake and there is acceptance among employees for incurring appropriate costs, such an insurance programme, although it has its limitations,[30] is possible.

Insurers also offer health insurance against very rare risks that affect a relatively small percentage of a given population. However, if such a risk occurs, the person concerned will not be able to cover the costs incurred by themself. Then having insurance makes sense, and the insurer is relatively easy to assess such a risk, as it does not occur as often as, for example, the flu. Such events include the risk of developing leukaemia. It is a very rare disease, but its occurrence is very costly (Berdine, 2011).

Insurance companies also play a very important role in the accumulation and allocation of capital in the economy. The creation and evolution of an insurance institution can also be associated with a low time preference. In the absence of insurance, a person may take action of gradual accumulation of certain amounts of money towards the uncertain future. The larger the amounts and if the accumulated capital continues to grow, the lower the time preference will be for a given person. On the other hand, insurance allows for a significant shortening of this process; they are more attractive, among others, because they allow for faster accumulation of the necessary funds in a certain group of people. Insured persons do not have to be afraid that the occurrence of an undesirable event will occur at a time when they have not yet managed to save adequate funds, as parallel payments of all insured persons significantly accelerate this process. Thus, insurance causes a significant intensification of the positive effects associated with low time preference. Insurance companies that conduct a reliable risk assessment, as a result, have significant capital, which they allocate (invest) appropriately depending on the type of risk. The lower the frequency of the events, the longer the investment will be. On the other hand, if there is a significant degree of consumption of insurance in a given insurance programme, then the time horizon of such investments is shortened. To some extent, it reflects the attitudes of the insured and the quality of the assessment and risk management of insurance companies. The positive contribution of insurance institution to the development of the capital structure of the economy was also noticed by Mises (2006, p. 86), who stated that:

> A great part of the capital at work in American enterprises is owned by the workers themselves and by other people with modest means. Billions and billions of saving deposits, of bonds, and of insurance policies are operating in these enterprises. On the American money market today, it is no longer the banks, it is the insurance companies that are the greatest money lenders. And the money of the insurance company is—not legally, but economically—the property of the insured. And practically everybody in the United States is insured in one way or another.

It is worth emphasizing that in the economic sense, insurance companies do not perform the so-called transfer of risk, both when accepting a given person for insurance and when investing the funds raised (net premiums). It is not true to say that the essence of insurance companies' activity is the transfer of risk. Conclusion of the insurance contract will not result in the insured person no longer having to worry about unfavourable events, as these have been transferred to the insurance company from the moment the policy was in force. The insurance does not eliminate or postpone the causes causing the given events. It only allows the reduction or elimination of negative effects resulting from the realization of a given risk. As already mentioned, the role of insurance is to cover the insured's losses. It is the insurer, not the insured person, who bears the costs related to the occurrence of a given event, but it is by no means a transfer of risk. Risk occurs over time; it is not a good that can be transferred from point A to point B. The expression risk transfer has a certain metaphorical meaning here and as such is used in the insurance industry – which is probably intended to be a simplified term for covering losses incurred by the insured due to the materialization of a given risk. However, it has no application for economics.[31] The functioning of insurers on the health insurance market requires the coordination of many complex processes. Individual insurance companies compete with each other for clients on many levels, ranging from the quality of economic calculation using probability, and ending with marketing or sales channels. However, it should be taken into account that despite the development of the health insurance market, there are still some factors that effectively prevent a given insurance product from entering the market. At times, these factors may be misinterpreted and misinterpreted. Such a case includes the arguments provided by Hoppe (2009) on the conditions necessary for the creation of health insurance:

> Private enterprise can offer insurance against events over whose outcome the insured possesses no control. One cannot insure oneself against suicide or bankruptcy, for example, because it is in one's own hands to bring these events about. Because a person's health, or lack of it, lies increasingly within his own control, many, if not most health risks, are actually uninsurable. 'Insurance' against risks whose likelihood an individual can systematically influence falls within that person's own responsibility.

While the arguments cited in the text by Hoppe regarding the elimination of state regulations in such areas of healthcare as medical universities educating future doctors or in the production of drugs and medical equipment should be considered correct, in the case of deregulation of the health insurance industry, the presented arguments are not appropriate. First of all, it should be noted, referring to Lipka (2013a, p. 87), that 'Modern methods of insurance risk assessment enable protection of 97–99% of people applying for insurance, including many people burdened with various health risk factors'.

Hoppe's arguments referring to having or not having control of the insured over their health as a prerequisite for health insurance are very imprecise. How can the insurer (and the insured themself) check when this control exists and when not? However, as it has already been presented, insurance companies create individual risk groups not on the basis of a clearly defined border defining some kind of awareness of the insured as to the control of their health, but on the basis of an appropriate risk calculation. Clients who deliberately try to deteriorate their health in order to receive an appropriate benefit are certainly characterized by pathological behaviours. However, their exclusion from insurance coverage is determined by economic calculation, namely the lack of acceptance of other insured persons who do not want to incur higher premiums. The abstract dichotomy has control – no control has no application here. On the other hand, how can you then explain people who were ill previously, but already accepted for insurance? Exactly the same principle as before. Of course, in this case it is no longer possible to talk about insurance risk, but about certainty, because the insurer is sure that such persons will immediately benefit from medical services. However, further, such an entity will calculate the risk due to having in its portfolio people with standard or sub-standard risk, who may voluntarily subsidize those who are already ill. Events covered by insurance are otherwise known as random events and, as Kowalewski (2001, p. 56) points out:

> What is a normal result of human action, in particular action taken to cause such an event, cannot be considered a random event. The random event must occur independently or against the will of the person affected by the event.

Perhaps this is what Hoppe meant, but his argument seems to be oversimplifying. For example, an insurer by offering insurance covering the costs of treatment abroad offers the client an additional extension of the insurance cover by random events resulting from the consumption of small amounts of alcohol. Therefore, the insured party consuming alcohol is aware that the probability of an accident is greater, and although it does not strive to cause it directly, the line between controlling and not controlling the risk begins to blur. In turn, the insurer can offer such an extension based on an appropriate risk calculation and a clear definition of the terms of its liability.

Therefore, in order for health insurance to arise, a given event must first be insurable, i.e. it must be possible to apply the calculus of probability. Otherwise, the event will be uninsurable, i.e. it will not be possible to rationally estimate the insurance premium. Subsequently, it is possible to indicate the insured risk and the uninsured risk. The insured risk occurs when it is possible to create a sufficiently large risk group. In the absence of a sufficient number of applicants, although a premium calculation is possible, the risk in question is not insured.

It seems that the use of an inadequate description of the rules governing the functioning of the health insurance market may lead to unnecessary misunderstandings with representatives of the insurance industry and ultimately hinder the introduction of necessary changes. The above remarks are particularly important as the individual stages of the health-care reform in the United States postulated by Hoppe are often eagerly quoted by Austrian School economists in various types of discussions and polemics. For example, Rothbard (2006, p. 133) points out that: 'Ludwig von Mises Institute, instead of offering its own 500-page health plan, sticks to its principled "four-step" plan laid out by Hans-Hermann Hoppe (Free Market, April 1993) of dismantling existing government intervention into health.' Therefore, for greater transparency of such activities, it is necessary to thoroughly analyse the arguments presented by Hoppe, which ultimately refer to the proposed changes on the health insurance market (in the United States of America).

Private and universal (public) health insurance

Insurance is a market institution, that is, one that was established and evolved on the basis of cooperation. Private health insurance cannot be confused with the so-called universal (public) health insurance, which is part of the social policy of states. In fact, there are a number of differences between private insurance and so-called public insurance.

First, insurance companies use advanced economic calculation using probability calculus to estimate risk and determine appropriate premiums for individual risk groups. Diversifying premiums, the scope of insurance, introducing exclusions and limitations is aimed at incurring costs in an adequate proportion to the obtained and invested premiums. The cooperation between the actuarial[32] and underwriting[33] departments allows for such risk management that enables profit. In the case of so-called public insurance, there is no risk calculation, selection, or classification. A uniform, compulsory premium is paid for all insured persons.[34] Public institutions responsible for financing access to healthcare do not have to fear the loss of insured persons. This situation makes the problem of moral hazard much more visible in public health programmes, especially when public authorities, in order to maintain them, often invoke the so-called right to healthcare of citizens.

Secondly, in the case of health insurance, it is usually unknown who specifically will need access to medical services. The insurance company is able to determine that, for example, out of 100,000 insured persons, 1% will develop a specific disease, but it is not known exactly who these people will be. In turn, in public insurance, in addition to such people, there is already a well-known, sick group of people. There is therefore no risk distribution, only certainty.

Thirdly, insurance companies, apart from financing access to a range of medical services for insured persons, invest some of the premiums obtained from them. As a result, the supply of savings increases on the market, which makes it easier for enterprises to raise the capital necessary to create more efficient production. Meanwhile, the so-called public insurance premiums are immediately consumed by the insured. Thus, the insurance market contributes to an increase in the supply of savings and their appropriate allocation in the economy,[35] while public insurance is nothing more than a redistribution of income. Compulsory transfer of funds between different groups of insured persons is not a source of investment.

Fourth, thanks to the limitations contained in the insurance contract, it is possible to rationally consume medical services. The insured know the limitations of such insurance, so they undertake other activities aimed at least maintaining their current state of health (e.g. they eat better). However, rational consumption of such services should not be equated with their rationing, which is characteristic of public programmes. In addition to insurance, there are many other forms of financing access to medical services and institutions offering them (e.g. medical networks, charities, or direct payments) in the unregulated market. Therefore, the lack of insurance does not mean that it is not possible to use medical services at all. Public insurance does not give the person in need of medical services a choice, and their situation worsens if they cannot avail themselves of these services through a public programme. For such people, only private insurance or other private institutions offering medical services are a real alternative.

Fifthly, in market conditions there are mechanisms contributing to the reduction of costs and improvement of the quality of medical services, which in the case of public insurance does not have to be so certain and often leads to an increase in costs or a decrease in the quality of services.

The above differences show that the so-called universal (public) insurance operates on extremely different principles than private insurance and there are, in principle, no common features between them, apart from the name. The first type of insurance is inextricably linked with interventionism. The second type is the result of market processes. Due to the above differences, it is not possible to combine these two types of insurance. Successive interventions in the health insurance market bring them closer to fulfilling a redistributive function in terms of financing access to medical services. The so-called universal (public) health insurance, which is an element of state policy, is not insurance in the true sense of the word. They have never been and never will be. Insurance, like money, is a market institution.

Notes

1 This is also true for sciences dealing with the past, such as history. While it is concerned with past events, the same study is an act of action. The uncertainty in this respect is therefore closely related to the desire to find answers (in the future) to the questions troubling historians. For example, what influenced the fall of the Roman Empire more? Barbarian invasions or internal (economic) problems? It is also a matter of historians looking for relevant information on this subject, which broadens their knowledge and reduces the aforementioned uncertainty.

2 Therefore, speculation should be broadly defined – as deliberate actions leading a person to achieve their goal under conditions of uncertainty. Therefore, this term does not have the colloquial and negative meaning so often ascribed to it.

3 Even if the trader made a mistake, the resulting loss would reveal it very quickly. Errors cannot be avoided, but the profit and loss mechanism, allows for their quick identification, which, at the same time, gives the competition a chance to take the place of those producers who were less able to predict the needs of consumers.

4 It would not even be compensation paid in money, but in abstract units of account. For more on this, see: Mises (1998, p. 250).

5 It is worth mentioning that Mises relied on the work of his brother Richard, an eminent mathematician. R. von Mises made an important contribution to the theory of probability. In his study 'Probability, Statistics, and Truth', he created an objective or 'frequency' theory of probability, so one that can be expressed numerically, which corresponds to L. von Mises' class probability. For more on this, see R. Mises (1981); Rothbard (1975).

6 It can be concluded that Shakespeare's 'To be or not to be? That is the question' perfectly captures the nature of Mises's case probability. Although, in this 'case', there are only two possible end results, the number of (unique) ways to achieve any of them cannot be estimated and grouped into appropriate classes.

7 This is a slightly modified version of the definition of risk used by M. N. Rothbard: '"Risk" occurs when an event is a member of a class of a large number of homogeneous events and there is fairly certain knowledge of the frequency of occurrence of this class of events' (Rothbard, 2009, p. 552).

8 For more on this, see: Hoppe (2007, pp. 1–20).

9 For more on this, see: Arrow (1971).

10 Thus, the benefits resulting from the creation of insurance allow better use of scarce resources in the economy. Thanks to the use of mathematics, it is possible to adjust the amount of premiums more appropriately to the risk represented by individual insured persons. Otherwise, it would be much more difficult to determine whether a given person pays too high or too low a premium.

11 Ferguson mentions several important achievements in mathematics which, in his opinion, contributed significantly to the establishment of the insurance institution. it includes, among other things: probability (B. Pascal); collection of statistical data on deaths and births to determine the average life expectancy (J. Graunt, E. Halley); the creation of the concept of statistical significance thanks to the work of J. Bernoulli or even the work of A. de Moive on normal distribution. Interestingly, Ferguson gives 17th-century Scotland for the first time that mathematical methods were used to calculate the premium. For more information see: Ferguson (2008, pp. 187–196).

12 An underwriter is the person responsible for assessing insurance risk.

13 It can also be stated that the insurer incurs 'normal' costs not related to the use of probability, such as administrative costs, commissions paid to agents and other intermediaries, costs related to the service of insurance already concluded, etc.

14 Therefore, the names class probability, risk, and objective risk can be used interchangeably. The division into objective and subjective risks is one of many in the literature and this may lead to some semantic confusion. Subjective risk can therefore be attributed more to uncertainty.

15 It is worth mentioning that there are different types of insurance on the insurance market. For example, in the case of life insurance, a distinction is made between individual life insurance and group life insurance (usually concluded through an enterprise and partially or fully paid for by the employer). However, this division is purely technical and relates more to the institutional conditions in which the insurance contract is concluded. Of course, also in the case of individual life insurance, risk classes are created.

16 If, on the other hand, in the case of concluding a contract between two parties, the calculation of probability does not apply, it is a bet. In the case of a bet, there is a case probability.

17 Insured persons often equate health insurance with medical insurance and use these names alternately.

18 The example below is for incapacity insurance, but the same rule is true for health and medical insurance as well.

19 Randomized controlled trials (RCTs) are particularly important for insurers.

20 Therefore, life insurance was created and developed earlier than health insurance precisely because of the availability of appropriate data enabling the calculation of insurance premiums.

21 That is, the part of the premium from which the relevant benefits under the insurance contract will be paid or financed. The total premium, in turn, is the gross premium and, in addition to the net premium, it includes, inter alia, administrative costs, commission for insurance agents, or the insurer's profits.

22 It can be concluded that the more information an insurer has, the more risk groups (classes) it is able to create.

23 Therefore, the so-called cherry picking, a term often pejoratively characterizing the actions of insurers, consisting in accepting only selected risks and rejecting others, should be criticized due to the fact that it does not reflect the essence of insurance and may lead to wrong conclusions.

24 Otherwise underwriting.

25 We can distinguish two stages of risk assessment: its selection, which consists in accepting or rejecting specific risks (and persons), and risk classification, where individual insured persons are assigned to previously created risk groups (classes).

26 Another name used is negative selection.

27 It is quite a general term as there are many types of co-payment. For more on this subject see: Kozber and Osak (2013, p. 96).

28 Or, in other words, insured persons with standard risk subsidize those with sub-standard risk.

29 Such statistics should not come as a surprise, however. Here, for example, the Pareto 80/20 principle can be recalled.

30 These include, among others: concluding a contract for a specified period, e.g. for one year, introducing an appropriate level of co-payment or increasing the amount of premium or limiting the scope of insurance, if a given programme generated too high costs for the insurer. Whether the premium increase applies to the employer or employees is of secondary importance here.

31 More on word criticism: *risk transfer*, see: Michalak (2008, pp. 135–147).

32 Dealing with the calculation of insurance risk.

33 Responsible for the insurance risk assessment, e.g. by analysing applications for insurance coverage of components by potential clients of the insurer.

34 From the economic point of view, it is nothing more than a levy or tax.

35 With the help of specialized financial institutions such as banks.

References

Arrow K. J., 1971, *Essays in the theory of risk-bearing*, USA: Markham Publishing Company.

Berdine G., 2011, *The economics of US healthcare*, https://mises.org/library/economics-us-healthcare (accessed: 22. 06. 2018).

Dziełak D.*et al.*, 2010, *Analiza korzystania ze świadczeń opieki zdrowotnej w 2009 r. i rozkładu indywidualnych wydatków Narodowego Funduszu Zdrowia związanych z finansowaniem tych świadczeń* [Analysis of the use of healthcare services in 2009 and the distribution of individual expenses of the National Health Fund related to the financing of these services], Warsaw: Centrala NFZ, Departament Świadczeń Opieki Zdrowotnej.

Ferguson F., 2008, *The ascent of money: A financial history of the world*, New York: Penguin Press.

Foss N. J., Klein P. G., 2012, *Organizing entrepreneurial judgment. A new approach to the firm*, USA: Cambridge University Press.

Guzel Z., 2013a, Organizacja i uczestnicy procesu ryzyka [Organization and participants of the risk process], in Z. Guzel, D. M. Fal, A. Lipka (eds.), *Medycyna ubezpieczeniowa: Underwritinig. Orzecznictwo. Ubezpieczenia zdrowotne* [Insurance medicine – underwriting, certification, health insurance], Warsaw: Poltext.

Guzel Z., 2013b, Ryzyko medyczne [Medical risk], in Z. Guzel, D. M. Fal, A. Lipka (eds.), *Medycyna ubezpieczeniowa: Underwritinig. Orzecznictwo. Ubezpieczenia zdrowotne* [Insurance medicine – underwriting, certification, health insurance], Warsaw: Poltext.

Hoppe H. H., 2007, The limits of numerical probability: Frank H. Knight and Ludwig von Mises and the frequency interpretation, *Quarterly Journal of Austrian Economics*, 1, 1–20.

Hoppe H. H., 2009, A four-step healthcare solution, https://mises.org/library/four-step-healthcare-solution (accessed: 22. 06. 2018).

Huber M.*et al.*, 2011, How should we define health?, *British Medical Journal*, 343, D4163.

Huerta De Soto J., 2010, *Socialism, economic calculation and entrepreneurship*, Cheltenham, Northampton: Edward Edgar Publishing.

Klimczak K. M., 2008, Ryzyko w teorii ekonomii ['Risk in economic theory'], *Master of Business Administration*, 6, 64–69.

Knight F. H., 1921, *Risk, uncertainty and profit*, New York: August M. Kelly.

Kostrzewski P., 2013, Proces oceny ryzyka w ubezpieczeniach zdrowotnych [The process of risk assessment in health insurance], in Z. Guzel, D. M. Fal, A. Lipka (eds.), *Medycyna ubezpieczeniowa: Underwritinig. Orzecznictwo. Ubezpieczenia zdrowotne* [Insurance medicine – underwriting, certification, health insurance], Warsaw: Poltext.

Kowalewski E., 2001, Ryzyko w działalności człowieka i możliwości jego ograniczenia [The risk in human activity and the possibilities of its reduction], in T. Sangowski (ed.), *Ubezpieczenia gospodarcze* [*Economic insurance*], Warsaw: Poltext.

Kozber M. M., Osak M., 2013, Współpłacenie bezpośrednie w bazowym systemie zabezpieczenia zdrowotnego – doświadczenia Szwajcarii [Direct cost sharing in the basic health system – Swiss experience], *Problemy Zarządzania*, 1, 93–111.

Light D. W., 2000, Sociological perspectives on competition in health care, *Journal of Health Politics, Policy and Law*, 25, 969–974.

Lipka A., 2013a, Prawo do ubezpieczenia a prawo do oceny ryzyka. Evidence based underwriting [The right to insurance and the right to risk assessment. Evidence Based Underwriting], in Z. Guzel, D. M. Fal, A. Lipka (eds.), *Medycyna ubezpieczeniowa: Underwritinig. Orzecznictwo. Ubezpieczenia zdrowotne* [Insurance medicine – underwriting, certification, health insurance], Warsaw: Poltext.

Lipka A., 2013b, Zasady oceny ryzyka w ubezpieczeniach na życie [Principles of risk assessment in life insurance], in Z. Guzel, D. M. Fal, A. Lipka (eds.), *Medycyna ubezpieczeniowa: Underwritinig. Orzecznictwo. Ubezpieczenia zdrowotne* [Insurance medicine – underwriting, certification, health insurance], Warsaw: Poltext.

Machaj M., 2013, *Kapitalizm, socjalizm i prawa własności* [Capitalism, socialism and property rights], Warsaw: Instytut Ludwiga von Misesa.

Michalak J., 2008, Przesłanki nieakceptowalności koncepcji transferu ryzyka' [Premises of unacceptability of the risk transfer concept], in J. Handschke (ed.), *Studia z ubezpieczeń gospodarczych i społecznych* [Economic and social insurance studies], Poznan: Wydawnictwo Akademii Ekonomicznej w Poznaniu, pp. 135–147.

Mises L., 1998, *Human action. A treatise on economics*, Auburn: Ludwig von Mises Institute.

Mises L., 2006, *Economic policy. Thoughts for today and tomorrow*, Auburn: Ludwig von Mises Institute.

Mises R., 1981, *Probability, statistics and truth*, USA: Courier Corporation.

Mowbray A. H., Blanchard R. H., 1961, *Insurance, its theory and practice in the United States*, New York: McGraw-Hill.

Osak M., 2008, Ryzyko zdrowotne jako podstawa wyodrębnienia ubezpieczeń zdrowotnych [Health risk as the basis for distinguishing health insurance], in J. Handschke (ed.), *Studia z ubezpieczeń gospodarczych i społecznych* [Economic and social insurance studies], Poznan: Wydawnictwo Akademii Ekonomicznej w Poznaniu, pp. 148–167.

Outerville J. F., 1998, *Theory and practice of insurance*, New York: Springer Science + Business Media.

Rockwell L. H., 2012, Freedom of association, https://mises.org/library/free dom-association (accessed: 22. 06. 2018).

Rothbard M. N., 1975, The correct theory of probability, *Libertarian Review*, 2, 9.

Rothbard M. N., 2006, *Making economic sense*, Auburn: Ludwig von Mises Institute.

Rothbard M. N., 2009, *Man, economy, and state with power and market*, Auburn: Ludwig von Mises Institute.

Sinek S., 2009, *Start with why: How great leaders inspire everyone to take action*, USA: Portfolio.

WHO, no date, What is the WHO definition of health?, http://www.who.int/suggestions/faq/en/ (accessed: 10. 06. 2018).

2 Alternative market forms of financing access to medical services

Direct payments

Direct payments (out-of-pocket) are currently not the most popular form of financing access to medical services – according to OECD data, in 2014, direct payments accounted for 15% of all expenditure on medical care among 28 European Union countries (OECD/EU, 2016, p. 123). However, they are of particular importance for decisions made by consumers. The creation and development of insurance or medical subscriptions undoubtedly allows the avoidance of a significant part of direct expenses, but this does not change the fact that these expenses are still incurred (in whole or in the majority) – in this case by the so-called third-party payer.

Direct payments are the basis of transactions in most markets. The amount of money allocated to individual goods and services is of great importance, because in the end, everything is subordinated to the judgements that consumers evaluate. Medical services are no exception in this case. The consumer is particularly attentive if they spend most of their funds on purchasing a given good or service. Their choices may turn out to be wrong at times, but they are never random. Even if they themself do not have sufficient knowledge about a given product, they often rely on the suggestions of other consumers (e.g. friends) or on the advice of specialized institutions. Price reductions and improvement in the quality of goods and services undoubtedly contribute to greater consumer satisfaction and allow producers to generate profits. However, good past performance by manufacturers is no guarantee that they will maintain their market position in the future. It depends on the ability to anticipate and meet the future needs of consumers.

Consumers allocating all or most of their funds to a given good or service cannot afford to consume them rashly, as this may worsen their situation in the future and, as a result, result in a loss for them. The

DOI: 10.4324/9781003258957-4

purchase of medical goods and services directly by the consumer should not be seen as a problem if it takes place in an unfettered market. Undistorted market competition effectively keeps costs and prices low, increases the supply and quality of the goods and services offered, and ensures their more diversified offer.

Purchasing certain goods and services has a direct impact on the rational behaviour of consumers. The situation is completely different if the consumer pays only a small fraction of the cost (as in insurance, for example). Then it is not able to fully estimate the direct cost for a given medical service, and its so-called price sensitivity is weakened or even eliminated. However, insurance contracts do not guarantee infinite access to medical services and are also subject to various types of restrictions. In health insurance contracts, the insured usually incurs part of the costs directly out of their own pocket (cost-sharing), which greatly helps insurance companies to reduce moral hazard and to keep costs and insurance premiums stable.

Currently, direct payments, which have been significantly marginalized by public healthcare, may be associated with the unpleasantness of incurring high costs, e.g. in the absence of insurance. However, in the case of problems with the availability of medical services through the so-called public health insurance is, inter alia, this form of payment that allows you to quickly access them. Importantly, thanks to direct payments, the consumer has the opportunity to purchase specific goods and services at a certain time and in the quantities they need from competing producers. There is no intermediation in the form of an insurer or a medical network. The power of the consumer making direct payments is as strong as it is in the health insurance market.

Medical savings accounts

Medical savings accounts (MSAs)[1] are also a form of direct payments. MSAs are a more institutionalized (i.e. introduced on the basis of new regulations) form of these payments, functioning within the framework of public systems, among others, in countries such as Singapore, South Africa, the United States of America, and China. Payments via MSA are made electronically (e.g. by debit card) and can be linked to health insurance as in South Africa or the USA, where the insured person pays some medical costs out of their own pocket before being able to use the insurance. In this case, the introduction of MSA made it possible to transfer funds faster or reduce the administrative costs of insurance companies.[2]

Undoubtedly, the appearance of MSA in these few countries can be read as a kind of attempt to relieve third-party payers and a step towards rationalizing the demand for medical services. One of the goals of this type of medical account is to try to influence the attitudes of consumers so that health insurance does not finance routine medical procedures that the insured can pay out of their own pocket. In addition, MSA can also affect the savings attitudes of the insured, and collecting funds for future medical (or more broadly health) expenses through a medical savings account is expected to help them in this.

The difference between MSA and regular direct payments can therefore be boiled down to the fact that in the first case, the purchase of specific medical services takes place from the funds previously accumulated for this purpose. Ordinary payments, on the other hand, may result through not purchasing other goods and services, selling some property, or voluntary savings. However, this state of affairs can be misjudged here. A person who makes a choice between saving for future medical (health) expenses and the current consumption of certain goods and services, in fact, chooses between a more or less desirable state. If such a person prefers to spend their resources on the purchase of a TV set, car, or a trip, it is a rational decision in terms of meeting urgent needs. The uncertainty of the future is not a proof of its irrational action – if it is not known what will happen in one day, and even more so in ten years, it cannot be said that current consumption (instead of saving) worsens the situation of such a person. In fact, most people can agree with the statement that having health insurance (e.g. against serious illness or accident) or saving for the so-called Black Hour is important and necessary, but it does not mean that they should all save the same amount or in the same proportion.[3] The responsibility of an individual for their own destiny is born of their freedom of choice, and only freedom of choice can teach them such responsibility to the greatest extent. For example, top-down determination of the portion of income to be allocated to MSA limits the individual's decision-making, depriving it of access to some of the funds. Therefore, an individual, after purchasing the desired goods and services (e.g. a computer), may have fewer funds that could be allocated to pro-health expenses if they had them (e.g. purchase of accessories for recreational running).

In fact, there have long been various types of medical savings accounts in the unfettered market, that is, simply savings, which did not have to be given that special name. The emergence of MSA should be considered a fairly important institutional stage of a gradual departure from financing medical services by a third party within the framework of more or less interventional public healthcare solutions. However, there are many countries where direct payments for specific medical services are made without the participation of MSA (e.g. Switzerland, the Netherlands, or Poland).

In summary, the emergence of the so-called MSA (or savings) is due to unfettered market processes enabling efficient capital accumulation and the freedom of consumer choice, and not to top-down institutional solutions. On this basis, it can be concluded that the creation and development of MSA are best served by lowering taxes and increasing tax reliefs, and not top-down regulations creating such solutions.

Medical subscriptions

Medical subscriptions as a form of indirect payments are an alternative to health insurance. Their development depends, inter alia, on institutional conditions in individual countries.

Medical networks that offer subscriptions do not, like insurance companies, assess risk with the help of insurance mathematics. Instead, they enter into contracts with doctors, nurses, and other health professionals to provide specific services within a single medical network. As a result, representatives of medical professions have a guarantee of employment and motivation to provide high-quality services. Everything is subordinated to the final consumer satisfaction. The medical subscription includes mainly outpatient services and diagnostic tests. Medical networks must therefore adequately anticipate the costs of providing such services. Unlike health insurance, the client's health does not play such a significant role. This does not mean, however, that medical networks guarantee unlimited access to medical services. Typically, when certain limits are exceeded, network customers also pay for these out of pocket. Therefore, also in the case of medical subscriptions, there are some forms of limiting the excessive consumption of medical services.

Medical networks focus on creating and developing appropriate human resources structures and procedures that enable them to generate profits with the appropriate frequency of consumption of medical services. They are first created and developed in large cities. They are favoured by a sufficiently high concentration of the population in a given area, access to qualified workers, and adequate infrastructure. These conditions favour the rapid establishment of new facilities within a given medical network.

Medical subscriptions, like health insurance, can be sold individually and in groups. In the latter form, they are often offered by employers as non-wage benefits and often compete with health insurance.

Insurance companies may, however, sign a contract for the provision of medical services to the insured with many entities, which do not have to be only medical networks. In addition, insured persons may go to other private institutions and, on the basis of presented bills, receive reimbursement up to certain amounts. On the other hand, a person with a medical subscription can usually only use the facilities of a given network.

Cooperation between medical networks and insurance companies brings benefits to both parties. Insurers do not have to incur large expenses to build their own facilities (although they can also create such a network) and can offer insured persons access to a larger number of medical facilities. On the other hand, medical networks also compete with each other for contracts with insurance companies. Thanks to such contracts, they can gain access to a wider group of clients, even if they directly lose their competition for clients with insurers. Then the insurance company monitors the quality of services provided by them on behalf of its clients. However, in the case of subscriptions, customer complaints are considered in specific medical facilities belonging to a given network. In addition, private medical networks, as a result of excessive consumption of medical services by customers, may incur higher costs than the revenues generated from subscriptions, which may result in actions on the part of the operator reducing its costs (e.g. longer waiting times and providing medical services or directing to less expensive research). In the case of group insurance, such risk may be lower, because the insurer transfers funds to a selected facility (network) as payment for medical services indicated by the insured and pays attention to their implementation, among others, at the appropriate time. Therefore, a given network which has a contract with an insurer cannot afford to extend the time of making an appointment – otherwise it may be replaced by more effective competitors.

However, medical networks will find it difficult to offer packages for relatively rare conditions that cover a small percentage of the population. In such cases, insurance companies are in a better position. In turn, medical networks will be more interested in extending their packages with medical services that can be provided to a larger group of customers – otherwise they would incur unnecessary costs.

To sum up, medical subscriptions to a certain extent both compete and complement each other with health insurance, which greatly benefits consumers (this is the case, for example, in Poland).

Charity

Charitable activity is an essential element of the market economy. Thanks to it, people who need it most can count on the help of the rest of society, which is able to work. However, such aid is possible thanks to the constantly growing production of goods and services, which is the result of the accumulation of capital. Such a developing economy improves people's living conditions and is responsible for the increase in their welfare, which in turn contributes to the intensification of charity activities. As Mises (1998, p. 833) put it:

> Within the frame of capitalism the notion of poverty refers only to those people who are unable to take care of themselves. [...] Capitalism, in improving the masses' standard of living, hygienic conditions, and methods of prophylactics and therapeutics, does not remove bodily incapacity. It is true that today many people who in the past would have been doomed to life-long disability are restored to full vigor. But on the other hand many whom innate defects, sickness, or accidents would have extinguished sooner in earlier days survive as permanently incapacitated people. Moreover, the prolongation of the average length of life tends toward an increase in the number of the aged who are no longer able to earn a living.
>
> The problem of the incapacitated is a specific problem of human civilization and of society. [...] The very existence of a comparatively great number of invalids is, however paradoxical, a characteristic mark of civilization and material well-being.

Such conditions affect people's attitudes. Asking for help is seen more as a last resort, and people who are able to work take steps to protect themselves in the event of an uncertain future, such as taking out insurance or limiting consumption. However, this is not an effect of dependence on the ruthless capitalist system, but actions that testify to their freedom of choice and independence. Units with insurance policies, their own savings, and other forms of protection in the event of uncertain events (e.g. accidents or diseases) do not constitute an economic burden for the rest of society. Through appropriate market institutions (commercial and non-commercial) they are able to take care of themselves. This state of affairs in the 1920s was well captured by American president C. Coolidge, who stated that 'There is no dignity quite so impressive and no independence quite so important as living within your means' (Maxwell, 2003, p. 101). This statement clearly contrasts with the contemporary calls of many politicians to increase the role of the state in providing society with the so-called social security.

It is important in this case that various market solutions create appropriate structures for financing access to medical services. Thanks to this, people involved in the production process have greater safety and can allocate part of their own resources to helping people in need. From the economic perspective, there are two basic conditions for providing assistance to those in need: the availability of appropriate resources and the will. People who voluntarily donate funds to those in need value the satisfaction with providing them higher than the preservation of these funds or their consumption. The benefits they obtain are therefore not of a monetary nature. Willingness to improve someone's situation motivates to action and gives a sense of satisfaction. Whether such an action is motivated by religious considerations, internal sensitivity to human harm, or other motives does not matter for the economy – the act of action itself and its effects count.

Even in modern economies, subject to many interventions damaging market productivity, one can observe an endless variety of charitable actions, on either an ad hoc or permanent (institutional) nature. Among other things, thanks to the development of the Internet, relatively quick collections of multi-million sums are possible. Such expenses are associated with the purchase of expensive drugs and/or the financing of expensive therapies, i.e. medical goods and services that are only affordable for very wealthy people. However, charity allows us to overcome this barrier, because in this case the founder is thousands of people providing support – even the most modest one. This has another positive effect. The additional demand for rare and expensive medical services encourages manufacturers to produce them more efficiently. The demand for these types of innovative and, in a sense, luxury goods and services no longer comes from only the highest-income people, which gives hope for their faster mass production in the future. Thanks to charity work, people with medium or low income also indirectly participate in setting trends or directions for the development of innovative medical goods and services.

An important feature of charity activity is its directness and informality. People who show such support are guided to a large extent by emotional criteria, which has many advantages. The situation is different in the case of various public programmes (non-market, non-charity), where there are clearly defined procedures. The sensitivity and good will of the donor is replaced by a formalized clerical decision leading to top-down selection of who is eligible for such assistance and who is not, which is a distortion of the act of providing assistance.

It is also important that market solutions enable the development of many charity institutions that improve these processes by quickly directing the attention of society to the cases of people most in need of support and by obtaining the necessary funds to improve their situation. In addition, thanks to such activity, the supporters also develop appropriate ethical attitudes and, at least indirectly, contribute to their promotion among the rest of society.

Notes

1 Another name used is health savings accounts (HSAs).
2 For more on the principles of MSA operation in selected countries, see: Goodman et al. (2004, pp. 110–111, 135–137).
3 This is due, inter alia, to the wide variety of needs for certain medical services – consumers do not report demand for one type of healthcare.

References

Goodman J. C., Musgrave G. L., Herrick D. M., 2004, *Lives at risk. Single-payer national health insurance around the world*, USA: Rowman & Littlefield Publishers.

Maxwell J. C., 2003, *There's no such thing as 'business' ethics: There's only one rule for making decisions*, USA: Warner Books.

Mises L., 1998, *Human action. A treatise on economics*, Auburn: Ludwig von Mises Institute.

OECD/EU, 2016, *Health at a glance: Europe 2016 – state of health in the EU cycle*, Paris: OECD Publishing.

3 The health system as an element of the market economy

Relationships between the various forms of financing access to medical services

When considering the functioning of market solutions in the field of providing consumers with medical (or health-related) goods and services, first of all, one should consider their appropriate definition. However, instead of describing these processes as market or private healthcare (as an alternative to public healthcare), it is more appropriate to use terms such as the private or market health system and the universal (public) health system.[1]

The very word 'healthcare' is very generalized and fuzzy. There is often talk of the need for people to have access to healthcare by the state, but there are no cases of countries having identical healthcare systems – on the contrary, there is a wide variety of them. However, healthcare is viewed as some kind of abstract, unified good that everyone needs. However, in reality no one consumes more or less units of the general healthcare resource. It is also confusing to talk about the so-called right to healthcare. It is not a right to use one homogeneous good. People differ both physiologically and psychologically. Additionally, they participate in random events causing undesirable effects (e.g. accidents or diseases). In fact, a person does not report a demand for healthcare in general, but for specific medical goods and services (or more broadly health services) aimed at reducing or eliminating their discomfort. The market (manufacturers) is thus responsible for meeting these diverse consumer health needs by providing heterogeneous goods and services, rather than one universal product under the misleading name of healthcare.[2]

The use of the term health system instead of the healthcare system has important economic and praxeological justification. Many people agree that if you get sick or have an accident, you should get treatment

DOI: 10.4324/9781003258957-5

as soon as possible. However, this intuitive agreement does not mean that they perceive these threats in the same way and take identical actions to prevent them. Contrary to popular belief, health does not have to be the most important thing – a lot depends on the human situation. For example, it is difficult to expect that young and unhealthy people will undergo thorough examinations every quarter or be interested in having a wide range of health insurance. Thus, they do not necessarily have to be willing to engage in this type of action. The situation is different in the case of people who are already ill – for them health will be ranked higher or highest in their hierarchy of needs. There is no rigid division or classification of needs here – everything depends on the judgements that value consumers and producers try to follow these needs. Therefore, a health need should be considered undergoing a complicated surgery, consultations, and examinations with a specialist doctor, taking medications as well as purchasing a gym ticket, walking in the forest, changing the diet, or going to bed earlier. Each individual meets their needs with the help of preselected means. So, they create their own plan or system to do this. Their needs are specific and often require the involvement of a set of complementary measures. Such a situation results in the emergence of specific complex market structures, reflecting decisions made by consumers.

Contrary to the universal (public) health system, its market counterpart does not have a single, institutionalized, rigid structure. The framework of the market system is not predetermined and is constantly changing. The health system, as an important part of the market economy, functions on the same principles as its other elements (markets). Perhaps due to the lack of this fixed 'shape' (or difficulties in defining it) the market health system may seem to be a less attractive solution than the public system. However, for economics and the economy, not only are the dynamics of market processes or their diversity important, but also the study of the effects that these processes bring. The market is not an abstract, changing entity that consumers must constantly adapt to. The market is the result of their actions. The essence of the market was well reflected by Mises (1998, p. 270):

> The market is not a place, a thing, or a collective entity. The market is a process, actuated by the interplay of the actions of the various individuals cooperating under the division of labor. The forces determining the – continually changing – state of the market are the value judgments of these individuals and their actions as directed by these value judgments. The state of the market at any instant is the price structure, i.e., the totality of the exchange ratios

as established by the interaction of those eager to buy and those eager to sell. There is nothing inhuman or mystical with regard to the market. The market process is entirely a resultant of human actions. Every market phenomenon can be traced back to definite choices of the members of the market society.

[...]

The direction of all economic affairs is in the market society a task of the entrepreneurs. Theirs is the control of production. They are at the helm and steer the ship. A superficial observer would believe that they are supreme. But they are not. They are bound to obey unconditionally the captain's orders. The captain is the consumer. Neither the entrepreneurs nor the farmers nor the capitalists determine what has to be produced. The consumers do that. If a businessman does not strictly obey the orders of the public as they are conveyed to him by the structure of market prices, he suffers losses, he goes bankrupt, and is thus removed from his eminent position at the helm. Other men who did better in satisfying the demand of the consumers replace him.

Although the entire production process is ultimately subordinated to consumers, they mainly come into contact only with producers of final goods and services. The so-called higher stages of production, although not of their interest, are also subordinate economically to them. The changes taking place there affect the final shape of the market only if consumers accept them.

This is one of the reasons why health insurance plays such an important role in the market health system. Due to reliable risk assessment of insurance companies, when the need arises, they are able to provide access to specific medical services under the previously indicated conditions. The fact that health insurance is not the only market form of financing access to such services is due to at least four reasons. First of all, health insurance has its limitations in financing access to these services – it does not guarantee unlimited access. Insurance companies try to limit the moral hazard in order not to increase premiums exceeding the expectations of the insured. Insured persons paying a fraction of the cost may use certain services much more often than if they incurred the costs directly. Secondly, not all events are insurable, that is, not all events can be accounted for in an economic calculation based on probability, and thus prices (premiums) can be determined. Third, not every person must feel the same need to adequately protect themselves against the adverse effects of losing health. Some people prefer to allocate their funds to other goods or services and, in the event of an accident or illness, pay e.g. directly for certain medical services. Fourthly, there may be substitutes for health insurance on the market, e.g. in the form of medical subscriptions, which to some extent offer access to the same medical services.

Moreover, it should also be emphasized that while insurance, to a certain extent, allows for relief from the burden of significant health expenses, their development should not be directly equated with the growing production of medical goods and services. The constantly growing demand for this type of good and service may be generated both by third-party payers (insurance companies, medical networks, and charities) and individual consumers (direct payments). One can imagine a situation where the production of such goods and services does not change or declines, but the demand generated by the growing number of insured continues to grow. In such a situation, premiums will also increase. The allocation of a fraction of the costs by the insured is possible thanks to the actions of insurance companies and the processes of competition. However, paying 10% of the cost in the form of an insurance premium, for example, does not result from a tenfold increase in supply, which is something to keep in mind. Falling health insurance prices may have their source both in the growing quality of risk assessment and in the ever-increasing supply of needed medical goods and services, but without this growing supply (and medical knowledge), the health insurance market would have very limited growth prospects despite the advances in insurance mathematics.

One can agree with the view that having health insurance or a medical subscription gives great comfort and these services/forms of payment may be of the greatest interest to consumers. However, direct payments will continue to play an equally important (or even fundamental) role in the market health system. Thanks to them, the consumer can easily estimate the cost of a given service, which affects the rationality of their decisions. The price system makes it easy for every consumer to find out about a given situation and make a decision about the amount of consumption. A consumer paying out-of-pocket will not be mismanaged. Direct payments are therefore a kind of anchor influencing the rational choices of the consumer and are a good alternative in the absence of insurance or medical subscription. As was mentioned before, nowadays they may be associated with incurring high costs, but this is the result of more interventions than in other markets. In addition, direct payments also allow for the development of innovation in the field of medical services, thanks to which specialized institutions providing innovative solutions are created. As indicated by Goodman et al. (2004, p. 248):

What Harvard University professor Regina Herzlinger calls 'focused factories,' providing highly efficient, specialized care, are becoming a reality. These health care businesses deliver lower prices, lower mortality rates, shorter stays and higher patient satisfaction.

For example, the Johns Hopkins Breast Center is a focused factory for mastectomies. The Dartmouth-Hitchcock Medical Center in Lebanon, New Hampshire, is a focused factory for heart surgery. The Pediatrix Medical Group, which manages neonatal units and provides pediatric services in twenty-one states, is another example. Focused factories also are cropping up around the country to provide cancer, gynecological and orthopedic services. One spectacular success story is Dr. Bernard Salick, a kidney specialist who has become a millionaire by pioneering a national chain of round-the-clock cancer clinics.

Insurance companies also often cooperate with many 'focused factories' by creating new insurance products, e.g. enabling coverage of significant costs of treatment (e.g. cancer) in highly specialized institutions operating in different countries. These 'focused factories' are therefore provided with an additional source of income. Despite the high sums insured, the premiums are not unattainable for the majority of those interested, inter alia, thanks to the creation of global, transnational risk groups by insurance companies. The greater the number of insured persons (and the available data), the easier it is to reliably assess and monitor the risk. Thanks to this, when, for example, an insured person, a Polish citizen, is diagnosed with a serious illness falling within the scope of such insurance, in the economic sense, their treatment in a specialized institution is in fact financed by the insured from all over the world. This is a good example of how entrepreneurial processes give people around the world the chance to better secure an uncertain future without them interacting directly. Tourist insurance that covers the costs of treatment abroad or medical tourism, which allows access to certain medical services outside the country's borders, also play an equally useful role. These examples show that a market-based healthcare system, at least in part, can be global in scope.

In addition, insurance companies or medical networks can also stimulate the development of the drug market, medical services, or medical equipment. Undoubtedly, insurers have an interest in ensuring that their clients enjoy good health as long as possible – this results in lower consumption of insurance and allows for a reduction in premiums. Taking 'uncertain' medications or using the services of 'uncertain' doctors may worsen the health of the insured person and, as a result, lead to more frequent use of health insurance. Of course, in a market-based healthcare system, there would be no compulsory licences required by public institutions. However, this does not mean that the licensing system would not function at all. On the contrary, a system of licences issued by competing institutions, such as associations of doctors, pharmacists, and other medical professionals, would be an excellent competitive advantage. Drug manufacturers or young, novice doctors would seek licences issued by various institutions, as these would increase their competitiveness.[3] In turn, the institutions issuing them would scrupulously evaluate the persons or enterprises applying for them for their products, because otherwise they would quickly fall out of the market, and their place would be taken by more reliable institutions. In an uninterrupted market where the consumer's power is not limited, the loss of consumer confidence has very serious consequences. Therefore, building consumer confidence in specific institutions or a given brand is gaining importance. This is also one of the reasons why insurance companies would be interested in their own activity in such markets, as they could have a greater impact on limiting health risk. If the insured would use the services of doctors recommended by insurance companies or take safe drugs, they would have a positive effect on their health. As a result, insurance companies could further develop the system of insurance discounts granted for the use of appropriate quality medical goods and services or even for active actions of the insured reducing the probability of disease or accidents (Tannenhill & Tannenhill, 2009, pp. 50–51). The insured persons could therefore lead a more active lifestyle which, if properly documented, would entitle them to receive a discount.

Insurance companies would thus contribute to the systematic improvement of the quality of medical goods and services, e.g. by holding shares in pharmaceutical companies or companies producing medical equipment. It can also be assumed that they would be very interested in supporting small, but innovative enterprises, which they would help in management and provide capital support. Such analysis shows the great potential of unrestricted market processes that do not create a rigid framework, but are constantly transformed, which benefits consumers – the final beneficiaries of the effects of these changes.

However, even in a private health system, it should be taken into account that the costs of financing access to medical services for a certain part of the society may turn out to be too high. On the one hand, people are not perfect and make mistakes, and on the other hand, it is very difficult to predict all possible developments in the future. These inconveniences can be (and are) effectively limited or eliminated by broadly understood charitable activities. Thanks to this type of activity, it is possible to overcome situations when basic forms of financing access to health services are not able to provide such access. An example is an extremely rare disease that is not insurable and, in addition, is very expensive to treat. In such situations, neither insurance nor medical subscription will help. The only option, therefore, is to finance expensive treatment in a specialized unit through the good will of other people. This may raise some concerns; for some, such application for help may even be considered derogatory – the lack of insurance or sufficient resources leads to a situation where it is necessary to turn to the last resort in the form of asking for help. However, insurance is also a kind of form of helping some people over others. The rules on which this support is provided are set by insurance companies, playing the role of agents caring for the interests of their clients. It should also be noted that the existence of predetermined solutions may not always be beneficial. If the subjects of support for charitable activities are rare, difficult cases, as well as those which give little chance of success, then establishing rigid rules of functioning for them will not be beneficial either for the helpers or for those who need this help. On what basis should it be determined in advance who is to help who and how much? That is why, thanks to various spontaneous initiatives and charitable institutions specializing in this type of activity, it is possible to provide the necessary support in a very short time. The greatest potential and at the same time value in this type of activity lies in the understanding that charity is an indispensable element of the market health system, and not just an unpleasant addition. Due to the fact that, in principle, every person can suffer great misfortune at any time, it is a rational and economic justification for society to direct its help to people who need it most.

An equally important effect of the market health system is the growing responsibility of individuals for their fate, which is why they will treat all kinds of charity as a last resort, and people who raise doubts about receiving this type of help will be carefully verified by charity institutions. Thanks to this type of action, society will become more aware that people who receive help really need it. An additional, positive effect will also be the development of appropriate ethical attitudes in the society. Maxwell (2003, pp. 23–24), referring to the Josephson Institute of Ethics, draws attention to the existence of two dimensions of ethics:

> The first involves the ability to discern right from wrong, good from evil, and propriety from impropriety. The second involves the

commitment to do what is right, good and proper. Ethics entails action; it is not just a topic to mull or debate.

At this point, it is worth paying attention to the important role played by the family institution in the market health system. Humans are beings who have recognized the benefits of the division of labour. Thanks to the existence of society, it is easier to meet your needs and the first social substitute in the life of every human being is the family. Therefore, in the discussion on the functioning of the market healthcare system, it should be noted that in a situation requiring support from the rest of the society, before this support occurs, the first costs and assistance are often already provided by members of the immediate or extended family. Therefore, the person needing help is not placed between their own decisions (e.g. paying for insurance or subscription fees or collecting savings) and the help of third parties. On this basis, charity work can be considered as a kind of extension of help from a neighbour to the rest of society. Also, therefore, family packages in the form of health insurance or subscriptions play an important role on the market. You can also see the benefits of using a medical savings account by one, previously authorized, family member in emergency situations, e.g. when such a person needs to urgently use an ambulance service.

The market health system and so-called market failures

When describing the aspects of the functioning of the market health system, one should also refer to the so-called market failures. The most important of these are the problem of asymmetric information, health-care as a public good, and the possibility of the formation of monopolies on the markets. These market defects are intended to prevent the effective provision of medical goods and services needed by the society on market terms and to justify the necessary state intervention.

Asymmetric information

In the case of the asymmetric information as a source of market fail-ure, the arguments contained in the works of Kenneth J. Arrow (1963, pp. 941–973) and G. A. Akerlof (1970, pp. 488–500) should be ana-lysed. Although they were established some time ago, they still form the basis of arguments against health market solutions. For example, it is believed that Arrow's article had a great influence on the creation of the so-called health economics and the development of other research areas such as public choice theory, sociology, banking, and education.[4]

It is also worth emphasizing that in 1963 the state's interference in the market healthcare system was much smaller than it is now, where third-party payers with public programmes such as Medicare or Medicaid (Savedoff, 2004, pp. 139–140) (in the case of the USA) dominate, and the content presented by Arrow was undoubtedly intellectual argument for introducing these programmes in 1965.

Treatment of the so-called asymmetric information as an alleged market failure is problematic for several reasons. Firstly, the mere fact that one of the parties to the transaction (usually the seller) has more information about the product or service does not necessarily mean that the other party (the buyer) will be cheated and receive a product that does not meet their expectations. To put it differently, the existence of asymmetric information does not have to and usually has no negative economic consequences. The very term asymmetry has an element of value and a pejorative overtone. Meanwhile, this disproportion in knowledge is nothing more than a differently defined division of knowledge and labour in the economy that enables trade and the development of markets. Asymmetric information results, among other things, from the fact that people have different skills, which results in a division of labour and a constantly deepening specialization. Also, natural conditions, such as the presence of raw materials, are not the same for the entire world. Moreover, even if it were possible to imagine a situation in which people have the same (in place and time) access to information, it does not solve the problem in any way, because they can interpret it differently and on this basis take different actions (DiLorenzo, 2011, pp. 250–252). People do not function as pre-determined algorithms or calculators, to which it is enough to enter the same data to give the same results. The same information does not imply the same actions or effects.[5]

Secondly, it is true that deepening knowledge, specialization, and the emergence of new professions lead to ever greater information disproportions, but this does not amount to unfair treatment of clients. If the assumptions about the asymmetric information were reduced to their logical consequences, producers would only achieve such benefits at the beginning, and then markets would experience stagnation. The shortcomings of the products would become apparent after a while. Competitive advantage would therefore have to rely on increasingly sophisticated ways of concealing information from naive customers who do not draw conclusions from defective products. In reality, however, the fact that the seller has more information about the product or service than the buyer does is more of a kind of problem for them, and certainly a challenge to best close this gap. The goal of any exchange is for both sides of the transaction to make a profit, i.e. a situation in which the benefits of the exchange exceed its costs. On the part of producers, this determines activities aimed at highlighting the benefits that buyers can bring to the purchase of a given good or service. To achieve this goal, they must not only offer a product of the right quality and price, but also dispel customer doubts arising from the lack of information that interests them, which in turn increases uncertainty. In market conditions, one of the sources of competitive advantage may be appropriate customer relations, such as providing information on the usefulness of the product or after-sales service. If the manufacturer can gain a competitive advantage thanks to this, it will be easier if the competitors' products have defects that they try to hide from customers.

Third, economists describing the alleged market failure in the form of asymmetric information do not seem to pay sufficient attention to how markets deal with this asymmetry. For example, Akerlof argues that manufacturers offering low-quality cars (so-called lemons) would become dominant in the used car market, as they would have more information about the goods sold. He did not notice, however, that at the time of the publication of his work, there were 30-day guarantees on the used car market. Continuing this line of reasoning, such a market should collapse, and at the same time, nothing like that has happened and is not happening. One might also wonder why similar practices of unfair sellers should only be carried out on the secondary market. Car manufacturers also have an information advantage, but the quality of their products and the state of the market do not confirm the predictions of Akerlof. Both on the primary and secondary market there is competition, insurance, guarantees, numerous advisory institutions, and knowledge resources in the form of internet portals evaluating both sellers and buyers. As Berdine (2017a, p. 66) points out:

> The market solution to information asymmetry is the market for asymmetric information. Experts sell advice. Advice that changes a decision to purchase something very costly is very valuable. The market solves the problem of information asymmetry by selling the advice for a much lower price than the price of the decision to be made.

All these solutions are aimed at meeting the needs of customers, including their demand for information. Both sellers and buyers are not omniscient and can make mistakes, but one of the advantages of market solutions is that they are quickly exposed through the profit and loss mechanism.

Another example of market failure caused by asymmetric information is the health insurance market. The person applying for insurance knows their health well and is better able to assess the risk of falling ill than the insurer. Moreover, they may deliberately not disclose the key information from the perspective of the insurance risk assessment in the medical questionnaire in order to obtain a lower premium or be covered by a given insurance programme at all. Such a situation means that people with a higher health risk than those with a lower risk are interested in joining the insurance. This phenomenon is called anti-selection. If such persons are insured (e.g. on standard terms instead of sub-standard terms), the costs will exceed income and an increase in premiums will be needed to cover this disproportion. This will lead to the resignation of some insured persons with lower health risk and there will be another increase. This process is known as the death spiral (Morris et al., 2012, p. 141). It is also interesting that in this case it is the insured (buyer) who has the advantage over the insurer (seller) and not the other way around.

However, such a presentation of the case would mean that insurance companies are not able to accurately assess insurance risk, which is in fact the core of their business. If insurance companies are unable to make an appropriate selection and classification of the insured, they suffer losses and give way to competitors. Moreover, it would be extremely naive to argue that these institutions are at the mercy of the ethical behaviour of insured persons. In fact, insurers have developed a number of solutions to properly assess and verify the insurance risk. These include, among others: medical surveys and examinations, access to information on the health condition of the insured person from various sources prior to the conclusion of insurance, exclusions and limitations of the scope of insurance cover, grace periods, or concluding fixed-term contracts. The use of the above tools along with the development of insurance mathematics has led to the development of the health insurance market, not its stagnation. Many diseases that were previously uninsurable or unknown are today in the field of health insurance. It is true that insurance companies are struggling with dishonesty and moral hazard on the part of the insured, but these are not problems that herald the collapse of this market. Insurers should be left free to act.

Interestingly, Arrow believes that the lack of many risks in health insurance and medical care services proves a market failure and if the market cannot provide health insurance to the whole society then the state should do so (Berdine, 2016, p. 60). This view should be criticized for two reasons. First of all, as has already been mentioned, the health insurance market is constantly developing and since 1963 it has been easy to see its progress, which is possible, among others, thanks to the development of medicine and the processes of competition. Second, you may agree that it is not possible to insure everyone against everything, but that is not evidence of an insurance market failure. For Arrow, the lack of insurance coverage is equated with market failure in general. Therefore, it should be emphasized once again that insurance is one of the forms of financing access to medical services, and the basis is direct payments, as is the case in many other markets: food, transport, computer, etc. The insurance institution allows you to free yourself from a part of significant health expenses but does not guarantee unlimited funding opportunities. Not all events are insurable or insured. The inability to perform an economic calculation based on probability does not necessarily have to be seen as a market flaw – if the premium (insurance price) cannot be rationally determined, then there is no basis for the economic use of scarce resources in the economy. That is why direct payments (and other forms of financing) are so important, because thanks to them the society easily receives information about the availability of rare goods and services through the price structure.

Public goods

Arguments for the existence of asymmetric information lead supporters of public healthcare to conclude that it is a special good, different from other goods and services provided under market conditions. On the one hand, there is a risk that the consumer (patient) will not be able to adequately assess the quality of goods and services, and sellers will use this situation to increase their profits. On the other hand, a lack of proper knowledge may turn against them and they may also take a light-hearted approach to, for example, buying insurance or paying for an examination that can detect a serious illness. Therefore, the only way out of this stalemate is state intervention to replace the flawed market solutions. The means for this is the creation of one (or more) public health programmes. It may be defined as public healthcare or otherwise, however, the principles of its operation and financing are predetermined by the state. It can then be concluded that a number of heterogeneous medical (health) goods and services with an appropriate price structure are replaced by public healthcare and treated as the so-called public good.

In this study, less technical (and rigorous) and earlier than Samuelson's, definition of a public good as a good produced by the state (government) and generally available for the benefit of its citizens was adopted. A more technical definition by Samuelson treats a public good as a good that, once produced for some consumers, can be consumed by others without additional, marginal costs of such consumption (the so-called non-competition in consumption) (Holcombe, 2007, pp. 2–3). The reference to a more general definition can be justified by the fact that the process of creating public healthcare systems or social welfare systems by states started at the end of the 19th century (Germany), i.e. before the publication of Samuelson's (1954, pp. 387–389) article in 1954. Also, earlier during World War II, Great Britain, on the basis of a Beveridge report, began to create a public healthcare system (National Health Service) which started operating in 1948. Public health systems became popular after the Second World War, and by 1949 they were already functioning in 36 countries (Monkiewicz, 2002, p. 388). Moreover, Samuelson cited national defence or lighthouses as classic examples of public goods. From the point of view of the Austrian School, one can agree as to the presence of goods with the characteristics indicated by Samuelson,[6] but this fact does not prevent their delivery on market principles (Kwiatkowski, 2010, p. 110).

For example, the use of private medical consultations and tests provides information about the patient's health and allows for earlier detection of the disease. So, the risk of infecting others with it decreases. Moreover, such a person, e.g. a company director, may not get sick at all or experience milder symptoms and return to work faster, which is related to its better functioning. The presence of the director means that important decisions can still be made on an ongoing basis. The company does not experience downtime resulting in delayed deliveries. Similar external benefits are shared by insurance companies, medical networks, and charities, and while they may differ, this does not in any way negate the fact that private institutions generate them.[7]

The need to provide society with a universal healthcare system may also be argued with equity or income criteria. The wealthier or less needy part of society should support the more needy. People should be sure that they will not be deprived of support in the event of illness or accident. It is believed that the state, through its activity in the area of healthcare, provides society with the so-called right to healthcare. However, the present meaning of the term has a strongly interventionist meaning.

In the conditions of voluntary relationships taking place on the market, the phrase having the right to something means a situation in which an individual has a choice that no one can (has the right) to impose on them by force, and they themself cannot use it to achieve their goals at the expense of other members of society. For example, the right to own a house or apartment means that a person can choose any offer from among those available on the market, guided by their own needs and financial possibilities. They have the right to decide how they will meet their housing needs. They are not condemned to the mercy of sellers, as they are also a seller in another industry, e.g. automotive, where the general principles of success are the same – customer satisfaction. The right to a house or flat of such a person will be limited, for example, when restrictive building regulations limiting the supply of houses and flats come into force or when higher taxes are passed to finance military operations. The principle is the same for healthcare. The right to healthcare means that a person has the choice between different, competing providers offering the goods and medical services they need. Its law materializes both when concluding such transactions and when refraining from them. The prices of certain goods and services that are too high for such a person do not deprive that person of the right to them, but only testify to their low availability and at the same time constitute an incentive for other entrepreneurs to produce cheaper, but adequately quality products. Examples of limiting this right include, for example, regulations limiting the supply of doctors, medical equipment, or drugs, which give the consumer a smaller choice. The modern right to healthcare means consent to forcing the greater part of society to provide it to others,[8] and any plans to limit state intervention in this area are treated as attempts to limit or deprive society of previously acquired privileges or the right to healthcare.

The modern right to healthcare cannot guarantee unlimited access to medical services, as the means of implementing this right are of an economic nature, that is, they are limited. By juxtaposing these limitations with the lack of market incentives to establish appropriate supply-demand relations, everyone (or a certain part of society) will try to exercise their rights in a world of limited resources without being fully aware of it. However, the lack of an adequate pricing structure, coupled with the ever-increasing demand, which stems from the right to healthcare, will be one of the main reasons why this target cannot be achieved. In the growing demand for financing medical services by the state, providers of these services will also benefit from their benefits, as they can thus guarantee a constant (non-market) demand for their services and limit competition through a dense network of regulations, requirements, and licences. In such circumstances, the constantly increasing costs must ultimately lead to limitations in access to healthcare. Society will see an increase in contributions and/or taxes and hence expenditure, which is an inherent feature of public health systems. If society accepts the higher costs, it will not be possible to pretend that the right to healthcare is cost-free – that is, the ever-increasing demand has economic consequences. This will be a non-market signal of resource constraints. An alternative is to introduce smaller or larger restrictions on access to healthcare, which may take various forms and names: cost (budget) control, queues to doctors, or extending waiting times for an appointment to the doctor or surgery. These various forms of rationing also show resource scarcity. What's important, however, is that their introduction essentially contradicts the fundamental assumption of unlimited right (and access) to healthcare – because it limits access to what, by definition, should be unlimited (Berdine, 2017b, pp. 25–26).

The above arguments also show that even taking into account Samuelson's definition of public goods, marginal (additional) costs are actually generated by public systems and also include those consumers who, by theoretical assumption, were not supposed to pay them at all. It is also visible in practice, as premiums paid by healthier and/ or professionally active insured persons are not able to adequately ensure access to medical services to all beneficiaries – hence the increase in the amount of premiums or regulation of services covering all insured persons. This is basically the case in all developed countries where people of retirement age, in an economic sense, do not bear any financial cost of health insurance. However, they bear other costs, e.g. in the form of longer queues to the doctor, a decrease in the quality of services, etc. This rationing is therefore a different form or reaction to the appearance of competition in the consumption of these services, i.e. a phenomenon that the definition and essence of public goods formulated by Samuelson had excluded.[9]

Moreover, even if some insured persons benefit at the initial stage – e.g. subsidized persons – this happens at the expense of groups with lower health risk, which, in order to avoid queues, may decide, for example, to purchase additional private insurance, etc.

In the discussion on the functioning of modern healthcare systems, too little attention is paid to possible market alternatives. The current shape of constantly expanded public systems, various forms of rationing, or constantly growing costs reflect well the consequences of abandoning rational market solutions. The market healthcare system is not able to use a magic wand to turn scarce resources into limitless ones, but thanks to human creativity and the processes of competition, it is able to increase the quantity and quality of the goods and services needed.

Monopolies

While the main arguments against market solutions focus primarily on asymmetric information or the perception of healthcare as a public good, there are also issues of monopoly formation in unfettered markets. The very concept of monopoly is not precise, however, and there are also some differences between the economists of the Austrian School.[10] In this study, the definition of Rothbard (2009, p. 669) was adopted, indicating (and justifying it accordingly) that:

> monopoly is a grant of special privilege by the State, reserving a certain area of production to one particular individual or group. Entry into the field is prohibited to others and this prohibition is enforced by the gendarmes of the State.

This definition is therefore closely related to interventionism. Other definitions of monopoly (or monopoly) as the sole seller of a given good, or the person to obtain the monopoly price, were thoroughly criticized by Rothbard.[11]

In this sense, on an unhampered market, monopolies do not arise, but properly functioning market structures or entities that better satisfy consumers' needs than competitors. They owe their dominant position or monopoly only to better anticipation of future market conditions. The consumer making their choice is not guided by sentiment, and if a new product that better meets their needs appears on the market, then the merits of the former producers do not matter. If a manufacturer is still trusted by customers and has achieved its position in the market through voluntary exchanges, there is no threat of a monopoly. Any market price is fair in the sense that it is determined by the sovereign decisions of buyers and sellers. Demanding state intervention to break up such a monopoly would be highly uneconomical, as part of the capital would go to entities that are not so well able to meet the needs of consumers, which would result in incurring losses and wasting capital.

The purpose of the market is not for countless small players to function. The market does not protect the big companies or exalt the small ones.[12] They are all subject to the same rules – in this sense, they have equal opportunities.

The arguments that representatives of the medical industry, for example doctors, can obtain very high prices or monopoly prices, demanding exorbitant amounts for treatment from sick patients, should also be considered untrue. The salary of a doctor or any other representative of the medical or health industry depends on the quality of their work (customer satisfaction) and competition. This was well presented by Mises (1998, p. 660):

> What produces a man's profit in the course of affairs within an unhampered market society is not his fellow citizen's plight and distress, but the fact that he alleviates or entirely removes what causes his fellow citizen's feeling of uneasiness. What hurts the sick is the plague, not the physician who treats the disease. The doctor's gain is not an outcome of the epidemics, but of the aid he gives to those affected.

Moreover, public health systems and private entities cooperating with them are much closer to the monopoly position. In this case, the consumer cannot choose the supplier. Regulations concerning manufacturers of drugs, medical equipment, or medical professions are above the power of the consumer, although they are introduced in the consumer's interest.

In this context, it is also worth paying attention to the issue of the so-called natural monopoly, which was supposed to mean a situation in which, among others, due to the substantial or massive scale of production, the producer concerned may have achieved a total unit cost lower than it would have been if there had been two or more competitors in the market. Thus, a single entity was to be more effective, which at the same time was to serve as a justification for granting it special privileges by the state. In this case, the existence of more entities would be ineffective and, paradoxically, would lead to higher prices. For example, in the history of the USA (at the turn of the 19th and 20th centuries), the recognition of a given enterprise as the so-called the natural monopolist was also seen as a way of restricting competition in a non-market manner (DiLorenzo, 1996, p. 43).

The economists of the Austrian School point out that the processes of competition are dynamic, which may lead to the existence of many competitors in a given market and several or even one entity. However, even the latter situation is not indicative of market failure. Such an entrepreneur could have achieved their position at any given moment by, for example, achieving the lowest costs, efficient management, and better anticipation of consumer needs. However, the success of the sole manufacturer attracts the attention of potential competitors that could quickly become real competitors (DiLorenzo, 1996, p. 44). Even if this does not happen, the current market leader must constantly develop its business if it does not want to go out of the market or significantly lose its position over time – it does not even have to be the result of the existence of many competitors, but the possibility of their appearance. That is why the lack of governmental regulations restricting these processes is so important.

Also, mergers, acquisitions, and trusts do not pose a threat to free competition and consumers. On the contrary, they testify to high capital accumulation and efficient management leading to lower prices. These processes also do not eliminate smaller entities, but integrate them into their own structures, while increasing their efficiency. For example, American trusts from the late 19th century, thanks to the scale of their operations, were able to increase production and lower prices faster than the rest of the economy.[13]

Standard Oil, developed and developed by J. D. Rockefeller, is a good example here. In 1899, Standard Oil refined 90% of the US crude oil. However, this did not translate into higher oil prices due to the company's use of its monopoly position. On the contrary, both refining costs and retail oil prices have been steadily falling. The latter fell to their lowest levels in history in 1897 – to 5.91 cents a barrel – at a time when Standard Oil had the largest market share (Reed, 2015, pp. 338, 343).

Many believed that such significant size and market share would lead to monopoly pricing. However, as Reed (2015, p. 353) points out:

> According to the notion that Standard's size gave it the power to charge any price, bigness per se immunizes the firm from competition and consumer sovereignty.
>
> As an 'efficiency monopoly,' Standard could not coercively prevent others from competing with it. And others did, so much so that the company's share of the market declined dramatically after 1899. As the economy shifted from kerosene to electricity, from the horse to the automobile, and from oil production in the East to production in the Gulf States, Rockefeller found himself losing ground to younger, more aggressive competitors.
>
> Neither did Standard have the power to compel people to buy its products.It had to rely on its own excellence to attract and keep customers.

This proves both the lack of establishing the so-called monopoly prices by entities with the largest market shares, as well as the fact that the potential recognition of Standard Oil as a natural monopoly would limit dynamic competition processes, which over time led to a decline in its market share, but continued to adequately satisfy the needs of consumers.

Notes

1 The justification for the use of the term 'universal health system' is described in more detail on pp. 00–00.
2 See also a comment by Prof. P. Klein (2013) on the definition of healthcare.
3 For example, medical networks could recruit only doctors with qualifications confirmed by appropriate certificates.
4 In this case, the authority or influence of Arrow can be compared, for example, to the authority of J. S. Mill, who in the 19th century argued for the introduction of public education, which resulted in the Education Act.
5 Moreover, eliminating the asymmetry of information would deprive an individual of what is their essence, i.e. the taste of life. Having exactly the same state of knowledge for everyone would make everyday reality completely predictable and monotonous. However, F. A. von Hayek and M. Polanyi showed in their works that equality of knowledge is impossible – both fundamentally and physically. For more on this, see: Hayek (1996); Polanyi (1962).
6 They can be called public goods or whatever.
7 For more on this, see also: Block (1983, pp. 1–34).
8 For more on this topic see: Riesman (1994).
9 For more on the Austrian critique of the theory of public goods see: Wiśniewski (2018).
10 For more on this subject see: Armentano (2005).
11 In this paper, due to the limited content, only some (general) arguments will be presented against the claims suggesting the emergence of monopolies in unfettered markets. For more information see: Rothbard (2009, pp. 661–704).
12 As the theory of perfect competition presupposes. For more on its criticism from the perspective of the Austrian School, see: Kuropatwa (2010, pp. 31–46).
13 For more on this, see DiLorenzo, 1985, pp. 73–90.

References

Akerlof G., 1970, The market for lemons: qualitative uncertainty and the market mechanism, *Quarterly Journal of Economics*, 84, 488–500.

Armentano D., 2005, A critique of neoclassical and Austrian monopoly theory, https://mises.org/library/critique-neoclassical-and-austrian-monopoly-theory (accessed: 24. 08. 2018).

Arrow K. J., 1963, Uncertainty and the welfare economics of medical care', *The American Economic Review*, No. 5, pp. 941–973.

Berdine G., 2016, 'Uncertainty and the welfare economics of medical care: an Austrian rebuttal: Part 1', *The Southwest Respiratory and Critical Care Chronicles*, No. 16, pp. 57–61.

Berdine G., 2017a, 'Uncertainty and the welfare economics of medical care: an Austrian rebuttal: Part 2', *The Southwest Respiratory and Critical Care Chronicles*, No 17, pp. 63–67.

Berdine G., 2017b, 'Uncertainty and the welfare economics of medical care: an Austrian rebuttal-part 3', *The Southwest Respiratory and Critical Care Chronicles*, No. 19, pp. 25–29.

Block W., 1983, 'Public Goods and Externalities: The Case of Roads', *The Journal of Libertarian Studies*, No. 1, pp. 1–34.

DiLorenzo T., 1985, 'The Origins of Antitrust: An Interest-Group Perspective', *International Review of Law and Economics*, No. 1, pp. 73–90.

DiLorenzo T., 1996, 'The Myth of Natural Monopoly', *The Review of Austrian Economics*, No. 2, pp. 43–58.

DiLorenzo T., 2011, 'A note on the canard of 'asymmetric information' as a source of market failure', *Quarterly Journal of Austrian Economics*, No. 2, pp. 249–255.

Goodman J. C., Musgrave G. L., Herrick D. M., 2004, *Lives at risk. Single-payer national health insurance around the world*, USA: Rowman & Littlefield Publishers.

Hayek F. A., 1996, *Individualism and economic order*, USA: University of Chicago Press.

Holcombe R., 2007, A theory of the theory of public goods, *Review of Austrian Economics*, 1, 1–22.

Klein P. G., 2013, The Mises view: 'Healthcare and the free market', https://www.youtube.com/watch?v=8lOC2itCc6g (accessed: 10. 06. 2021).

Kuropatwa A., 2010, Problemy neoklasycznej teorii konkurencji [Problems of the neoclassical theory of competition], in M. Machaj (ed.), *Pod prąd głównego nurtu ekonomii* [Against the tide of mainstream economics], Warsaw: Instytut Ludwiga von Misesa, pp. 31–46.

Kwiatkowski S., 2010, Teoria dóbr publicznych i rynkowe mechanizmy ich produkcji [The theory of public goods and market mechanisms of their production], in M. Machaj (ed.), *Pod prąd głównego nurtu ekonomii* [Against the tide of mainstream economics], Warsaw: Instytut Ludwiga von Misesa, pp. 95–123.

Maxwell J. C., 2003, *There's no such thing as 'business' ethics: There's only one rule for making decisions*, USA: Warner Books.

Mises L., 1998, *Human action. A treatise on economics*, Auburn: Ludwig von Mises Institute.

Monkiewicz J., 2002, Prywatne ubezpieczenia zdrowotne w Unii Europejskiej [Private health insurance in the European Union], in J. Monkiewicz (ed.), *Ubezpieczenia w Unii Europejskiej* [Insurance in the European Union], Warsaw: Poltext.

Morris S., Devlin N., Parkin D., Spencer A., 2012, *Economic analysis in healthcare*, Great Britain: Wiley.

Polanyi M., 1962, *Personal knowledge: Towards a post-critical philosophy*, Chicago: University of Chicago Press.

Reed L. W., 2015, Rockefeller's standard oil company proved we needed antitrust laws to fight market monopolies, in L. W. Reed (ed.), *Excuse me, Professor: Challenging the myths of progressivism*, USA: Regnery Publishing, pp. 337–357.

Riesman G., 1994, *The real right to medical care versus socialized medicine*, USA: The Jefferson School of Philosophy, Economics & Psychology.

Rothbard M. N., 2009, *Man, economy, and state with power and market*, Auburn: Ludwig von Mises Institute.

Samuelson P. A., 1954, The pure theory of public expenditure, *Review of Economics and Statistics*, 4, 387–389.

Savedoff W. D., 2004, Kenneth Arrow and the birth of health economics, *Bulletin of the World Health Organization*, 2, 139–140.

Tannenhill L., Tannenhill M., 2009, *The market for liberty*, USA: Cobden Press/Fox & Wilkes/Laissez Faire Books.

Wiśniewski J. B., 2018, *The economics of law, order, and action: The logic of public goods*, London, New York: Routledge.

Part II

Universal (public) health system as an effect of state interventions

Introduction

The second part of the study deals with issues related to the functioning of universal (public) health systems and their characteristics. The analysis covered primarily issues related to the appropriate definition of such a system, the goals it is to pursue, the sources of its financing, and the concept and importance of health in the individual and social dimension.

This is to help better understand the principles of its functioning and the impact on the availability of medical services, health, or even the doctor–patient relationship. Thanks to this, it will also be possible to compare such a system more easily with market solutions characterized by a more diversified structure of financing access to medical services.

In order to better understand this issue, at the beginning, the theoretical aspects of interventionism are also analysed, starting from its definition and the type of individual interventions, and ending with their possible effects (consequences) for the market health system.

DOI: 10.4324/9781003258957-6

4 Interventionism in the health system

The definition and essence of interventionism

The issue of interventionism was gradually developed by successive representatives of the Austrian School from single interventions to a coherent general theory. The first economist to use the term in an economic sense was Mises (Huerta de Soto, 2009, p. 292). Successive interventions in the market economy over the years (including the health system) required appropriate analysis, which also influenced the development of the theory.[1] An important contribution in this regard must also be attributed to Rothbard, who, inter alia, made an appropriate classification of the various interventions.[2] For Rothbard (2009, p. 877), intervention is: 'the intrusion of aggressive physical force into society; it means the substitution of coercion for voluntary actions.'

This definition is very broad and has a praxeological character. From this perspective, it doesn't matter who intervenes: single bandit, mafia, or state. The fact that the economic analysis of interventionism concerns mainly state actions is because this institution has a monopoly on the use of force (or the threat of its use) in voluntary market relations. The institution of the state is not the subject of an ideological attack for the economist, but a subject of study, as was the case with the market economy or socialism. Economics as a science strives to best understand the effects of actions taken in various economic systems, and this means that assumptions must be objective if it is to perform its function well.

As a rule, interventionism allows for the existence of a market economy in order to control its specific spheres. Interventionist measures used, for example, by political groups or key decision-makers in the country may take very different forms, which can ultimately be classified into three types of intervention: autistic, binary, and triangular. The first type of intervention means forcing the *intervener* [3] (e.g. the state) to force

DOI: 10.4324/9781003258957-7

an individual or a group of units to behave in a specific manner relating to that entity (group) or its assets at a time when no exchange is made with other market participants. Examples of such intervention include, for example, murder, ban on expression, or religious practices. Importantly, this type of intervention does not lead to a forced transfer of goods or services to the entity making the intervention. The second type, binary intervention, consists in forcing such a transfer. The individual must surrender some of their goods or services, under threat of force by the *intervener*. Examples of this type of intervention include, for example, taxes, conscription, and slavery. On the other hand, a triangular intervention takes place when the intervener forces an exchange (or prohibits it) between two parties to the transaction but does not itself participate in it – it boils down to the role of a kind of intermediary influencing the terms of the exchange. Examples include price control (e.g. setting a maximum or minimum price) or licensing a profession. A common feature of these interventions is the existence of a hegemonic relationship between the *intervener* and the individuals they concern. The intervening entity always benefits at the expense of individuals, only in the third case it is possible to benefit from one of the parties to the transaction, e.g. as a result of restriction of competition by state regulations – then the harm will be suffered by consumers and entities willing to enter a given market (Rothbard, 2009, pp. 877–878).

Economics does not presuppose the existence, activity, or function of a state that is excluded from these considerations. Therefore, the legitimacy of certain actions taken by the state should also result from economic premises. As Mises (1998a, p. 718) put it:

> The problem of interventionism is not a problem of the correct delimitation of the 'natural,' 'just,' and 'adequate' tasks of state and government. The issue is: How does a system of interventionism work? Can it realize those ends which people, in resorting to it, want to?

This applies to every aspect of state activity: road construction, national defence, pension systems, and healthcare. From the economic point of view, it is unacceptable to say that a given activity of the state in the economy should be excluded from economic analysis, as it is generally not recognized as the domain of the market and market (and economic) laws do not apply here.

Individual interventions are measures taken to achieve the intended goals. However, these measures or plans for their use may (and usually are) very different from each other. While the goal remains basically the same, the desire to improve the welfare of a society or a country, the variants of its implementation remain quite different. The basis for the political struggle between particular groups is precisely the manner and scope of the use of interventionist measures. In fact, each grouping has more or less different plans, which is the basis for the political struggle and the object of soliciting votes. Mises (1998a, p. 727) described the problem as follows:

> All this passionate praise of the supereminence of government action is but a poor disguise for the individual interventionist's self-deification. The great god State is a great god only because it is expected to do exclusively what the individual advocate of interventionism wants to see achieved. Only that plan is genuine which the individual planner fully approves. All other plans are simply counterfeit.

It can therefore be concluded that individual interventionists do not support interventionism at all, but their specific plans. They can unite for a common goal when, for example, a part of society begins to consciously and increasingly actively undermine the sense of making any interventions in the market economy. However, there are also cases where it is quite easy to discern some internal contradiction in the actions or plans of interventionists. An example should be social/health insurance. If a certain political grouping today demands, for example, extending the scope of public health insurance or lowering the retirement age, pointing to the fact that it is the domain of the state and a human right, such postulates constitute a hidden criticism of its initial activities in this area. In the late nineteenth and early twentieth centuries, when the first public social security programmes were established, they did not contain any extensive coverage. These programmes were very modest and today, if another group wanted to limit the modern, extended ranges to their original size, it would certainly be criticized by their political rivals (and perhaps part of society as well). Nor can it be argued that the previous solutions were adapted to the social needs of the time. For example, in the Bismarck system, retirement privileges began to be granted from the age of 70, while the average life expectancy was about 40 years, and the minimum contribution period was 30 years (Pieńkowska-Kamieniecka & Rutecka, 2014, p. 20). Also, healthcare only guaranteed access to specific medical services in the event of loss of capacity for work due to an accident or disease.[4] It is a paradox that initial social security systems or programmes would be unacceptable today. The reason they are not criticized is that the modest momentum in their introduction allowed the achievement of certain political goals at relatively low cost. However, this did not prevent them from growing to an exorbitant size over the course of many decades.

If the direction to a more extensive range of such programmes (and interventionism) is considered to be the subject of economic analysis, then the opposite direction should also be – from interventionism to a pure market economy.[5] There are many different examples of interventions. Each of them requires appropriate analysis and often brings different results.

One of the more famous examples is the milk price control case described by Mises.[6] In a given economy, there is a milk market that is not subject to intervention. However, the government believes that the price of milk is too high, so that part of the population, especially children, cannot consume enough of it. In order to improve the situation, the government introduces a maximum price (below the market price). The government is counting on the fact that by artificially lowering the price, more people will be able to afford milk. However, the effects of this intervention are quite different from those assumed. The milk market consists of many enterprises (milk producers) who try to meet the needs of their customers in the best possible way. So, they employ primary and secondary factors of production and, as a result, incur costs. The amount of these costs is not the same for everyone. The most efficient producers achieve the highest profits, others lower profits, and the rest of them lose and, as a result, they fall out of the market. However, artificially lowering the market price, the part of the producers who have the highest costs but remain in the market will not be able to cover all costs from falling (artificially) revenues and will eventually fall out of the market. In addition, some of the more efficient producers may switch to the production of more profitable goods, such as butter or cream – there is no price control in these markets, so the achievable profits may be higher than in the milk market. Ultimately, the supply of milk on the market decreases and the number of people willing to buy it at a certain price increases. The price, although lowered thanks to the government, did not contribute to the increase in milk consumption. The government, of course, sees this problem. The situation after the intervention is less desirable than that before the intervention. The government may admit its mistake and withdraw from its plans – then the situation will return to normal relatively quickly. However, if the government continues to achieve its goal, it will have to introduce further interventions. This may be, for example, the introduction of maximum prices among suppliers of milk producers, e.g. feed producers, and then among suppliers of feed producers, etc., up to the owners of the primary factors of production. In addition, the government will have to introduce similar regulations in other markets, otherwise the capital will go to less regulated related markets or, for example, to luxury goods markets. This example shows that the initial, single intervention gives rise to another, and as a result, the government begins to control other parts of the economy, even though it had not planned it before. Of course, the government can backtrack on its decisions, but it usually doesn't. This may be due to a reluctance to admit a mistake, the belief that political competitors will point out the government's mistakes and want to introduce their own, more interventionist programmes, or blame a deteriorating market economy (e.g. producers). For economic analysis, the reasons why governments decide to intervene again are irrelevant. What matters is the very fact of making them and their effects.

The process of making subsequent interventions can be very long, but it will not last forever. Eventually, the government will be forced to control the entire economy. The price system, and hence the profit and loss mechanism, will not fulfil its useful function in the appropriate allocation of capital and in satisfying the needs of consumers. The government will have to properly instruct producers what to produce and in what quantities and to whom to sell. Naturally, the purpose of the example above is not to prove that intervention in the milk market leads to socialism. It is led by the consistently applied interventionism, or in other words, the system of the (increasingly) hampered market economy. Mises's important contribution to the development of the theory of interventionism was precisely the demonstration of the dynamic nature of interventionism. The maintenance by governments of isolated and non-widening interventions in the market economy is not possible due to different effects than assumed, which is a kind of moral hazard for governments in the form of a desire to improve the situation. As Mises (1998b, pp. 77, 91) stated:

> Interventionism is not an economic system, that is, it is not a method which enables people to achieve their aims. It is merely a system of procedures which disturb and eventually destroy the market economy. It hampers production and impairs satisfaction of needs. It does not make people richer; it makes people poorer. [...]
>
> Interventionist measures lead to conditions which, from the standpoint of those who recommend them, are actually less desirable than those they are designed to alleviate. They create unemployment, depression, monopoly, distress.

The analysis of the effects of interventionism is not easy due to, inter alia, constantly changing and complex market conditions and the emergence of subsequent interventions that have a direct or indirect impact on these conditions. Following Rothbard, however, it can be said that free exchange leads to the maximization of social utility understood as all utilities achieved by individuals on the market. Under market conditions, both parties to the transaction, by definition (ex-ante) benefit from the exchange, otherwise it would not take place. Intervention, on the other hand, consists in forcing people to take actions that they would not have taken otherwise. Therefore, interventionism always leads to a decline in the utility of the individuals it covers. On the other hand, the entity making the intervention and, possibly, in the case of a triangular intervention, one of the parties to the transaction gains. Since utility is subjective and cannot be represented in numbers, the state cannot prove that social utility increases. For example, it is not possible to prove that taxes imposed on the rich cause less loss of utility in them, and greater loss in people with relatively lower income or wealth. Of course, people make mistakes and it may turn out that after the transaction (ex post) their usefulness has decreased or has not increased as much as expected. However, in a free market, people can take measures to avoid a similar situation in the future. And in the case of subsequent interventions, the individual has very limited possibilities to counteract them (Rothbard, 2009, pp. 878–891).

Another important feature of interventionism is also worth mentioning. Very often, interventions that appear at first sight to control producers are in fact intended to influence consumers indirectly. For example, if the state wants to reduce the consumption of carbonated sweet drinks and increase water or juice, it may impose additional taxes on the sale of this product, introduce regulations limiting its supply, or subsidize producers of healthy drinks. The fact that a given intervention does not directly concern the consumer may be caused by the fear of a decrease in support or the awareness of the lower effectiveness of such intervention. Moreover, they perceive the effects of interventions involving consumers much more easily than interventions involving producers. Due to the large number of interventions and the complexity of market processes, it is usually difficult for consumers to see cause-and-effect relationships. Also, favouring lobbying producers at the expense of competition (e.g. through a licensing system, capital requirements, safety standards, etc.) is an indirect influence on the decisions of consumers, for whom the costs of lost opportunities in such a situation are not noticeable.

Selected possible interventions on the healthcare market and their effects

The dynamic nature of interventionism can also be demonstrated in the market health system. The proliferation of interventions does not lead to the establishment of socialism in the health system,[7] but to increasing state control of markets that provide society with the medical (health) goods and services it needs. The scope of such interventions can vary greatly, from single interventions to integrated, predetermined health plans designed to provide comprehensive and (mostly) free access to these goods and services. The dynamics of interventionist processes can therefore be considered both from the stages of individual interventions leading ultimately to public healthcare (a single payer system) or from such a system, if it has already been fully implemented, to subsequent actions of the state aimed at maintaining its functioning. Subsequent interventions, as mentioned earlier, do not prove the success of previous interventions, but their failure.

Due to the large variety of universal (public) health systems in individual countries, the case of each of them should be subject to a thorough cause-and-effect analysis. For example, the United States of America does not have a single payer system like European countries or Canada. The history of successive interventions in the US health system shows, however, that they create an increasingly integrated (although not planned top-down) structure limiting market processes and directing the US health system to the state-funded single payer system. An important task of economics is to demonstrate the effects that subsequent interventions bring or may bring.

The introduction of a more or less extensive universal (public) healthcare system has very serious socio-economic consequences. One of the most serious is the disturbance of the relationship between direct and indirect (through third-party payers) purchasing of medical goods and services by consumers. The state, instead of the consumer, makes a lot of decisions, including: what goods and services are to be included in the scope of such a system, whether and what the level of payment is to be, what are the standards for approving drugs, technologies, or particular medical professions for use, or medical facilities providing the services (under the general system) are to be public or private, etc. The effects of these interventions are primarily such that the consumer who does not pay the bills out of their own pocket has a problem with real cost estimation. It is not able to accurately assess whether a given good or service is easily or difficult to access. On the market, they could, for example, insure themself against certain events, and pay the rest out of their own pocket with competing suppliers. However, they would be aware of the consequences of their choices. In addition, any norms or standards for approving drugs or technologies on the market replace the subjective opinion of the consumer regarding their suitability. Also, regulations on medical professions (e.g. through a system of non-market licences) limit the consumer's choice and knowledge of alternative treatments. The activities of producers and suppliers are then aimed at meeting these top-down requirements, which also generates higher costs and extends the time of introducing new goods and services to use. The development of innovative solutions is either eliminated or limited. Producers no longer estimate the potential demand reported by consumers based on their value judgements (or at least to a limited extent) but try to predict what action the state (given government) will take. Disrupting the processes of consumer evaluation by subsequent interventions negatively affects the satisfaction of their needs and contributes to the problems of economic calculation – arising when the state tries to take over the role of the market. However, the price structure in the market for final and capital goods and services was originally subordinated to the consumer's sovereignty. In a market economy, each participant is both a consumer and a producer. On the one hand, everyone sets their own requirements for the goods and services they are willing to buy and, on the other hand, as an employee or entrepreneur, they try to meet them towards other consumers. As Mises (2012, p. 20) put it:

> Now, in the economic system of private ownership of the means of production, the system of computation by value is necessarily employed by each independent member of society. Everybody participates in its emergence in a double way: on the one hand as a consumer and on the other as a producer. As a consumer he establishes a scale of valuation for goods ready for use in consumption. As a producer he puts goods of a higher order into such use as produces the greatest return. In this way all goods of a higher order receive a position in the scale of valuations in accordance with the immediate state of social conditions of production and of social needs. Through the interplay of these two processes of valuation, means will be afforded for governing both consumption and production by the economic principle throughout. Every graded system of pricing proceeds from the fact that men always and ever harmonized their own requirements with their estimation of economic facts.

The artificially stimulated demand for medical services leads to social pressure to spend more and more money on their delivery. The state therefore raises taxes (or premiums) on the basis of the right to healthcare. However, it is not possible to constantly raise taxes or incur debts for these purposes. First, the non-net beneficiary part of society begins to express its dissatisfaction with the ever-increasing levies.[8] Secondly, the state has other competing goals that also require resources (taxes), e.g. road construction, pension insurance, national defence, etc. Third, if the consumer spends only a fraction of their cost on certain goods and services, they will not abstain from consumption. At the same time, the illusion of free healthcare creates the illusion of its abundance. However, when the almost unlimited right to healthcare of one citizen meets the same law, successive citizens begin to compete with each other for, as it turns out, rare goods and medical services. In response to these actions, the state introduces various forms of rationing, which may further accelerate the use of (still) available resources.

So it is a version of the so-called tragedy of the commons, a case described by Hardin (1968, pp. 1243–1248), where dairy farmers, in order to increase their profits, over-exploited the common resources (pastures), not caring for the interests of other farmers and ultimately leading to the degradation of pastures. The solution to this problem was to separate private property through a fencing system, so that each farmer had an interest in the proper exploitation of their pastures.[9] Thus, private property introduces order to social relations and enables rational decisions based on economic calculation. Often, in order to deal with similar problems, the necessary state intervention, e.g. in the form of issuing appropriate regulations or imposing taxes, is also indicated. However, considering the use of such measures in relation to universal (public) health systems, it should be said that it is such interventions that are the main cause of problems (tragedies), not the solutions to them. If the state creates its insurance programme for all members of society, then, unlike real insurance, taxes and regulations abolish the limits of using a common healthcare resource. Under market conditions, insurers create specific risk groups consisting of members with similar probability of using medical services. The premium paid (net) reflects the insurance risk. Therefore, these are the boundaries that insurers set for individual members of risk groups, ensuring their relative homogeneity, which is a condition for effective assistance to their members when the need arises.

Also, local communities can create various quasi-insurance programmes. In the past, for example, fraternal associations were very popular. These institutions brought together city residents or people working in a given profession and provided them with access to various benefits, such as payment of funds as a result of an accident or the death of a member.[10] Their advantage was, among other things, that local communities have an interest in supporting each other and at the same time making sure that no one tries to excessively use the benefits they are entitled to. Joining a new, anonymous member was associated with their acceptance of the prevailing rules. To simplify it, it can be said that the principles of operation of such associations were similar to those of modern mutual insurance companies.

Meanwhile, public insurance makes the restrictions created by insurance companies or other associations disappear, while at the same time extending the scope of anonymity of such programmes, which creates the illusion of a real possibility for unhampered use of medical services. A resident from the east of Poland will not wonder if their frequent use of such insurance does not limit funds for a resident of the western part of Poland. They will focus on satisfying their needs in the best and fastest way (at an artificially low price), which is evidence of a kind of competition in general (public) health systems and a result of state interventionism.

If the price of a given goods and services has been artificially low-ered or is unrelated to the rational pricing of risk, there is pressure to increase them. Due to the fact that patients cannot pay the doctor directly from their own pocket, they try to do it through other forms of payment or, in other words, bribes in exchange for preferential treat-ment. From an economic point of view, a bribe testifies to the failure of public institutions to provide needed medical goods and services. The fact that a person received the medical services they needed thanks to a bribe at the expense of another person does not change the fact that the supply-demand relations have been disturbed. Even if such a situation did not take place, someone would not ultimately gain access to medical services. In the marketplace, this problem is solved by rising prices and profits, which encourages suppliers (and competitors) to increase supply and reduce costs

Producers also treat this type of payment as an effective means to achieve the goals. Instead of being subject to the laws of the market, they start to take a defensive stance. In order to maintain the current market position, they undertake numerous lobbying activities aimed at limiting competition, often under the pretext of providing high-quality services in order to care for the health of patients. This is one of the reasons why the medical industry has so many licences, quality stan-dards, product control, and other regulations that are a substitute for consumer sovereignty and competition processes.

Part of society, dissatisfied with the functioning of the universal (public) healthcare system, reaches for market alternatives: direct payments, health insurance, medical subscriptions, or, as a last resort, charity aid. In this way, you pay double for the goods and services in question, in a sense subsidizing defective public systems and, in part, camouflaging their problems with ensuring adequate availability of medical goods and services. However, the number of people willing to purchase private alternatives is relatively smaller. Additionally, government regulations hinder the functioning of these market processes, increasing manufacturers' costs and limiting competition and innovation. Therefore, the prices of certain goods and services are relatively higher than they would be in the case of unhampered market processes. Interestingly, politicians are often among the first buyers of market alternatives. A good example here is Sweden, where politicians were among the first beneficiaries of having private health insurance as an alternative to the many months of waiting for, among others, specialist services such as surgery (Bylund, 2014).

The society uses market alternatives and is aware of the problems of public systems, but at the same time has a problem with recognizing that market solutions are not only an addition or supplement to public systems, but a condition for the efficient provision of the necessary medical goods and services to society. Interventionism in the healthcare system leads to the consolidation or even deepening of the asymmetry of information. The consumer does not make decisions on their own behalf, choosing among competing suppliers and advisers. All decisions about what is to be produced and which entities are to approve e.g. drugs or technologies are made without their participation. Moreover, rising costs and concerns about the spectre of expenses exceeding the financial capacity of a single person, to some extent, consolidate the belief in society that a universal (public) healthcare system is necessary – despite its shortcomings. This leads to successive interventions, this time to remedy the unintended effects of previous market economy interventions.

Notes

1 For more on the development of Mises's theory of interventionism, see: Lavoie (1982, pp. 169–183).
2 Some differences can be found between the definitions of interventionism in Mises and Rothbard, but they are not significant for the issues discussed in this book.
3 Other names Rothbard uses are *invader* or *aggressor*.

4 Fr. von Bismarck, de facto, pursued political goals by successfully adapting the postulates of his political opponents as his own, thus depriving them of some of their arguments in the struggle for power. The various social security programmes were thus introduced, at least in part, for political reasons.

5 If an interventionist criticizes the analysis of a pure market economy as an impossible or even imaginary state, then at the same time they should have the same position towards the other extreme system, i.e. socialism. For various reasons, however, this is often not the case, because de facto socialism also uses force against, or threatens to use, individuals.

6 Interestingly, this is not only a good academic example with little economic impact. In fact, during World War II, many countries used product price controls in response to inflation induced to finance the increasing war spending. It is also interesting to note that in the US price controls have led to a non-market increase in health insurance demand, which is an interesting example of the 'interface' of economic theory (in Mises's example) with economic reality and this work.

7 This term refers to the economy as a whole in which there is no private ownership of the means of production.

8 It may also lead to a slowdown in the growth rate of expenses.

9 It is also worth mentioning that other solutions to this problem have been described by E. Ostrom. For more on this subject see: Ostrom (1990).

10 Northern Italy in the late nineteenth and early twentieth centuries can be indicated as an effective historical example of this type of initiative. For more on this subject see: Tedeschi (2015, pp. 47–64).

References

Bylund P., 2014, The market is taking over Sweden's health care, https://mises.org/library/market-taking-over-sweden's-health-care (accessed: 28. 08. 2018).

Hardin G., 1968, The tragedy of the commons, *Science*, 3859, 1243–1248.

Huerta De Soto J., 2009, *The theory of dynamic efficiency*, USA, Canada: Routledge.

Lavoie D. C., 1982, The development of the Misesian theory of interventionism, in I. Kirzner (ed.), *Method, process and the Austrian Economics essays in honor of Ludwig von Mises*, Lexington Books, Lexington: DC Heath and Company, pp. 169–183.

Mises L., 1998a, *Human action. A treatise on economics*, Auburn: Ludwig von Mises Institute.

Mises L., 1998b, *Interventionism: An economic analysis*, New York: The Foundation for Economic Education.

Mises L., 2012, *Economic calculation in the socialist commonwealth*, Auburn: Ludwig von Mises Institute.

Ostrom E., 1990, *Governing the commons: The evolution of institutions for collective action*, Cambridge: Cambridge University Press.

Pieńkowska-Kamieniecka S., Rutecka J., 2014, System emerytalny w Niemczech – analiza aktualnych tendencji na tle dotychczasowego procesu reformowania [Pension system in Germany – analysis of current trends against the background of the reform process to date'], *Ubezpieczenia społeczne. Teoria i praktyka*, 6, 19–33.

Rothbard M. N., 2009, *Man, economy, and state with power and market*, Auburn: Ludwig von Mises Institute.

Tedeschi P., 2015, A new welfare system: Friendly societies in Eastern Lombardy from 1860 to 1914, in B. Harris (ed.), *Welfare and old age in Europe and North America: The development of social insurance*, London, New York: Routledge, pp. 47–64.

5 Universal (public) health system

Definition of the universal (public) health system

The universal (public) health system is not the result of independent consumer decisions, but the result of a regulatory framework defined by the state. Perhaps this openness of public institutions indirectly speaks in favour of interventionism. The perspective of the state's responsibility for the fate of an individual, to some extent, frees them from decision-making and responsibility in the area of their own health by creating a system to ensure their safety. The goals of the universal and market-based health system remain the same – to provide the society with necessary medical (health) goods and services. The question that economics is trying to answer boils down to the legitimacy of the measures that are to serve this purpose and the effects of their application.

One of the features of interventionism is that it is quite difficult to identify examples of identical interventions applied across countries in the field of public health systems (or universal health systems). While the very definition of an intervention is quite broad, there are many examples of it. The same is true of the concept of healthcare in the literature on the subject defined as: 'Goods and services used as inputs to produce health. Some analyses consider people's own time and knowledge used to maintain and promote health, in addition to conventional health care inputs' (Folland et al., 2012, p. 551).

However, as mentioned earlier, basically each of the beneficiaries imagines these outlays differently. Of course, this image is about their needs, not the rest of society. Healthcare is not one-size-fits-all. These are a variety of medical goods and services that everyone needs depending on their needs. An elderly and chronically ill person needs a different set of goods and services than a young and healthy person. Moreover, each entity or person making the intervention has its own

DOI: 10.4324/9781003258957-8

plan for their implementation. Therefore, individual public health systems, more or less, differ from one another. However, the question may be asked whether the state cannot finance access to healthcare only to those most in need of it. Why, as world prosperity increases and economic development continues, is there no minimum public health system for the poorest? When trying to answer this question, one should take into account the economic consequences of this state of affairs. The question of the functioning of such a minimal system is not limited only to itself, but de facto, it also concerns the entire economy. It can be concluded that then two health systems would function: minimal (state-owned) and comprehensive (complementary, market-based) – covering the rest of the society. It should be noted, however, that in such an arrangement the state does not undertake only and exclusively to refrain from intervening in the market healthcare system, but also in other parts of the economy.[1]

If it is recognized that only a small part of society cannot or does not have sufficient resources to take care of itself, the rest of society can do it. In order for the majority of society to take appropriate action to this end, it must have certain resources at its disposal. Markets, too, must therefore be subordinated to their decisions. The state, wishing to introduce, for example, new taxes in order to implement an ambitious investment programme limits the amount of funds at the disposal of an individual. It is not possible to conduct an experiment whether a given entity wants to allocate its resources to health insurance or, for example, to purchase a computer, and to tax it or not. Even if its decisions do not concern the purchase of medical goods and services, in the name of respect for its freedom and responsibility for its own decisions, it cannot be prohibited from doing so. Such a society will therefore not be willing to accept new taxes. Hence the conclusion that the market health system is an element of the market economy and any state interference, also in its other areas, has an indirect impact on this system. The existence and proper functioning of the market health system depends not only on the lack of state intervention in itself, but also (indirectly) in other parts of the economy.

It can also be stated, with some simplification, that the universal health system is to some extent complementary with other state interventions in the economy. The universality of this system results, inter alia, from the fact that by embracing every member of society, it gives the state the means both to create a universal health protection system and, indirectly, it can serve as a justification for other interventions in the economy. It is not only a theoretical case. Often times, the public fails to see that a state's withdrawal from one area of intervention does not have to be sufficient. Due to the disturbed supply-demand relations, it is currently difficult to state what expenditures on healthcare are needed. In which segments are they too high and in which too low? Of course, unhampered market processes in the health system can bring very positive results also if the state does not withdraw from its interventions from other parts of the economy. However, the purpose of this argument is to draw attention to the fact that individual parts of the economy cannot be treated as isolated islands. Therefore, instead of talking about the public healthcare system (and its economy), it is more reasonable, from the economic perspective, to use the term universal (public) health system, which can be defined as:

> Systematic use by the state of interventions (binary and triangular), involving consumers and producers of medical (health) goods and services, aimed at forcing them to make decisions that would not be made by these entities in the consumption and production of these goods and services, if the interventions did not take place.[2]

The economic aspect of the above definition draws attention to the existence of opportunity costs for interventionism. Therefore, one cannot focus solely on the analysis of interventionism in the healthcare system without any reflection on the effects on the rest of the economy or society.[3] As Hazlitt (2008, p. 5) stated: 'The art of economics consists in looking not merely at the immediate hut at the longer effects of any act or policy; it consists in tracing the consequences of that policy not merely for one group but for all groups.'[4]

Interventionists may, however, argue that failure by the state to intervene can have dire consequences due to market failures. The problem of asymmetric information is particularly often pointed to as its alleged failure in the market healthcare system. Criticism of individual cases of market failure has already been presented in Part I. However, in the context of the problem of asymmetric information, it is worth paying attention to the internal contradiction of the arguments cited. According to them, state intervention in the market health system is necessary due to the fact that producers (sellers) have more knowledge about their products and thus they will be able to deceive unaware consumers. Without specialist knowledge, a consumer will never be sure whether a given good or medical service will improve or maintain their health. Therefore, state intervention is necessary to effectively protect society against dishonest producers (sellers). However, if the consumer does not have sufficient knowledge to determine from which manufacturers they should purchase the given medical goods or services, they will also not be able to determine whether experts hired by the state are acting in their favour or not. It will not be able to say whether the solutions (interventions) of party X are better than those of party Y. The information gap will still exist. Society will not be able to assess the justification and effects of the intervention. Therefore, it should be considered a paradox that politicians consider citizens competent to elect them during elections, at the same time stating that they are not competent enough to freely decide about the purchase of the medical goods and services they need. In other words, citizens are guided by wisdom and insight and caution in their elections, qualities that unexpectedly disappear after the elections are completed.

The above argumentation can also be extended by asking the question why the problem of asymmetric information should concern only the producer–consumer relationship. In the market conditions, in principle, every producer of final goods and services has its suppliers who also have their suppliers, etc. There are markets for factors of production. There is no single large enterprise that directly manages all stages of production within a large organizational structure. Each company has a specific specialization that is constantly deepening. Therefore, accepting the theory of information asymmetry, one should agree that it also occurs in the producer X (seller) – producer Y (buyer) relationship. The markets for the factors of production would then have to undergo constant collapses, as a last resort, preventing the emergence of final goods and services of adequate quality. Producers of lower-order goods would be at the mercy of producers of higher-order goods. Reducing the above claims to their logical consequences would mean that the state must also deal with strict control of the factor markets.[5] The state would have to decide for entrepreneurs what products are to be purchased, in what quantities and at what *prices*. The image of such an economic system is nothing but socialism.

Of course, there are no such collapses (crises) in the factor markets. This is because unhampered market processes do not lead to the creation, but to the removal of asymmetric information, which is one of the conditions for satisfying consumer needs adequately.

It can also be concluded that the problem of asymmetric information (or uncertainty) may also be exacerbated by announcements and reforms of public health systems. In fact, no one, apart from the initiators of these reforms, is able to find out in the maze of regulatory changes, let alone their exact impact on access to specific medical services.

General principles of operation and goals

The general principles on which universal health systems have been based have remained the same since their inception – the use of systematic interventions. Only the means by which one tries to achieve the set goals can change. The means for their implementation are individual interventions, which, according to Folland et al. (2012, p. 398) are manifested in three activities (groups): 'provision of goods and services, redistribution, and regulation. Governments have pursued each of these activities in the health economy.'

On the other hand, the basic, general purpose of the existence of such a system can be defined as an attempt to systematically provide the society with the necessary medical (health) goods and services, the purchase of which under market conditions (in the opinion of the governing bodies) would not be possible in the scale of the entire society. There are causal relationships between the three above-mentioned interventions. In order to provide the society with medical goods and services, the state must first produce them or purchase them from private suppliers, first specifying the requirements (for consumers) that they must meet. In order for these activities to be possible, the state must have adequate funds from private sources – without them it will not be possible to maintain appropriate institutions and redistribute funds between individual members of society. For this purpose, appropriate legal acts (subsequent regulations) are created, imposing the obligation to transfer some private funds (income) to previously set purposes, e.g. in the form of taxes or contributions (premiums).

Due to the fact that the universal health system is non-market, the methods of assessing its results also differ from the market ones. On the market, it is easy to assess the degree of meeting consumer needs, e. g. on the basis of the profit and loss account or taking into account rankings of institutions or people working in a given profession, created on the basis of opinions expressed by consumers. Meanwhile, in the case of the universal health system, other criteria are used – inter alia, due to its compulsory nature. Frequent examples are the size of public expenditures allocated to healthcare (e.g. in relation to GDP or the state budget) or the number of insured persons. However, these criteria are not at all synonymous with getting better results. Very often, in order to improve the functioning of such systems, it is recommended to increase the expenditure. However, it is a mistake to equate an increase in financial resources with an increase in the supply of necessary medical goods and services – and these are often missing due to the disturbance of market relations. Medicines, medical equipment, or doctors are not idly waiting for patients in warehouses and offices due to lack of funds. The amount of drugs, medical equipment, or doctors is insufficient due to artificially stimulated demand or artificially limited supply. Therefore, increasing outlays only exacerbates the shortcomings of public systems without contributing to the improvement of their performance, much to the disappointment and confusion of the public. It is also a good example of where means are confused with ends, leading to further interventions and even greater statism. Moreover, even if increased inputs improve results, this does not at all prove the need for public systems. In this case, economics draws attention to the ratio of inputs to outputs, which is rare in political debates where participants focus especially on the first variable.

In the market conditions, the producer who suffers losses (which does not adequately meet the needs of consumers) falls out of the market and is replaced by more enterprising competitors. However, in the case of the universal health system, there is no such alternative. It is only possible to replace the plan of one party with the plan of party y, but the principles under which this system operates remain the same. It also often happens that the issues of improving the functioning of such systems are a hot topic of pre-election discussions, and no actions are taken after their completion. This is so, inter alia, because any changes could be associated with a decrease in the support of a part of the society[6] for the government planning such changes.

In some countries (e.g. Switzerland or the Netherlands) it was decided to involve private entities more. However, it should be emphasized that it was the implementation not so much of market solutions as private entities into the framework of public systems. Private entities supplying society with medical goods and services do so based on top-down guidelines, not market laws. They are not market systems as they are sometimes referred to. Further systematic interventions are made in them. The benefits offered by private institutions may be related to e.g. better resource management or management which results in lower costs, but they are still subject to many regulations.[7] Interestingly, the introduction of such solutions[8] was intended more to maintain public systems than to transform them into a market alternative. A good example is the reform of the Dutch healthcare system in 2006. As Gorajek (2013, p. 305) points out:

> The Minister of Health of the Kingdom of the Netherlands, speaking about the goals of the health reform introduced in 2006, did not focus on such items as putting the patient at the center of the system or improving satisfaction with the perception of the

health system, as we often hear in discussions of our politicians. The Dutch reform was introduced in order to: 'create a chance to maintain universal access to medical services at a level not significantly different from the scope before the reform'. In short, its aim was to maintain the status quo and prevent the deterioration of access or exclusion of a large group of citizens from the health care system.

The side effect of these processes is therefore a permanent monopoly (or quasi-monopoly) as the state continues to claim the right to take action to improve the situation despite previous failures. Such systems are not well prepared for the major demographic changes that are already taking place in societies. There is often talk of new challenges or goals for public systems, but these are merely nice-sounding semantic statements. The state, for its part, can only propose further interventions.

Sources of funding

To implement their objectives, specific public institutions must have adequate funds from private sources. To this end, the state must also determine on what terms the redistribution of funds between specific members of the public is to take place. The transfer of funds is also one of the basic differences between individual public systems. Already the first two public systems differed in this respect. In the British system, the source of financing the universal health system was taxes while the German system used premiums. The third option is a combination of the two. However, from the economic perspective, the form of taxation is secondary. What matters the most is the amount of taxation. What matters for an individual is the amount of funds they will be deprived of and what they can receive for it instead. Whether for example 2,400 USD per year is being taken from Smith in the form of a tax or contribution has less (or even none) meaning for him than the amount of the tax. Hence if Smith disagrees with such a state of affairs, he will be dissatisfied not so much with the form of taxation as with its amount.

Some may argue, however, that there is a difference. For example, a tax relief can be obtained from the collected premium; thanks to that Smith will be able to maintain some money, and that is not possible in the case of a tax. In fact, this is the confirmation of the above argument. A tax credit may cause that even the taxpayer is still charged 2,400 USD per year for healthcare, it reduces taxes paid by them (e.g., by 1,200 USD per year).[9] What is extremely important, Smith (or speaking more in general, society) will keep these 1,200 USD annually only when the state will not compensate for this reduced tax revenue and introduce new taxes or incur new debts. Thus, the tax credit system makes sense only then, if it reduces the total public expenditure and do not cause new budget deficits. In this situation, the state will have less funds for the implementation of its other purposes and if it does not give up on some of them, new taxes will be created to compensate for the tax credit. So, Smith will lose in the new taxes everything that he saved due to tax credit. In this situation, the redistribution of income will be made no longer only by the premium, but also through new imposition. Its reach will expand. New imposition, although directly not related to healthcare, in an economic sense, will serve to further fund it at a specified level. The state is not usually interested in reducing the total level of expenditure, i.e., it agrees on tax credits, but at the same time introduces new impositions so that the previous level of total expenditure can be maintained. This also leads to a dangerous situation in which it seems that the costs of healthcare incurred by individual members of society are falling (thanks to the tax credit and payers of the third party), which may result in even greater demand combined with constantly growing general level of healthcare expenditure. This is because the new impositions are spread over the entire society and beneficiaries of health systems may not even perceive their growth. For when society bears only a fraction of costs or expenses it does not pay sufficient attention to their constant growth.

Employer's participation (obligatory or voluntary) in financing employee's access to healthcare is confusing as well. And it does not matter whether the healthcare is public or private. Because in the economic sense, employees (not the employer) finance this access (e.g., through insurance). When hiring a new employee an employer is guided by economic calculation. They expect that additional (extreme) revenues related to this employment will be higher than additional (extreme) costs; otherwise, the employment of an additional employee would not make sense. If the state imposes an obligation on the employer to finance health insurance for the employee (e.g., in the amount of 50% of the premium), this does not lead to a nominal growth of the employee's salary, in the amount of this share, but it reduces the employee's net income instead. The employer's financial contribution is visible only from the point of view of the regulations (i. e., on paper). The employer may increase the nominal remuneration of the employee only if they reduce other costs — for example other employees' remuneration or costs of other factors of production. Also, in the case of group private health insurance constituting the so-called expansion employee benefits, the employer bears their costs from sources that could be spent on higher remuneration (or other objectives). The fact that this is not happening often results from the fact that employees' private group health insurance, through a workplace, gives much better insurance conditions than they could get as individual clients. For employees, for example, 100 USD per month for such insurance gives greater benefits than the increase in net pay by the amount mentioned. For the employer, in turn, offering such programmes constitutes an additional form of competition for employees, affects better working conditions, and therefore produces a good image for the company.

Increasing expenditures for the universal health system may also take place without the growth of taxes or increasing the deficit. In this situation, the state would have to limit expenditures for other purposes. Various goals that the state tries to achieve are therefore, in a certain sense, competitive. For example, resignation from one goal comes at the expense of the other one and resisting one social group brings support from the other one. The state is constantly facing the dilemma of achieving specific objectives at the expense of others. Should funds be allocated to improve road infrastructure or healthcare? If the state considers that the expenditure should be increased for healthcare, it must determine specifically which objectives will be funded: on the increases to pay doctors and nurses or maybe for the construction of new medical facilities? However, even in the case of assigning funds for relevant purposes, public institutions that do not have access to a profit and loss account will not be able to correctly specify whether the expenditure is sufficient or not. Without the freedom of consumers' choice and their value judgements, it will not be possible to check if the amount of tax or premium is too high, too low, or adequate. In the first two cases, this leads to increasing discomfort (reduction of utility) of individuals.

In fact, budgets that have public institutions financing access to specific health goods and services should not be considered as reliable because they are not the result of market economic calculation. Under the market conditions, economic calculation is possible due to the existence of the prices of final goods and prices factors of production. On this basis, you can easily determine profits or losses and take appropriate action in the future. Although prices expressed in money do not replace the valuation of consumers, they do constitute an easy tool for entrepreneurs, through which, on the basis of profit and loss account, they can specify whether they meet their needs sufficiently. Economic calculation also allows for easier investment. If the entrepreneur provides for consumer needs, the involvement of certain factors of production will allow them to achieve profits; otherwise, they will incur losses. Even if entrepreneurs are not discourage with initial losses, they surely cannot incur them indefinitely. The long-term losses cause difficult situation for such entrepreneurs and this should be understood. However, the resulting losses should not be negatively received. Eventually, they are the result of consumer decisions and a signal that rare resources are used in the wrong way — that is, they do not contribute to better satisfying their needs, including these medical (health) services.

However, the budgets of public institutions are not established on the grounds of independent consumer decisions made on the basis of prices and other measures. In this case, speaking about budgets, revenues, or costs is much imprecise. Such institution must distribute available means to specific purposes. It spends funds, but this is not identical to bearing costs under the market conditions. Among other things, due to the artificially stimulated demand, it is very difficult to determine what amount of funds should be directed to individual goals. Public institutions do not have funds (revenues) voluntarily transferred to them by consumers. With their top-down decisions, they must also replace consumers; therefore, above all, they have a problem with determining the correct hierarchy of goals and the scale of the necessary measures. Unhappy consumers cannot resign from paying contributions or propose a higher price for better quality services. Also, decisions regarding investments are becoming problematic. It is not possible to determine the profitability of a given project due to the lack of capability in establishing revenues based on prices (Fuller, 2018). Therefore, obtaining funding for providing access to specific goods and medical services and the investment has little to do with rational targeting of rare resources.

Concept and significance of health in individual and social dimensions

It is very difficult, if not impossible, to achieve an optimal level of goods and medical (health) services which should be provided to individuals to preserve their health. There are at least three reasons for this. First, there is no clear and easily discernible line between health and disease. Second, as a result of the development of medicine and technologies, new and more effective treatment methods, medicines, or medical equipment increase the amount and quality of goods and medical services (health services) and increase choice. Third, for an individual health does not have to be the most important thing. Therefore, a person takes decisions, resulting in a more or less intended use of rare funds for medical (health) services. Under market conditions, this has implications, among other things, for the formation and development of relations between consumer (patient) and physician. The patient knows their body better than the doctor. In turn, the physician has much greater medical knowledge about the patient. There is a specific relationship between them whereby the patient better understands the doctor's recommendations. Because of this, the patient return to health and work more quickly. In this case, the encouragement of adequate trust in the doctor is of special importance, and it also takes time. Building trust is so important, because the patient shares with the physician their personal information. But this is necessary knowledge for the doctor to choose effective treatment methods. In principle, each case is unique due to the fact that people differ in terms of their physiological or psychological makeup. It should also be emphasized that one of the basic conditions for the creation of trust and, subsequently, an appropriate relationship is the voluntary nature of contracts.

These conditions look completely different in a universal health system, which is a system built upon coercion. As indicated by Hayek (1978, p. 300):

> There are so many serious problems raised by the nationalization of medicine that we cannot mention even all the more important ones. But there is one the gravity of which the public has scarcely yet perceived and which is likely to be of the greatest importance. This is the inevitable transformation of doctors, who have been members of a free profession primarily responsible to their patients, into paid servants of the state, officials who are necessarily subject to instruction by authority and who must be released from the duty of secrecy so far as authority is concerned. The most dangerous aspect of the new development may well prove to be that, at a time when the increase in medical knowledge tends to confer more and more power over the minds of men to those who possess it, they should be made dependent on a unified organization under single direction and be guided by the same reasons of state that generally govern policy. A system that gives the indispensable helper of the individual, who is at the same time an agent of the state, an insight into the other's most intimate concerns and creates conditions in which he must reveal this knowledge to a superior and use it for the purposes determined by authority opens frightening prospects.

Under the market conditions, the patient is free to dispose of their funds and with appropriate doctors' recommendations, allocating them the necessary goods and medical services. Doctors' profit depends on customer satisfaction. Meanwhile, in the case of a universal health system, the doctor is obliged to comply with the guidelines imposed on them and faces the problem of permanent shortage of funds and medical services. Additional problems occur when they have to resolve which patients should first be directed to examination or treatment: working people (i.e., those paying premiums) or people who in the post-production age. From the perspective of a public payer, the first group finances the budget (Fund) and the second is only a recipient of collected funds (i.e. do not supply the budget with its own funds). The second group expects adequate treatment, among other reasons because they had also paid premiums before. However, the number of contributions was not related to their former health and present needs. Also, the first group waits for access to medical goods and services. In the market health system, both groups and individual persons may take action to secure their health in ways that do not interfere with the interests of other people. On the other hand, in a universal health system, there are inevitable problems with the distribution of funds between its participants, which may lead to social conflicts. The second group is in a less favourable situation, in the sense that the medical (health) needs of its members are much greater and its economic contribution to financing this system remains negligible. Another problem is the phenomenon of aging societies.

Therefore, the governments are trying to solve this problem through various forms of limiting access to goods and medical services, which comes down to an arbitrary decision what health conditions should be insured in the first place. From this perspective, more arguments might favour focusing on those of working age, because this group can recover faster and pay for contributions. Such people can be easier restored to health than the elderly. In addition, public institutions (e.g., hospitals) can follow their own interest during the treatment process of patients deviating from market conditions. This may be expressed, for example, in an artificial extension of the patient's residence in the hospital, because it gives the hospital additional influences from the Fund. Another example is the pressure on shortening the hospital time for patients requiring a longer stay due to their relatively high costs. In this situation, it is not entirely clear whether the patient is discharged only and exclusively from medical premises. Naturally, market solutions do not consist in the treatment of patients regardless of costs. However, they allow for the effective adaptation of needed and scarce goods to demand (through the price system), thanks to which individual members of society can better understand the situation and take appropriate actions.

Notes

1 Alternatively, also for minimal intervention.
2 This definition is based on the terminology of intervention used by Rothbard.
3 At the same time, changes in other parts of the economy affecting the universal or market health system cannot be ignored.
4 It is also worth noting that economists had already drawn attention to the problem of opportunity costs much earlier. For more on this, see: Bastiat (2010); Sumner (2009).
5 You can also ask the question: if the state knows better than entrepreneurs what the consumer and producers need, why not become an entrepreneur itself?
6 For example, people in post-working age.
7 On the other hand, an example of an attempt to translate market solutions into the public system is the obligation to bear some of the costs directly by the insured, which, in a sense, confirms the usefulness of market solutions by the rulers.
8 From the point of view of governments, they could be referred to as market based.
9 The level of spending on healthcare remains the same.

References

Bastiat F., 2010, *That which is seen, and that which is not seen: An economic essay*, USA: WLC.

Folland S., Goodman A. C., Stano M., 2012, *The economics of health and health care*, USA: Routledge.

Fuller E. W., 2018, Socialized medicine: An accounting perspective, https://mises.org/wire/scocialized-medicine-accounting-perspective (accessed: 13. 09. 2018).

Gorajek M., 2013, Rynek prywatnych usług medycznych w Polsce i na świecie [Private medical services market in Poland and in the world], in Z. Guzel, D. M. Fal, A. Lipka (eds.), *Medycyna ubezpieczeniowa: Underwritinig. Orzecznictwo. Ubezpieczenia zdrowotne* [Insurance medicine – underwriting, certification, health insurance], Warsaw: Poltext.

Hayek F. A., 1978, *The constitution of liberty*, USA: University of Chicago Press.

Hazlitt H., 2008, *Economics in one lesson*, Auburn: Ludwig von Mises Institute.

Sumner W. G., 2009, *The forgotten man*, USA: Sparks Media.

Summary

Increasing the role of the market in the provision and financing of medical goods and services requires not only appropriate institutional solutions limiting the influence of the state. In the first place, the path to such changes must have solid support on the basis of economic theory. That is why creating a theoretical basis for the functioning of a completely market-based health system is so important.

Private health insurance is often presented as a viable alternative to insurance or the public system. At the same time, it is pointed out that such insurance has a number of disadvantages that effectively limit universal financing of access to medical services. In the market system, many people could not take out insurance and would, in a way, be forced to incur significant direct expenses.

However, this presentation of the matter overlooks many important aspects of the market system. The insurance institution is not intended to guarantee universal access to such benefits for everyone. It may cover persons representing the risk accepted by the insurer. Thanks to this, part of the society can free themselves from the problem of relatively high expenses in the future.

However, market solutions are not limited to offering health insurance only. As in most markets, many transactions are done using direct payments. Therefore, the problem lies not so much in the insurance or direct payments themselves as in the regulations limiting the supply and appropriate competition between suppliers. In fact, for example, when making everyday purchases, we do not use 'food insurance'. Although direct payments dominate in such transactions, consumers are not struggling with shortages of food and other goods or services.

Therefore, one of the most effective ways to ensure adequate access to medical services is, inter alia, deregulation of the medical professions and the pharmaceutical industry or greater trust in private institutions that guard the quality. In this case, market processes lead to the

DOI: 10.4324/9781003258957-9

free formation of a rational structure of financing the structure of access to medical services with a significant (and non-conflicting) role of both insurance and direct payments.

It is important because a better understanding of the principles of operation of market solutions increases the chances of their more and more courageous implementation in individual countries.

Moreover, it is not only theory that speaks of the legitimacy of applying market solutions. At the turn of the 19th and 20th centuries, before the emergence of public health systems, there were many market solutions in this area. These were, for example, the so-called fraternal associations – voluntary mutual aid organizations, especially popular with the working class. As late as 1920, more than 25% of American adults were members of such organizations, and the proportion was even higher in the UK and Australia. Such organizations were financed from the monthly or annual contributions of their members, and in return, when necessary, the accumulated funds were transferred to meet individual needs (e.g. financing a doctor's visit). However, over time, a well-functioning market has become the subject of state interventions.[1]

It is worth remembering, especially in times of large and problematic public systems.

Note

1   For more on this subject, see, among others: Long (no date); Harris (2015).

References

Harris B. (ed.), 2015, *Welfare and old age in Europe and North America: The development of social insurance*, London, New York: Routledge.

Long R. T., no date, How government solved the health care crisis, http:// freenation.org/a/f1213.html (accessed: 10. 03. 2021).

Index